NOTES ON

LABOR PROBLEMS IN NATIONALIST CHINA

By

ISRAEL EPSTEIN

With a Supplement by

JULIAN R. FRIEDMAN

International Secretariat
INSTITUTE OF PACIFIC RELATIONS
1 East 54th St. New York

1949

$2.25

PREFACE

The two separate reports presented in this volume are not intended to serve as definitive studies of labor problems in wartime and postwar China but simply as interim compilations, based on often fragmentary material, for the convenience of research workers interested in the evolution of the Chinese labor movement. Since the publication by the China Institute of Pacific Relations in 1933 of Facing Labor Issues in China by Dr. Lowe Chuan-hua and the more recent short book by Miss Nym Wales, The Chinese Labor Movement (1945), there has been no substantial report on modern Chinese labor problems. It is therefore hoped that the present studies, independently prepared by two experienced writers with first-hand experience in China during the wartime and postwar years, will provide a useful body of reference materials pending the time when a more comprehensive book can be written.

Such a book will of course have to take into account the profound changes likely to occur in the Chinese labor situation as a result of the policies to be initiated by the Chinese Communist administration. The present volume does not discuss these new developments nor does it include any account of labor conditions or policies in the older Communist-controlled areas of Manchuria and North China. Nevertheless, the account which the two authors give of conditions in wartime and postwar Nationalist China provides a valauble background for understanding and evaluating the policies to be followed by the Communist authorities.

For convenient reference a number of documents have been included in the appendix and here it has been possible to include the text of a few important laws and policy statements recently issued by the Communists administration in North China and Manchuria.

Mr. Epstein served for many years as a journalist in wartime China and is well-known as the author of The Unfinished Revolution in China (1947) and The Peoples War (1939). Mr. Friedman is now Lecturer in Colonial Administration at the London School of Economics and was formerly Labor Attaché at the United States Consulate-General in Shanghai in 1946. Though the volume is issued under the auspices of the International Secretariat of the Institute of Pacific Relations, it should be noted that the authors are solely responsible for all statements of fact or opinion expressed in their respective reports.

William Holland
Secretary General

New York

June 7, 1949

PREFACE

The two separate reports presented in this volume are not intended to serve as definitive studies of labor problems in wartime and postwar China but simply as interim compilations, based on often fragmentary material, for the convenience of research workers interested in the evolution of the Chinese labor movement. Since the publication by the China Institute of Pacific Relations in 1933 of Facing Labor Issues in China by Dr. Lowe Chuan-hua and the more recent short book by Miss Nym Wales, The Chinese Labor Movement (1945), there has been no substantial report on modern Chinese labor problems. It is therefore hoped that the present studies, independently prepared by two experienced writers with first-hand experience in China during the wartime and postwar years, will provide a useful body of reference materials pending the time when a more comprehensive book can be written.

Such a book will of course have to take into account the profound changes likely to occur in the Chinese labor situation as a result of the policies to be initiated by the Chinese Communist administration. The present volume does not discuss these new developments nor does it include any account of labor conditions or policies in the older Communist-controlled areas of Manchuria and North China. Nevertheless, the account which the two authors give of conditions in wartime and postwar Nationalist China provides a valuable background for understanding and evaluating the policies to be followed by the Communist authorities.

For convenient reference a number of documents have been included in the appendix and here it has been possible to include the text of a few important laws and policy statements recently issued by the Communists administration in North China and Manchuria.

Mr. Epstein served for many years as a journalist in wartime China and is well-known as the author of The Unfinished Revolution in China (1947) and The People's War (1939). Mr. Friedman is now Lecturer in Colonial Administration at the London School of Economics and was formerly Labor Attaché at the United States Consulate-General in Shanghai in 1946. Though the volume is issued under the auspices of the International Secretariat of the Institute of Pacific Relations, it should be noted that the authors are solely responsible for all statements of fact or opinion expressed in their respective reports.

William Holland
Secretary General

New York

June 7, 1949

C O N T E N T S

S U P P L E M E N T

APPENDICES

APPENDICES

(Compiled by Israel Epstein)

TABLES

INTRODUCTION

I

The history of Chinese labor during the war with Japan in 1937-45, of which this regional study covers only a part, cannot be understood without reference to the whole development of industry, labor and the labor movement in pre-war China -- and indeed of the place China has occupied in the world system of economic and political relationships during the past century.

This background, in turn, cannot be adequately studied with the tools of the conventional labor or trade union specialist. The only fruitful approach is that of the political, economic and social historian. As distinct from the trade union movements of the West, which developed institutionally under more or less stable political conditions already established by thorough-going political revolutions, the Chinese labor movement grew as part of the revolutionary cataclysms through which Chinese society still seeks a forward path.

The reasons why the Chinese labor movement could not and did not arrive at the trade-unionist pattern of economic association for collective bargaining under an evolving system of labor law lies in the difference of its environment from that of contemporaneous labor movements in the West.

Trade unions, with or without corresponding political organizations (labor and socialist parties, PAC, etc.), arose in Western countries long after these had established themselves as independent nation-states. In these countries, capitalism had won already its economic and political battles with feudalism. Urban economy based on mechanized industry had become decisive for their entire national economies. Modern means of transportation provided physical access to both a nationwide and a worldwide market for the products of industry. Parliamentary institutions were an essential part of government, giving labor the ballot and other forms of legal political pressure as weapons in its own interests.

The society in which modern Chinese wage-labor grew did not exhibit these conditions. It does not now.

Chinese national sovereignty was severely curtailed by forcibly-imposed treaties throughout the period after 1840. Treaty limitation of China's right to set import tariffs at rates consonant with her own interests, imposed in 1858 and not relaxed for seventy years, made it possible for foreign goods to saturate her available internal markets when the first domestic industries were fighting for emergence.

Extraterritoriality and administrative concessions in China, not abandoned by foreign powers until 1942, made it possible for foreign-owned factories to establish themselves in many Chinese ports where they were subject neither to Chinese law nor to Chinese taxation. Coupled with higher capitalization and greater technical and management experience, these advantages made it possible for foreign firms to beat down Chinese competition and survive periods of depression with greater ease. As late as the 1930's, foreign interests owned more than half the textile industry in China and an even greater proportion of manufacturing properties in other fields, as well as mining and shipping. The same circumstances gave a tremendous head-start to foreign-owned banks and credit institutions, which even enjoyed the right of currency emission for several decades.

In the meantime, agriculture, the chief Chinese industry, remained unmodernized. This stifled industrial growth in two ways. It provided a higher return on capital invested in land, in the form of rent, than was available as profit from industrial investment. Moreover, by keeping the peasantry impoverished, it prevented the development of a home market for industrial products. Old-style imposts and tools on inter-provincial transport, such as likin and its successors, aggravated technical transport difficulties in impeding commodity circulation.

Urban population never exceeded 20% in China. Even in the cities, the vast majority of the people were not employed in industry. The number of workers in modern manufacturing, mining and transport in China (including Manchuria) has never been above 3 million -- or less than 1% of the total population.

China was poorly supplied with modern transportation. Peak railway mileage was 13,000, or 27 miles per million people. By comparison, the United States has 1,940 miles of railway per million population, besides being served by a highway system hundreds of times as great as that in China and over 1,000 times as many motor vehicles. It was not until after World War II that China came to possess a single ship or airplane engaged in transoceanic service.

China has never had a functioning parliamentary system or labor law . Prior to 1924, all forms of labor organization were without legal status, and generally repressed as illegal. Full trade union rights were recognized by national law for only three years during the past century, 1924-27, and even then were effective only in parts of China south of the Yangtze dominated by the revolutionary Kuomintang-Communist united front of that period. The aim of all National Government labor laws subsequent to 1927 was to prevent independent labor organization, and to control labor through official regulation (see Chapter VII).

II.

The scope and structure both of China's industry and of her modern labor force were conditioned by the restrictive circumstances described above. Both Chinese industry and labor were impeded in their growth and ambitions by the semi-colonial and internally backward condition of the country. Politically, this situation expressed itself in repeated alliances of Chinese domestic capital and labor against foreign privilege and repressive rule. This provided sharp contrasts to the early history of industry and labor unionism in the West, where two forces early organized themselves as counterweights and antagonists one to the other. So strong were the factors of colonialism and feudalism in China that they played a greater part in stimulating labor organization than the abuses suffered by labor in Chinese-owned enterprises. This was all the more striking because exploitation in such enterprises was generally greater than in foreign-owned industries; the technically backward and relatively under-capital-ized Chinese firms were able to compete only by such methods.

Both the earliest and the greatest strikes in Chinese history were directed against foreign administrators and owners. The first on record, the Shanghai wheelbarrow strike of 1897, was called by employees of the extra-territorial Shanghai Municipal Council and suppressed by foreign volunteers and naval landing parties. The two great seamen's strikes of 1922 and 1925 in Hong Kong, both of which developed into general strikes, had the British colonial administration of that port as antagonist.

Backward warlord administration, supported in each case by foreign patrons, were the second great enemy of Chinese labor. The first major economic railway strike, the Peking-Hankow line walkout of 1923, pressed its demands on a foreign-capitalized railroad and was broken by the warlord Wu Pei-fu, who massacred its leaders. The Shanghai (political) general strike of 1927 passed into an armed workers' uprising which unseated the warlord Sun Chuan-fang and made it possible for Kuomintang forces under Chiang Kai-shek to enter the city. The same Shanghai strikers were afterwards put down by military force, supplied both by Chiang Kai-shek and by the foreign authorities of the International Settlement, with whom he collaborated after his entry. These Shanghai events split the one important alliance between Chinese capital and labor. They served at the same time to consolidate the alliance of Chinese labor with the progressive forces of peasant revolt.

A third category of Chinese strikes and demonstrations represented labor's share in combined pressures applied by all anti-imperialist groups to Chinese governments regarded as subservient to foreign pressure or complacent toward foreign aggression. The strike movement of 1919 supported demonstrations of students and other middle-class elements against Peking government tendencies to accede to the award of Shantung to Japan under the Treaty of Versailles. Sixteen years later, in 1935-6 textile workers in Japanese-owned mills in Shanghai and Tsingtao walked out in support of nation-wide student demonstrations calling on the Kuomintang government to abandon civil war and resist Japanese aggression. After World War II, Shanghai workers demonstrated to protest against renewed civil strife and to demand withdrawal of U. S. troops from China.

It will be seen from the above that major economic strikes by Chinese labor have always ended in political clashes with the forces that kept China backward, and that mass political strikes have charac-terized every period of Chinese labor development. Organizationally, the "movement" rather than the western-type union has been the recurring highlight of Chinese labor history. Chinese labor, too weak to with-stand combined pressure by foreign interests, Chinese landed interests and Chinese capital at periods when these reached some mutually satis-factory accommodation, has always erupted in large-scale struggles against governments which have alienated the middle classes as well as the workers by too many surrenders to foreign or backward influences.

The coincidence of Chinese labor struggles and organizational advances with nationwide political revolutionary and protest movements of which labor formed only a part is corroborated by strike statistics. 1/

_____

1. Nym Wales, The Chinese Labor Movement, New York, 1945.

- iii.-

Year	Participants in Strikes	Remarks
1918	6,455	
1919	91,520	1919 student movement
1924	61,680	
1925	784,821	"May 30" movement
1926	539,285	Northern Expedition
1934	135,656	
1935	323,884	
1936	258,672	Nat'l Salvation Movement

The prominence of Chinese labor at such periods and its relative inability to act when labor's immediate economic interests alone are in dispute points up both the weakness and the strength of the Chinese working class during past years.

The weaknesses of Chinese labor might appear, at first sight, to be overwhelming. Labor in China has represented a tiny proportion of the people. Its ranks have included a high proportion of women and children. The feebleness and inability to compete of Chinese industry itself have led to recurrent crises in which continuity of employment has been broken and a large part of the labor force has returned to the villages. The predominance of small industrial enterprises has contributed to a fragmentation of labor's forces, making organization difficult. The constant presence of unemployed masses of refugees driven to the cities by military upheavals, social shifts, and natural catastrophies in the countryside, has made defense of labor standards by bargaining well-nigh impossible. The Chinese working class has remained semi-peasant in character, with consequent division along local and craft lines. Illiteracy has always been extremely high. These reasons, combined with undemocratic government, have impeded the development of organizationally or financially stable trade unions.

Nonetheless Chinese labor has always proved ready to launch large-scale organized struggles, many of which have been successful. Its power has been feared both by foreign invaders and reactionary Chinese governments. As between the two main new political forces generated by the repeatedly thwarted development of a capitalist economy in China, labor has always been stronger than native capital because the working class grew in both locally-owned and foreign-owned enterprises while native "free enterprise" was frequently decimated by foreign and bureaucratic competition and ultimately by Japanese invasion. Small in relation to China's population, labor nevertheless represented the most numerous and powerful group brought into organized motion by the changes in Chinese society prior to the tremendous unrolling of the Chinese peasant revolution during World War II under Communist leadership. That leadership itself acquired its first mass roots and experience in the labor movement of the 1920's.

Convinced by repeated and often bloody experience that normal improvement of labor standards was impossible while China remained semi-feudal and semi-colonial, Chinese workers were most readily moved by the idea of revolutionary change in both the internal and external

relations of Chinese society. Possessing the tradition of early
achievements in the fight for such changes, they were not long content
merely to follow the sporadic and wavering political leadership of
Chinese middle-class groups who also wanted change but only within
limits dictated by their own interests. Instead they gravitated toward
leadership by Chinese Marxists who, while frequently themselves of
middle-class intellectual origin, saw labor as the vanguard force in a
revolutionary process whose ultimate, though not immediate, objective
was socialism.

III.

Any student who follows the history of Chinese labor organizations will find that attempts to form non-political economic associations of the Western trade union type always remained small in scope and
ended in withering-away, suppression or conversion into instruments of
control manipulated by anti-labor elements (gangsters of the Tu Yu-sen
type, government bureaus, etc.). Unions which were really revolutionary
mass organizations, on the other hand, have always re-emerged in one
form or another despite apparent annihiliation, and have continued to
pursue their original aims. In periods of upsurge, they have repeatedly
incorporated the entire rank and file of purely economic and even
government-controlled "yellow" unions.

Thus, China's first workers' mutual benefit and wage-bargaining
agency, the Canton Mechanics' Union, remained a more or less isolated
example of labor organization for more than a decade. In strong contrast, the railway and miners' unions organized in 1918-19 by political
"groups of ten", composed of Socialist intellectuals from Peiping
universities, grew very quickly. With the formation of the Chinese
Communist party, which most members of the "groups of ten" joined, the
Peking-Hankow railway and Tangshan miners' unions embarked on large-
scale strike activity. They were soon supplemented by a Communist-led
Chinese Seamen's Union, which conducted the two great Hong Kong strikes
and became the strong shield of Sun Yat-sen's Kuomintang government in
Canton.

The subsequently organized national Labor Secretariat and All-
China Labor Federation, based on the new type of union, embraced
clerical, "coolie" and agricultural wage workers as well as those in
industry and transport. It instituted the practice of linking all
organizations in a given city into a General Labor Union, whose joint
action could make up for the weakness of scattered locals in small
factories and among non-industrial workers. The Second All-China Labor
Congress, in 1925, was attended by delegates representing what were
variously estimated at from 200,000 to 570,000 organized workers. The
Fourth Congress, in 1927, collected representatives of almost 3 million
organized unionists (the lowest estimate is 2,800,000). This was the
high tide of the Chinese labor movement, suppressed by Chiang Kai-shek
in the same year at the cost of over 30,000 workers' lives. The Fifth
Congress, held secretly, had delegates from only 70,000 organized
workers in outlawed underground organizations in Kuomintang territory
and open unions in areas that had rebelled against the Kuomintang. The
latter were to survive and multiply through the period of the Chinese
Soviet Republic and the wartime Communist-led Liberated Areas.

The stormy growth of organized labor in China in 1921-27 has conditioned all the subsequent labor history of the country. Fear of the movement's resurgence dictated Kuomintang labor legislation from 1929 to 1947, including such otherwise incomprehensible safeguards as the requirement that government officials be present at the smallest union meetings and the prohibition against union federations (See Chapter VII.). On the other hand, labor's hope that its power might once again reach the 1927 heights never died. After the Kuomintang-Communist united front was renewed on an anti-Japanese basis in 1937, workers in Changsha and Hankow began to talk of a restoration of "Northwestern expedition unions". In 1938 the Kuomintang government put its foot down firmly against the revival even of the name of the All-China Labor Federation, though this was proposed by an agency it had itself created, the then shadowy Chinese Association of Labor. A fuller account of these events will be found in Chapter VIII of the present study.

The All-China Labor Federation was finally reconstituted, by the combined action of unionists in the warring Kuomintang and Communist areas of China, in August 1948 -- on a program calling for, among other objectives, the overthrow of the Kuomintang regime. Significantly, the Harbin conference at which it was reformed was called the Sixth All-China Labor Congress, the fifth having been held almost twenty years previously in 1929. This nomenclature was not merely a semantic device to satisfy the claims of tradition. Many of the men who attended and addressed the Harbin congress had been active leaders in the All-China Federation of the 1920's and had spent the intervening years commanding guerilla armies, organizing peasants and shaping the Chinese Communist party and the coalition of social forces it now leads to the point at which it became the effective heir to the 1924-27 revolution on a nationwide scale. In the rank and file of labor itself, as we have already seen, the tradition remained much more than a matter of words.

The labor movement in the North China Liberated Areas, which elected a majority of delegates to the Sixth Congress, came to it as the direct but much more developed counterpart of such organizations as the Canton and Wuhan General Labor Unions, which had formed a main source of power for the combined Kuomintang-Communist revolutionary government of the middle 1920's, and indeed had provided a good measure of its military force ("picket guards", workers'battalions,etc.). Interestingly enough, the Communist-led Liberated Area unions of 1948 were helping lead a regional economic reconstruction program which involved participation in production councils and a limitation of wage and hour demands in the interest of greater capital re-investment and plant expansion by both publicly and privately-owned industries.

Liberated Area hours (8-10 daily) and basic wages (a minimum per worker sufficient to support two persons) represented working conditions better than any achieved elsewhere in China. Labor's political strength in these areas was very great. On the other hand, the policy of the union movement there was to withhold its full economic power from the wage-and-hour bargaining field so as to hasten industrialization. Here we see a much more advanced stage of the traditional orientation toward achieving changes in Chinese society by its own resources. Under Liberated Area conditions, in which the political battle was regarded as won, the main effort was directed at the increase and modernization of production rather than at battling social and political obstacles that barred the way.

The Chinese Association of Labor and unions officially outlawed in Kuomintang territory were also represented at Harbin. They came in roughly the same capacity as the North China unions of the 1920's, struggling for the destruction of the warlord power there, had come to the All-China Labor Congresses of the earlier period. The watchwords of the Kuomintang territory delegations in 1948 were the overthrow of Chiang Kai-shek and the preservation of industrial plant from "scorched earth" destruction by his retreating armies. Dispatches from China at the end of 1948 reported many examples in which these tasks were actually accomplished, as in the Kailan mines, the Kaifeng, Chengchow and Suchow railroad workshops and depots, etc.

The Process that brought the Chinese Association of Labor to this role from its original character as a Kuomintang government labor agency is sketched in Chapter VIII. Other chapters in the current study provide clues as to how and why that government came to alienate and antagonize all Chinese labor, and why no "reformist" or "Third Force" group ever achieved vitality in its ranks. President Chu Hsueh-fan of the CAL, indeed, had been the Chinese personification of a "Third Force", both in his personal ideas as to the most desirable road for the labor movement to follow and in his long association with non-revolutionary Western union leadership. Chu's difficulty was that the Chinese situation in its essence, and the Kuomintang government in its actual policies, made such a line of development quite impossible. So Chu, too, came to Harbin, with a Kuomintang warrant of arrest hanging over him from a time long before he made his ultimate decision. Significantly, Chu's disgrace with the government dated from his strong advocacy of General George C. Marshall's truce plans for China.

In the face of the facts outlined above, stretching over almost thirty years, we can see clearly what has been the main channel of the Chinese labor movement as determined by modern Chinese history.

IV.

The study that follows is of much more limited scope than the above introduction. It describes mainly the composition, conditions, legal situation and organization of workers in Kuomintang China during World War II. It deals with only one portion of the wartime Chinese labor scene, in a geographical setting far removed from the main centers of Chinese industry. It does not cover the equally important wartime experiences of Chinese labor in the Japanese-occupied and Communist-led areas.

Nonetheless, the author believes that the partial treatment adopted offers certain advantages and leads to some conclusions valid for the Chinese scene as a whole. Observation even of this narrow field confirms the thesis that industrialization in China, and the solution of related problems, is impossible under any government that does not assail the traditional economic relationships of the old Chinese society -- however modern its ambitions in the sphere of administrative practice and however good the education of its technicians. While war-

time Kuomintang China labored under extraordinary material difficulties, it was also relatively free from some pre-war obstacles to the
growth of Chinese production, such as the influx of foreign goods
backed by extraterritorial advantages. Moreover, wartime difficulties alone cannot explain why even essential war industries were
stifled in their growth, and why factory work in Kuomintang China
exercised so little attraction -- even for poverty-stricken peasants --
that they entered industry mainly out of greater fear of conscription
into an army in which death from starvation and neglect was the commonest form of casualty.

Consideration of labor conditions in wartime Kuomintang China
also shows that, within the framework of old Chinese society, such
names as "trade unions", "labor policy" and "labor legislation" have
served only to cover the realities of sham and suppression. It
explains why even labor leadership of the CAL type had to return to
the conclusion reached by a previous generation of Chinese unionists --
that only the completion of the long-drawn-out unfinished revolution
in China could clear the way for any expansion of Chinese labor's
numbers, opportunities, productivity, and share in the fruits of its
toil.

CHAPTER I.

THE WAR AND INDUSTRY

1. ### Loss of Plant

The earliest battles of the Sino-Japanese war were fought along the coast, where more than 80 per cent of China's modern industrial capacity were located. Production was halted almost immediately. At the end of the first 14 months of hostilities, all major industrial centers in China were in enemy hands.

Of the 5,526 factories and mechanized workshops in Shanghai, 5,255 were destroyed or under Japanese control by November 1937. Units destroyed in the International Settlement alone included 136 textile mills, 72 metal works and 410 machine shops. Machinery in many plants which had weathered the fighting was later broken up for scrap by the conquerors.

The textile industry of Wusih and the silk filatures of Chekiang were wiped out. Before they retreated, the Chinese themselves blew up Japanese-owned cotton mills in Tsingtao, with 250,000 spindles and 4,000 looms.

In North China the well-developed railway network, the main modern coal mines in China (accounting for 13,035,000 tons of her total production of 22,250,000 in 1936), and many other industries fell to the enemy intact.

The industrial position of unoccupied China in the "Wuhan period," (December 1937-October 1938) while the capital was in Hankow, was roughly as follows:

Table 1

Modern Industry and Transport
in Pre-war China (excluding Manchuria), 1937

Population (est.)	450,000,000
Cotton spindles	5,821,122
Cotton looms	66,509
Flour mills (output, sacks)	79,930,518
Coal (output, tons)	22,250,000
Iron ore (modern mines, output, tons)	1,340,220
Railway mileage	7,309
Steamship tonnage	541,128

By the spring of 1938 the Chinese government had lost control of areas containing one-third of the population of the country excluding Manchuria. The loss of industrial and transport facilities was out of all proportion greater, the Japanese having captured approximately 80 per cent of the cotton-spinning capacity listed in the above table; 90 per cent of the cotton looms, 75 per cent of the flour milling capacity; 60 per cent of modern coal mines by output, and 60 per cent of the railway mileage and

70 per cent of shipping tonnage. The majority of iron resources remained in its hands, but they were largely out of production.

No figures are available on munitions plants, but the Hanyang arsenal was in production and some of the machinery of the Nanking arsenal had also been moved to Wuhan.

Although industries in Wuhan and Changsha were working, those of Canton and Chengchow (a cotton and flour center in Honan) were very early paralyzed by bombing, and Hsuchow was lost in May 1938. Wuhan was not severely bombed at any time, but after the fall of Hsuchow it, too, was slowed down by evacuation preparations.

After the fall of Wuhan and Canton and the great Changsha fire, all in late 1938, Free China's modern industries were cut even more drastically. They remained negligible, even with the re-installation of removed factories and the construction of some new ones in such places as Chungking, Kunming, Kweilin, Sian, Paochi and Lanchow.

By 1943, the Chinese government controlled areas with a population of perhaps 45 per cent of pre-war. The industry and transport at its disposal, even after transplanted factories had been put into operation and some new industries and railroads built, were roughly as follows compared to July 1937: modern cotton-spinning facilities, 4.2%; coal mining, 22%; railway mileage, 16%; steamship tonnage, 19%. The main iron mines along the middle Yangtze had also been lost.

Apart from direct war losses, this low level was aggravated by inflation and government economic policies inimical to production. The remaining two years of hostilities (1944-45) brought new surrenders of railways and territory, including Kweilin, where new industries had been developed in wartime. Moreover, they were characterized by acute industrial crisis, with closures of many of the small private factories so important to Chinese war production (60 machine shops in Chungking in early 1944 alone). Just before V-J day the industries of Free China were at a virtual standstill.

2. Loss of Industrial Workers

The loss of industrial workers to Chinese resistance was proportionate to that of plant. Less than 20% of the workers in modern factories in China in 1937 were available for production and construction of new industries in the unoccupied sections of the country a year later.

Figures on the number of workers coming within the scope of the Chinese Factory Law 1/ published by the Central Factory Inspection Bureau of the National Government in 1936, listed no less than 131,628, or 72%, of the national total of 181,461 living in areas occupied by the Japanese by late 1937. The proportion would be much

_____

1. Factories using mechanical power, employing more than 30 workers and situated in areas under full Chinese administrative control (not including those in foreign concessions, or under foreign ownership).

- 2 -

greater were we to take into account all workers in foreign-owned factories or foreign-administered areas, as well as those engaged in mining, transport, and shops employing less than thirty persons. Some sources estimate the total of such workers in the coastal areas at from 1,100,000 to 1,200,000, which brings the proportion to those in all China closer to ninety than seventy per cent.

Aggravating the loss was the fact that the average of skill, habituation to industrial life, and labor productivity were much greater along the coast than elsewhere in the country. A further factor was the absolute loss represented by deaths and deprivation of employment in the battle areas themselves. The 1937-38 issue of the China Year Book concludes from "various figures" that a total of 605,000 workers became jobless in the lower Yangtze valley as a result of the war devastation, 300,000 of them in Shanghai, and 100,000 each in Wusih and Chekiang. In North China, 20,000 lost their livelihood in the blown-up Tsingtao cotton mills.

While a large proportion of the displaced workers were women and children employed in textiles, the destruction of hundreds of Shanghai machine shops cost China dearly in highly-skilled lathe operators, mechanics and fitters. All authorities agree that even the subsequent rapid reconstruction in the International Settlement, where the erection of new factories and transfer of older plants to the neutral area brought employment up from 27,000 in December 1937 to 237,000 in December 1938, did not restore the bulk of the displaced workers to industry. The China Year Book reported that "the overwhelming majority of the unemployed ... returned to their native places and became dependent on their relatives or the public."

The same process was repeated in Hankow and Canton when they fell to the Japanese in the following year, and in cities like Changsha and Chengchow which, though they then escaped occupation, were scorched by the flames of war. Finally, in 1944-45, similar disasters overtook Loyang, Kweilin and Liuchow.

3. "Boom and Bust" and the Bureaucratization of Industry

The years 1939-41 witnessed a fair measure of industrial reconstruction in the rear provinces. Just before Pearl Harbor, however, building slowed down and cutbacks and bankruptcies began in existing industries. By 1943 inflation and unfavorable government policy had brought about a state of crisis from which interior industry was never to emerge -- despite the efforts of Chinese managers and technicians and the advice of an American mission headed by Mr. Donald Nelson. The characteristic features of this crisis were declining production, diversion of private capital from industry to speculation and hoarding, and a shift in industrial ownership from private hands to those of the government and individual officials -- the so-called "bureaucratic capitalists."

A Chinese expert gave the writer the following succinct account of these developments as they applied to industries in Chungking:

"More than 200 industrial units moved from the coast in 1937-38 and were set up in the city. At first they did very well. The demand for goods was high. Food prices, and consequently wages, were low. In 1941, however, they began to suffer from inflation.

"The government gave little assistance to private plants. Its attitude was that 'industry must take care of itself,' and that 'there are too many small factories.' All it did was to buy up small plants as they went bankrupt. These were seldom returned to production though their machinery was sometimes distributed to larger units. By 1943, no less than 20 per cent of plants functioning in 1941 had gone out of business. Private industry as a whole was facing ruin.

"Afterwards, only government industries, with access to government raw material stockpiles, could look forward to continued work. The same advantages were enjoyed by provincial enterprises with 'mixed' government-private capitalization. The 'private' share in these was almost invariably monopolized by government officials functioning as individuals.

"The chief concern of all these 'government' and 'mixed' concerns was to show a money profit. Consequently both they and the government banks began to de-emphasize production and concentrate instead on cornering various raw materials and manufactured goods, which were piled up in their warehouses and released gradually as prices rose. Such tactics only aggravated the inflation. As a result, production of actual goods fell sharply from 1941 to 1943, though the money value of industrial products, recorded in official statistics, was 140 times greater.

"Private bankruptcies mounted and even affected production directly essential to war. Sixty machine-shops closed down in Chungking within three months. One arsenal suspended operations. The government's National Resources Commission, controlling practically all steel production, turned out only 10,000 tons in 1943. But even this was considered 'excessive' because costs of domestic production were 'too high.' To import American steel by air on lend-lease account was considered 'cheaper.'"

The Chairman of the Association of Factories moved to Kweilin, Kwangsi, told the newspaper Ta Kung Pao on December 23, 1943, that, while early wartime troubles had included shortages of labor and raw material, later difficulties bore all the earmarks of industrial depression. Curtailed operations had made the raw material lacks less acute, although stocks were largely hoarded and very expensive. There was a surplus of labor, resulting from large-scale dismissals of workers. Capital, however, was hard to get. Many small factories were "trying hard to carry on with their own resources, and had to sell machinery each month to meet payrolls."

The Central Government had appropriated Chinese $2,000,000,000 for loans to industry, but not a penny of this had been seen in Kweilin. In any case, applications for loans involved so much red tape and delay that inflation would wipe out much of their value before they were actually received. Planning and cost-accounting had become impossible.

- 4 -

The nation-wide tendency toward bureaucratic monopoly was over-whelming. In 1935, according to figures of the Ministry of Industries in Nanking, government holdings in Chinese industries amounted to 11% of their total capitalization. During the war and the immediate post-war months when enemy-owned enterprises were officially taken over, the figure rose to more than 70% of the whole, 2/not so much through additional investment as through shifting of control.

As to the "private sector", the China Industrial Reconstruction Corporation, headed by Dr. H. H. Kung, who was Finance Minister through most of the war, alone came to own 35% of the capital invested in the 399 largest factories in Szechuan province, the main wartime industrial base. In the two largest "mixed" (nominally half-government, half-private) provincial development companies, the Bank of China (T.V. Soong) and the Farmers' Bank (CC group of the Kuomintang) came to own 68% of the Kweichow Enterprise Company. Dr. H. H. Kung was the leading "private" investor in the Hunan Industrial Company. Chen Li-fu, "CC" group leader, acquired heavy interests in the West China Reconstruction Company, the China Industrial and Mining Reconstruction Corporation, the Ta Hwa enterprises and other major wartime concerns.

It must be noted that government organizations and officials were throughout interested in control of supplies rather than in production. Almost half of the U. S. loan of 1942, for example, was devoted to buying and storing Japanese goods from the occupied areas, while an infinitesimal portion went into industry.

Already depressed for almost three years, industries established in the deep rear during the war were almost entirely abandoned in the scramble to get back to the recovered coast after V-J day. The earlier hope that they would serve as seeds of future industrialization in the interior did not materialize. Although much of their plant remained, very few of these enterprises had re-opened even by 1947. Having been founded by temporarily sojourning government organizations and private individuals, without any real effort to attract local investment and participation, they did not survive the departure of these elements.

All in all, the self-sacrificing and promising efforts of the early war period were virtually nullified after 1942. Monopoly increased, but production fell. Far fewer wheels were turning in the interior, and far fewer workers were employed, at the end of the war than in the middle years. This applied to places where there was no physical destruction as well as to others. Although the government, and its senior officials "privately", had come to own most of industry, they did not use the resources at their disposal to preserve wartime gains. All that continued to function in the rear provinces were the new railways and highways, which were in poor condition.

The fortunes of labor in wartime Kuomintang China were largely conditioned by the ruling party's industrial policies and their results, and still more by the fact that the government and its officials were rapidly becoming the direct employers of most workers in Chinese factories.

_____

2. Ta Kung Pao, Chungking, June 1, 1946.

CHAPTER II

HOURS AND WAGES

The wage-and-hour picture in the industries of wartime interior China was extremely confused. It varied with location, types of enterprise, and the history of the individual factory (whether newly established or migrant, originating in Shanghai or in other cities.) Two constant features were, however, evident as regards wages. Firstly, with the progress of the inflation, the all-money wage tended to be replaced by a mixed wage, including such items as staple foods, quarters, special allowances, etc. Secondly, the trend of real wages was sharply downward. There was no industry in China at the war's end in which real wages (and total real earnings) had not declined by at least 50% from the pre-war level, already among the lowest in the world.

1. Chungking

Since it was the chief wartime industrial center, we shall begin our survey with Chungking.

Hours: According to an article which appeared in Kweilin in April 1942: 1/

"In most factories in Chungking, the working time is at least 12 hours. The workers arrive at 5:30 a.m., have a half-hour break at 11:30 and leave the plant at six.

"Government regulations lay down a working day of eight hours, with three hours permissible overtime, which may be extended to six under certain circumstances."

A Chungking investigator wrote some eighteen months later: 2/

"Owing to differences of conditions and customs, working hours are uneven. Generally speaking they range from 10 to 16 hours a day. Although certain factories fix a nominal working day of 8 hours, night work brings the average to ten or more. Most workers in state and military factories work longer, 11 hours or more on the average."

He gave the following detailed figures on some of the larger government "mixed ownership" and private plants.

---

1. "Study of Chinese Industrial Labor", by Hsu Sheng-tze, in Wen Hua Tsa Chih, (Culture Magazine), Kweilin, April 25, 1942.

2. "Conditions of Workers and Employees in Chungking", by Shu Hwa (pseud.), unpublished MS., December 1943.

Table 2

Hours of Work in Chungking Factories, 1943

Plant	Hours
Ordnance Ministry, 22nd Arsenal	16
Mei Yi Silk Factory (private)	14
China Reconstruction Electrical Engineering Factory	13
Hsing Kuo Company	13
Talai National Reconstruction Factory	12½
Ordnance Ministry, 20th Arsenal	12
China Enterprise Co. Steel Mill	12
Szechuan Sericulture Company	12
Minsheng Construction Company	11½
Experimental Ceramic Factory	11½
Ordnance Ministry, 10th Arsenal	11
Ordnance Ministry, 5th Arsenal	11
Some War Ministry plants	8
Municipal Power Station	8

The investigator further remarked that "technical workers in both state and private factories are willing to do night work owing to the fact that wages received from daytime work alone cannot maintain their livelihood."

In simpler industries, such as glass blowing and electric battery-making, where the piece-work system was adopted, workers had no fixed hours but had to turn in a daily production quota.

Composition of Earnings: Under inflationary conditions, the mere statement of a money wage is meaningless unless a great many other factors are taken into account. Some figures given by Shu Hwa for the period October-November 1942 show the variation in money payments and the composition of a worker's total earnings in a few Chungking enterprises. They illustrate his statement that "while wages received by technical workers in the state factories are far lower than in the private factories, other terms of treatment are better."

Table 3

Composition of Earnings in Some Government, Mixed and Private-owned Plants in Chungking, 1943

Plant or Industry	Monthly wage of highest-paid worker	Monthly wage of lowest-paid worker	Factory also supplied
Ordnance Ministry Arsenals (government)	$600 av.	$300 av.	Factory meals for $50 per month; also rice for family use, coal, oil and rent at nominal rates.
Mei Yi Silk Factory (private)	2,100	1,575	Factory meals at $12 per month only.

Plant or Industry	Monthly wage of highest-paid worker	Monthly wage of lowest-paid worker	Factory also supplied
Hsing Kuo Machine Shops (mixed)	1,620	960	Food and lodging for worker
National Reconstruction Machine Shops (mixed)	1,100	790	Food and lodging for worker for $10 monthly pay deduction.

In this situation the relative attractiveness of the factory for the worker depended more on the subsidiary services and allowances offered in each case than on the "take home pay."

Arsenal workers, for instance, could buy 3 tou of rice each month for their own sustenance at $3 a tou, which was only a small fraction of the open-market price. They were also allowed additional rice for family use at $6 a tou, likewise a very low price. This privilege alone was worth more than a money wage differential of several hundred inflated dollars. The word "lodging" covered a multitude of qualitative gradations from a bunk in a barrack to a detached cabin in which a family might live. "Food" covered a range that was almost equally wide.

These factors cannot appear in any brief table but they were decisive in causing the worker to prefer one employer over another and made a very great difference to his additional expenditures.

Purchasing Power: A Chinese monograph on "Wartime Wages", written in the summer of 1943 by Mr. Su Chuan-po of the National Mobilization Council of the Central Government, provided a very clear analysis of the purchasing power of wages. Mr. Su quoted the following index figures issued by the Szechuan Provincial Government Reconstruction Bureau, the Municipal Bureau of Social Affairs and the Statistical Bureau of the Ministry of Economics.

Table 4

Chungking Wholesale and Retail Price Indices, July-August 1942
June 1937 = 100

	Gen'l Index	Food	Clothing	Fuel	Metal & Elec.	Elec. Fixt.	Bldg. Materials	Misc.
Wholesale	5081.8	4080.6	5720.2	5872.2	11332.1		3730.5	4771.9
Retail	5304.4	4165.2	8269.8	4504.7	-		-	6958.0

Table 5
Actual Earnings and Cost of Living of Industrial Workers in Chungking
July-August 1942
June 1937 = 100

	Actual Earnings		Cost of Living
General Index	2055.6	General Index	4318.71
Machinists	1925.7	Food	4155.41
Printers	2152.8	Clothing	9720.56

	Actual Earnings		Cost of Living
Flour millers	2393.8	Fuel	7084.04
Textile workers	2408.0	Rent	1134.57
		Miscellaneous	4529.96

The present writer is not familiar with the exact data from which these indices were computed. It must be said that lack of coordination and unified standards among various statistical organs were extreme in wartime Kuomintang China, where different ministries, provincial governments, departments and municipalities were apt to hire a group of university graduates and let them go on by themselves in accordance with any system they preferred and with a degree of thoroughness dependent entirely on their energies and the usually meager budgets allowed. This had its positive as well as its negative side since the absence of uniform control also made it difficult to engage in systematic distortion.

So far as the basic situation was concerned, however, the above figures undoubtedly give a true idea. The tremendous and widening discrepancy between earnings and the growing cost of living of industrial workers in wartime China has been remarked on by all observers.

The fact that the growth of wages in heavy industries -- those most essential to the waging of war -- lagged behind that in light industry has also been widely noted.

Real Wages: The trend of real wages is shown by the following table taken from the regular mimeographed reports published by the Ministry of Social Affairs (for restricted circulation).

Table 6

Wage Indices of Industrial Workers in Chungking, Feb.-Mar. 1943

(First half of 1937 = 100)

Description	Rates of Wages		Actual Earnings		Real Wages	
	February	March	February	March	February	March
General Index	1557.6	1556.7	3065.2	3244.9	43.5	48.5
Machinists	1444.9	1433.7	2960.2	3123.9	42.0	46.7
Printers	4212.5	4270.3	3507.6	3823.5	49.8	57.1
Flour Millers	8129.6	9338.2	3581.9	3825.7	50.8	57.2
Textile Wkrs.	1695.6	1691.2	3203.8	3417.1	45.6	51.1

The main information in this table is that real wages were slashed by half in the first five years of the war.

The other figures show the effect of the differing wage systems in the respective industries. The highest wage index is that for flour millers in March, 9338.2. The lowest is that for machinists in the same month, 1433.7. But the corresponding actual earning indices are 3825.7 for millers and 3123.9 for machinists, a much smaller discrepancy. This corroborates statements already quoted on the composition of wartime wages and the greater extra allowances in government-operated industries. But it also confirms that wartime Kuomintang China never followed the lead of other countries in increasing the relative reward for the skills most essential to national survival. The real wages index for flour millers, who are not essential food-processors in rice-eating Szechuan province, stood at 57.2, in 1943 as compared with 1937. That of machinists fell to 46.7 during the same period.

The machinist was almost always a migrant from the more developed coast and an older man, often with a family to support. It is probable that the real return for his labor declined even more than these figures indicate, because the cost-of-living figures are much more accurate with regard to quantity of consumption than with regard to quality. Thus, a skilled worker in heavy industry who had lived in a room with a wooden floor and electric light in a brick house in Shanghai might have had to content himself with a corner of a dormitory, or a mud-floored, unlighted bamboo shed in Chungking. Such factors go far to explain the moods, working habits and high degree of mobility of skilled workers in the wartime interior which is discussed in other sections of this study.

The following table also from Ministry of Social Affairs and Chungking Municipality sources, shows the real wage position of industrial and non-industrial workers in the city between 1937 and 1943.

Table 7

Real Wages in Chungking, 1937 to March 1943

(January-June 1937 = 100)

Factory Workers	1937	1938	1939	1940	1941	March 1942	March 1943
Machinists	101.7	166.7	114.2	77.1	53.1	41.1	46.7
Printers	98.1	123.6	113.1	85.3	59.6	54.7	57.1
Flour millers	108.4	150.4	141.6	92.7	51.0	58.6	57.2
Textile workers	99.7	115.1	127.7	81.6	64.6	62.2	51.1
Handicraft Workers							
Carpenters	98.2	122.1	158.8	187.1	98.0	90.4	94.4
Stone-cutters	104.3	194.1	347.9	208.4	126.4	210.8	231.1
House builders	102.7	108.1	165.9	141.5	102.7	87.0	90.6
Coolies							
Rickshaw pullers	100.3	306.4	437.3	254.2	163.3	113.3	102.3
Sedan chair-bearers	97.7	116.7	148.7	130.8	65.8	47.1	47.0
River ferry men	101.4	110.6	111.5	98.3	99.6	83.8	69.8
River boatmen	111.2	140.7	225.0	153.1	110.8	122.6	98.6
Stevedores	102.5	119.9	117.3	88.0	61.6	56.0	49.3
Cart pullers	98.3	232.5	247.3	166.3	84.4	83.4	66.4
Water carriers	96.0	137.6	151.3	127.1	60.9	54.5	50.3

The comparison here is even more striking. Handicraft workers and coolies maintained their standards better than industrial workers. It must be remembered, however, that these standards were very low in Szechuan and that they remained low; also, the trades were largely seasonal and part of the old-style worker's wage was generally pocketed by a contractor. The decline of the factory worker's income brought him to a level very close to that of the toilers in the backward interior.

The years 1938-39 were Chungking's most prosperous period. The continued relative prosperity of the stone-cutters, who were tightly organized in a feudal guild, was due to the incessant building of air raid shelters. Boatmen, builders and rickshaw coolies all enjoyed a temporary "boom" as a result of the city's increased population, but by 1943 they were falling behind. Stevedores, who worked under a barbarous contract system, enjoyed no good times at all. The situation of cart-pullers was probably unfavorably affected by the influx of motor transport and by the fact that much of their work was done for official and military organizations with whom one could not bargain successfully.

2. Kunming

Hours: Kunming labor standards were just as varied as those in Chungking. The report of the Municipal Social Affairs Bureau for March 1943 revealed the following situation as regards working time in big and small factories in the city.

Table 8
Hours of Work in Kunming Factories Employing 30 or more persons, March 1943.

		Hours worked during month by:			
	Official hrs. worked daily	Skilled Workers	Semi-skilled Wkrs.	Unskilled Workers	No. of workers in Factory
1. Yung Kwang Glass Works (Private)	12	375	248	240	30
2. Yaolung Electric (Nat'l Power Plant Gov't)	10	316	321	280	167
3. Central Machine Works (Nat'l. Gov't.)	9	287	287	220	1,639
4. Chao Pao Printing Co. (Private)	9	279	-	234	63
5. Yunnan Spinning & Weaving Mill (Provincial)	9	252	252	221	1,128
6. Yunnan Silk Corporation (Nat'l. Gov't.)	10	238	280	280	93
7. Central Chemical Works (Nat'l Gov't.)	9	230	230	265	127
8. Kunming Copper Refinery (Nat'l. Gov't.)	8	226	239	237	181
9. Kunming Electric Power Plant	9	225	225	225	249
10. Yunnan Printing Works (Provincial)	8	218	218	208	158
11. Central Elec. Works (Nat'l. Gov't.)	9	213	220	212	738
12 Yunnan Leather Factory	8	208	-	214	123
13. Yunnan Tobacco Company	8	200	201	197	151
14. Yunnan Scientific Glass Works (Private)	8-11	192	198	207	32

- 11 -

Working time in two of the 14 factories listed exceeded 300 hours a month. It was over 250 hours a month for all or part of the workers in five others. Every plant showed more than 200 hours for at least one category of workers. Out of the total of 4,879 workers investigated, no less than 3,247 were in plants that worked over 250 hours monthly.

The complete Social Affairs Bureau table also noted the average paid overtime in each factory. The highest figures given were 24 hours per skilled worker during the month in Factory No. 1, 18 hours per semi-skilled worker in Factories No. 4, 9 and 14, and 25 hours per unskilled man in Factory No. 14, which was not working at full capacity. Persons employed in Factory No. 4, with a nine-hour day, worked 279 hours and recorded no overtime, indicating continuous labor without a single holiday during the 31-day month. Factory No. 1, with 375 hours for skilled workers, likewise reported no overtime. The workers in these two plants were on the job for more than twelve hours every day in March 1943 - at regular rates of pay.

Nominal Wages and Actual Earnings: The wages and actual earnings of workers in the same fourteen factories showed a variety of systems of computation, as will be seen below:

Table 9

Wages and Actual Earnings in Fourteen Kunming Factories, March 1943

Factory	Skilled Workers		Semi-skilled Workers		Unskilled Workers		Method of Payment for Overtime
	Nominal Wage	Actual Earnings	Nominal Wage	Actual Earnings	Nominal Wage	Actual Earnings	
1	$600	$1,060	$570	$ 646	$ 450	$510	Unreported
2	201	1,643	129	1,268	96	906	Double pay
3	240	2,839	100	2,400	90	1,167	7 hrs. paid as full 9-hr. day
4	440	890	-	-	200	200	Double pay
5	63	734	59	304	50	227	Double pay
6	150	1,900	70	970	40	870	Double pay
7	540	1,073	450	878	120	504	4 hrs. paid as full 9-hr. day
8	108	926	65	563	60	547	6 hrs. paid as full 8-hr. day
9	167	1,232	90	875	80	688	Double pay
10	305	844	259	510	280	346	5 hrs. paid as full 8-hr. day
11	180	833	86	741	58	585	2½ hrs. paid as full 9-hr. day
12	707	740	-	-	382	407	Unreported
13	1,170	1,170	770	700	800	800	Unreported
14	2,000	2,000	1,000	1,000	500	500	Unreported

Notes: Workers eat in factory and pay for food at factory rate.

The term "actual earnings", as used above, includes total value received by the worker in wages, overtime pay, allowances, bonus if any, etc. All the above figures were supplied to the Social Affairs Bureau by the respective factories. They may or may not have been checked by Bureau investigators.

Shih Kuo-heng, in China Enters the Machine Age, reported the development of the hourly wage system in wartime government-owned factories in Kunming. This was a method of getting the worker, rather than the factory, to pay for all interruptions of production including those due to air raids. Computation of such wages was complicated and aroused the distrust of the worker. It inconvenienced him by deferring the day of payment, and enraged him because he often received less cash than he had expected for reasons that were not sufficiently explained.

In the Central Electric Works (Factory No. 11 in our table), which Mr. Shih studied, fines were imposed for tardiness and leaving early. The penalty for absence without permission was double the wage for the working time lost. Deductions were also made each pay day for goods purchased by the workers in the factory canteen. On the other hand, workers who had been neither absent nor tardy for a month were given a bonus equivalent to two days' extra pay.

Mr. Shih stressed that wages for the factory's work week of six nine-hour days were not sufficient to support the worker, who therefore sought overtime work. In emergencies he had to borrow money from the factory's loan department. Money so borrowed was repaid by further deductions from the fortnightly wage.

Mr. Shih concluded his consideration of wages with a statement which suggested a good deal more than it explained. He wrote:

"After the workers have worked additional hours their wage approximate the normal wage which does not include additional hours. (According to statements made by the management) although the workers may work three additional hours, totalling twelve hours a day, they normally accomplish nine hours' work.

"The real purpose of introducing the additional work is not so much to speed up production, but is first, as the management explained to me, to keep the workers out of trouble by occupying their time in the evenings; second, owing to the rapid progress of inflation, the real wage of the workers is decreasing; by giving them additional work they receive more money.

"The effect, however, is to lessen the workers' interest in efficiency. Some told me that work which could have been accomplished during the day is postponed until ... evening. The twelve hour day decreases the efficiency of the three additional hours as well as of the whole day's work. This method of making up workers' earnings seems undesirable both from the point of view of the factory and of the worker."

We may therefore infer that the "nine-hour day" in this factory was really purely fictitious in 1940, when Mr. Shih made his study, as was the reported system of calculating overtime. Keeping this in mind, let us look back at Table 9, which refers to the situation in 1945. At that time Factory No. 11 reported only 213, 220 and 212 hours spent on the job by respective categories of workers, which allows for no overtime and seems credible in the light of the general curtailment of production then affecting all interior industry. But such an explanation does not jibe with the factory's assertion that it was reckoning overtime at the rate of a full 9-hour day wage for every 2½ hours, suggesting a much greater demand for extra labor than three years earlier, when Mr. Shih reported a rate of only time and a half for week-day overtime and double time on Sundays. Mr. Shih's information was secured at first hand and can be trusted. One suspects, therefore, that the officials of the Central Electric Works who supplied the 1943 figures to the Social Affairs Bureau either "rigged" them for some purpose or simply told the investigators the first thing that came into their minds.

Real Wages: The writer has no detailed real wage figures for Kunming such as were available to him for Chungking. Mr. Shih's testimony is that real wages in Kunming industry had already begun to fall in 1940. He quotes the following figures to illustrate the decline in relation to the pre-war wage level in Shanghai, from which city most of the workers he studied in the Central Electric Works originally came:

Table 10

Percentage of Total Earnings Spent on Food
by Industrial Workers With Families

Shanghai (pre-war)	53.2% (a)
Kunming, 1940 (skilled only)	74.1% (b)

(a) From Standard of Living of Shanghai Laborers, published by the Shanghai Municipal Government (quoted by Mr. Shih, who gives no date.).

(b) Calculated by Mr. Shih himself in China Enters the Machine Age, pp. 79, for skilled workers with families in the Central Electric Works.

Previous to the war, the highest food expenditure reported by any category of workers was 71.2% by ricksha coolies in Peiping. In other words, the wartime skilled worker in a "first class" government-owned factory in Kunming in 1940 was worse off in this respect than one of the lowest categories of urban unskilled labor in pre-war China.

The further decline of real wages in Kunming after 1940 can be assumed from the fact that the Kunming price level was fairly consistently above that in Chungking, and that Chungking workers, whose average real wages had fallen to 48.5% of pre-war by March 1943, showed no significant tendency to migrate to industries in Kunming.

3. Kewilin, Liuchow, and Hengyang

Hours: A questionnaire sent out by Miss Liu Wu-kou to enterprises along the war-built Hunan-Kwangsi railway was answered by five heavy industry plants employing 2,934 workers. Of these workers 922 had a 9-hour day and 2,012 worked ten hours or more. Sunday was a holiday in most of the plants.

Miss Liu also gave the average daily working time in textile workshops in Kewilin during 1943 as 10 hours, and the average number of working days per year as 306 for male workers and 310 for women. In 37 cigarette-making enterprises in the same city the average daily time was 8 hours, but some shops worked 350 days a year.

Nominal Wages and Actual Earnings: The factories queried reported earnings for skilled workers varying widely in composition. The biggest plant, the Kweilin arsenal, which employed 1,831 persons, paid a basic monthly wage of $700 for skilled and $590 for unskilled workers but also provided free food, lodging, light and two suits of clothing a year. The second largest, the government-owned Kweilin Radio Factory, with 782 workers, paid $1,400 monthly for skilled men and $900 for unskilled, but provided no free facilities at all. A small private steel plant at Liuchow, with 125 workers, paid an average wage of $1,000 a month to skilled hands and $700 to unskilled, with supplementary monthly cost-of-living allowances of $500 in both categories and an annual bonus of 20% of the company's net profit divided at the end of the year among all workers employed throughout that period.

One small textile factory in Hengyang reported a very low basic wage, $450 monthly for skilled and $300 for unskilled workers, free lodging and food for skilled workers only and a substitute monthly allowance of $500 for the unskilled and an annual bonus of "twice the annual basic wage at the end of each year of uninterrupted work." This arrangement actually amounted to withholding of a substantial part of the wages, which benefitted the company in two ways, by increasing its available operating capital during the year and preventing labor mobility. Workers leaving during the year forfeited the withheld wages.

The income of 699 workers employed in the cigarette industry was as follows:

Table 11.

Earnings of 699 Cigarette Workers in Kweilin, December 1943

Workshops	Workers		Income (Incl. Wages & Allowances)		
			Lowest	Highest	Average
37	Men	352	$300	$2,125	$1,575
	Women	228	250	1,900	1,275
	Children	119	315	675	515
	Total	699			

Note: Workers feed in shop, paying moderate canteen prices.

Real Wages: The real-wage situation of workers in the Kweilin area can be seen from a comparison of pre-war wages and prices with those prevailing at the time of the investigation.

Table 12.

Money Wages of Kweilin Workers, 1937-43

	Machinists			Wages Printers			Textiles			Retail Price Index (1937=100)
	Low-est	High-est	Aver-age	Low-est	High-est	Aver-age	Low-est	High-est	Aver-age	
Pre-War (a)	$20	$140	$45	$15	$30	$20	$3	$11	-	100.00
Dec.1943 (b)	60	3,000	2,500	300	2,000	800	40	450	$300	18,291.50

(a) Pre-war wages from Kwangsi Provincial Government Yearbook.
(b) Figures by Liu Wu-kou.

In all cases covered, both wartime and pre-war, the factories supplied dormitory space and food. The worker, however, invariably had to eke out factory meals by his own purchases if he was not to suffer from malnutrition. While the average wage of machinists rose 55 times, that of printers 40 times and that of textile workers 30 or more times, retail prices jumped 182 times. Even if we take into account the very substantial increase in wartime allowances, it is clear that the real wages of workers in the Hunan-Kwangsi area, like those in Chungking and Kunming, had fallen to considerably less than half of those before 1937.

The meaning of this can be grasped from a consideration of pre-war (1933) budget studies of Kwangsi workers. 3/ Of 353 families of men employed in provincial government factories, where conditions relatively "good", more than 60% then reported expenditures in excess of income. An average of 55% of these expenditures went for food, with 10% each for rent, clothing and fuel. The average sum of money spent by a family each month was around $40.

In December 1943 the retail price index by items (1937 = 100) was: food, 144,662.60; clothing, 27,714.60; fuel, 24,174.50. The general index, as already given, was 18,291.50. If a family had spent $40 in 1933 (or in 1937 when prices were not much higher), it would need $7,316.60 in December 1943 to live on the same level.

An average machine-shop worker in Kwangsi in 1933 received a wage of $45 a month. He needed to spend $46.30 to support himself and three dependents, divided as follows:

Table 13.

Family Budget of a Machinist in Kweilin, 1933

Food	$24.90
Clothing	4.90
Rent	3.70
Fuel	5.00
Others	9.90

An average machinist in 1943 received $2,500 a month. If his family situation was the same as that of his pre-war confrere, to

3. From Kwangsi Provincial Government Yearbook.

maintain a household on the same scale would cost him:

Table 14.
Family Budget Needs of a Machinist in Kweilin, 1943

Food	$3,602.12
Clothing	1,848.00
Fuel	1,208.72
Others (incl.rent)	1,457.36
Total	$8,116.20

4. Kweichow Province

There was no modern industry in Kweichow before the war. After 1938 a number of plants were established there by the National Resources Commission and the Kweichow Provincial Government. The writer has no detailed statistics on this area, but scattered figures indicate that wage and hour conditions there paralleled those in state enterprises in Chungking, Kunming and Kweilin.

An article by Ting Tao-chien printed in the organ of the Chinese Association of Labor 4/ in 1943 listed nineteen factories operating under the aegis of the provincial government holding company -- the Kweichow Enterprise Corporation -- and employing a total of 2,658 persons.

The article contained the following remarks on the wage system:

"Wages in Kweichow are of two kinds. They are paid in goods, such as rice and flour, or purely in money. The latter is increasingly practiced, especially in places with good communications.

"The wage period varies. The traditional annual wage, though now rare, still exists. The commonest form is the monthly wage. The daily wage exists for comparatively well-paid workers on short term jobs. Computation of wages by the hour, as for skilled workers' overtime, is rare.

"Piece work wages have been introduced in newly established industries (for instance in the printing factory). Rates are determined by skill, seniority, social custom and the bargaining power of labor, as well as by supply and demand.

"There are no labor unions. Conflicts are settled by compromise. Working hours and the treatment of labor need to be formally regulated."

5. The Kuomintang Northwest

Industry in the Kuomintang Northwest was concentrated in Sian, Paochi and Lanchow. Of the 106 factories working in Lanchow in 1942,

---

4. Chungkuo Laotung, (Chinese Labor) Vol. IV (1943), No. 5.

only 25 had been in existence before the war. Most of them were officially owned or controlled. The Central and provincial governments owned 71.9% of industrial investment in the city. 5/ Kinds of industry, in the order of their importance, included flour, paper, glass, matches, soap, textile, leather and metals. The neglect of heavy industry can be seen from the fact that metal and machine works represented only 3% of the total capital in Lanchow factories. Flour mills accounted for 34% of the investment, textiles for 16% and leather for 15%.

In October 1942, the total number of workers employed in Lanchow's 106 plants was 1,526, showing the small size of individual units. Working hours were from 9 to 10 daily. Wages were generally paid monthly. Most factories lodged their workers.

The Lanchow Industrial Survey gives the following table:

Table 15.

Wages of Factory Workers in Lanchow, October 1942
(In Chinese national currency)

Branch of Industry	Highest	Lowest	Average
Leather	$750.00	$200.00	$475.00
Spinning & weaving			
Workers	300.00	150.00	225.00
Apprentices	50.60	00.00	40.00
Medical supplies	300.00	150.00	225.00
Glass	260.00	200.00	230.00
Machine & metal	400.00	30.00	215.00
Flour	200.00	180.00	190.00
Paper	200.00	180.00	190.00
Chemical (scrap, etc.)	120.00	40.00	80.00
Match	320.00	120.00	220.00
Printing	280.00	30.00	155.00
Tobacco	500.00	70.00	285.00
General Averages	$306.67	$117.50	$212.08

These figures only show the relationship of wages in different industries. A comparison with contemporary wages in other parts of China, however, indicates that rates in the Northwest were even lower than elsewhere. In the year covered by the above table (1942) wages in Chungking averaged 1½ to 4 times those in Lanchow. The cost of living in the capital was somewhat higher but by nothing like so much. This explained Northwest industry's inability to attract and retain skilled workers from the coast, of which the Industrial Survey complained bitterly.

---

5. All figures in this section are from the Lanchow Industrial Survey, compiled by the Lanchow Industrial Experimental Station of the Ministry of Economics, the Research Cabinet of the Kansu Provincial Bank, the Bank of Communications (Lanchow Branch) and the Construction Department of the Kansu Provincial Government, October, 1942.

6. Conclusion

There was a sufficient lack of uniformity in wartime wages in different parts of China, and at different times, to cause a high degree of labor mobility. The general level of wages was constantly falling. After 1942, real wages all over China were less than half of what they had been in 1937. This discredits the many loose statements made in wartime Kuomintang apologetics that industrial workers did not suffer to any considerable degree from the inflation, which was pictured as wreaking hardship chiefly on the salaried middle class.

Wartime hours were generally little different from those usual in pre-war coastal factories. The main exception was in some branches of the ordnance industry, which lengthened their working time to 16 hours daily. Some factories working with local interior labor also had a sixteen-hour day -- and no holidays of any kind.

In plants with an official day of only eight or nine hours, and which allowed weekly or fortnightly rest-days, the workers themselves were compelled by low wages to seek overtime and Sunday work, either in their regular places of employment or elsewhere.

CHAPTER III.

MIGRANT SKILLED WORKERS

1. Factory Removals

Skilled workers were a rare and precious asset to China at war. There had been hardly any, before the hostilities, in the interior of the country. After July 1937 efforts were made to attract them inland from the relatively industrialized coast, and to provide facilities for their transport and placement.

Over 12,000 such workers were actually brought to the government's new bases in the first fifteen months of the war (1937-38), before the loss of Hankow and Canton. Most of them came by special boats and trains with the movable equipment of enterprises in which they had previously worked -- predominantly state-owned arsenals and other defense plants. A very few privately-owned textile and other light-industrial factories were also moved. The total number of industrial units transferred to the rear up to October 29, 1938, was officially stated to be 229, with machinery weighing 45,306 tons. Workers participated enthusiastically in solving the technical problems involved in shifting plant, guarded it en route, and sometimes carried it on their own backs. Particularly notable in this respect was the voluntary workers' "Factory Removing Movement" set up for the evacuation of Hankow.

After the government established itself in Chungking in late 1938, there was considerable confusion in industrial policy. Despite Chiang Kai-shek's declarations that the war would be protracted and fought out to the end, the ideas of possible defeat, or of half-way compromise with Japan, was present in many official minds. Although facilities for importing machinery still existed (by way of the Indo-China railway) and workers could be transported both along this route and through many gaps in the front, efforts made to utilize these possi-bilities were half-hearted. Both the government and private indus-trialists invested funds and energy in building new plants in the International Settlement of Shanghai and the British colony of Hongkong (to which some old Shanghai factories also were removed), reliance being placed on Anglo-American protection. This was the easy way out, offering what seemed to be the greatest security for opera-tions and profits. Instead of productive personnel and equipment, it was the products themselves that were brought in. Industrial construc-tion in the interior suffered accordingly, being confined, in practice, to some development in the output of arms, fuels and telecommunica-tions equipment.

Political trends also had their effect. The patriotic indoctrina-tion of workers in the initial war period, and the organization of the "Factory Removing Movement", were largely the work of democratic non-Kuomintang elements. From 1939 on these elements were virtually outlawed. Much official repression and ingenuity was thereafter applied to isolate them from the people and from effective participation in the war effort, whether at the front or in the rear.

2. Conditions of Workers Migration

In the next period, the Industrial and Mining Readjustment Commission of the Ministry of Economics, the Chinese Association of Labor and some private factory owners continued to interest themselves in importing needed workers from the occupied coastal cities. Contact work was entrusted largely to the underground Kuomintang party organizations and secret service. During the first flush of the united front the hostility of the workers toward these historic enemies of their welfare and liberties had not played any great part. With the whittling down of unity it reasserted itself once more. The estrangement was aggravated by corruption and dishonest promises to the workers on the part of many agents.

Shih Kuo-heng described the operation of these factors in an excellent but necessarily very carefully phrased study. 1/ He wrote:

"Before the fall of Indo-China, laborers recruited in Shanghai were sent to Haiphong in Indo-China by steamboat (steerage) and then to Kunming by train (fourth class). From the beginning to the end, this way involved many social difficulties and the cost is considerable. Under the peculiar circumstances of Shanghai's Settlements the factory representative found it wise not to advertise anything openly. Recruitment had to go on through private individuals and organizations under cover, so to speak.

"From tales of black labor recruiting in the past, Shanghai laborers are naturally suspicious of such behavior. This provides good occasions for middlemen to exact a commission as a condition for their safe introduction. One private agreement even provided that the laborers pay from 7 to 20% of their monthly wage to the introducer from the date of their starting work onwards. This agreement was responsible for the ultimate failure of workers to come to Kunming."

Japan's seizure of both Hongkong and the Shanghai International Settlement at the outset of the Pacific War in 1941 meant the total loss of the Kuomintang's investment there and the bankruptcy of the concept that had given rise to it. There was now no question of salvaging equipment from these cities and much of the rear economy tied to it came to depend on the output of plants fully controlled by the Japanese (hence the development of "smuggling" into an approved trade with occupied zones in which the enemy held all the trumps).

Skilled workers were the only productive force that could possibly be saved from the ruin. Some traveled inland after 1941 under their own power or with employers' assistance, especially from Hongkong. The Industrial and Mining Readjustment Commission and the Chinese Association of Labor also tried to remedy previous neglect in assisting migrants, the latter successfully appealing to American trade unions for necessary funds.

---

1. The Labour Situation in Wartime Interior China, Yenching-Yunnan Station of Sociological Research, Kunming, January 1943. (This was the preliminary study for his China Enters the Machine Age.)

Very little was achieved, however, because recruitment procedures were not revised, and the workers were more distrustful than ever, through much bitter experience. By 1942 there was a serious industrial crisis in the interior itself. Unemployment appeared and grew. A counter-movement of skilled workers back to the occupied areas began under economic pressure and did not cease till the war's end. Although no figures are available, it is the general opinion that this movement balanced, and even over-balanced, all immigration after 1943.

3. Defects In Utilization And Planning

Official appeals addressed the skilled worker as a most important person for the war economy. He was exhorted, as a patriot, to undertake the arduous and sometimes dangerous trip to the interior, which often involved leaving his family for an indefinite period. But he had only to make the first steps of the journey to find himself regarded not as an honorable participant in national resistance but as an object of chicanery and exploitation.

This impression was not dispelled if he overcame all hurdles, as many did, and came to the rear. Here again he encountered bureaucracy, indifference, and bad treatment. Worst of all, the worker frequently discovered that nobody had any use for his abilities. Although many paper plans were drawn up, the industries for which he was recruited often never got under way, or stopped soon after they began. The official organs responsible for placing him did not function properly. He generally had to look for a job - in strange places where he had no connections -- by the ordinary method of personal introduction. Once on the job, he was given no protection by official organs or trade unions. If he became unemployed, he faced starvation.

The only workers who were actually guaranteed employment, and that only in the first years of the war, were those in the arsenals. Certain other workers in state enterprises, as for instance the railways, had been evacuated en masse and never went off the payrolls. These received maintenance even when they were not used. But because of rigid departmentalism they were not made available to other industries unless they sacrificed their seniority and sought outside employment themselves.

An economic survey made under the auspices of the Kwangsi Provincial Government in 1943 described one group of railwaymen living in Liuchow. They were receiving an allowance of CN $1,500.00 a month, which was somewhat below the prevailing skilled-labor wage. They "did not work, because there was nothing to do, and had to provide their own food."

The conditions found by workers who went to the northwestern provinces in 1943-44 were described as follows:

"The Industrial and Mining Readjustment Commission have offices in Paochi and Sian which are supposed to help private industry in various ways, including procurement and placement of skilled workers. But in fact they are only interested in the Yumen Oil fields, in Kansu, a government enterprise.

"As regards conditions, government industries are under military law. In private plants wages are higher but there is no security, workers who have come hundreds of miles being laid off anytime things get slack. Only government unions, under the San Min Chu I Youth Corps, are allowed. They teach the workers to be loyal to the party and to work as hard as possible, but do nothing for them and are in close contact with the owners and managers. The Ministry of Social Affairs does not help the workers either. It used its welfare funds to open 'Worker's Restaurants' (Lao Kung Shih T'ang) and hostels, which are good enough but so high priced that no workers can use them. Government and factory officials and foremen eat and sleep there.

"Lately (early 1944) there has been much unemployment among skilled workers through the closing of factories or reduction of schedules. Many spend their time cutting and selling firewood. Some are drifting back to the occupied territories." 2/

An informant from Southeast China stated in late 1943:

"In 1938-39 there was a boom and competition for workers. Now there is unemployment. Even truck drivers come to ask for jobs where a couple of years ago you had to beg them to work for you. After the fall of Hongkong, skilled workers came into the interior, moved from place to place, could not find anything, so made their way to Shanghai. Private business is in a bad way. Honest enterprises unconnected with some high official cannot survive." 2/

4. Labor Poaching and Mobility

While newly-arriving workers had difficulty in finding jobs, there was great mobility among those already employed. This became such a serious problem that many local and national decrees were promulgated to cope with it. 3/

In 1939-41, a major cause of mobility was labor poaching. This was partly connected with the chaotic situation with regard to placement of skilled workers, discussed in the preceding section. Factories with openings for such men did not know how to find them, and tried to entice them from other enterprises. An official of the National Resources Commission in Kunming told the author:

"The Central Machine Works here needs mechanics, but private plants offer more wages. The only way we can get a man is by asking one we already employ to find a friend who may have come with him from the coast, and who may be working in some other place."

_____

2. From author's notes of interviews with informed individuals in the area concerned.

3. See Chapter VII, below.

Private factory-owners, on the other hand, complained that government plants attracted their workers by promising greater immunity from military conscription.

An equally important cause, however, was the dissatisfaction of workers with wages and job conditions, and with the absence of satisfactory procedure for adjusting grievances. Despite administrative enactments tying workers to their places of employment, large numbers were constantly on the road, going to places where they heard things were better. Liu Wu-kou wrote in 1943:

> "The workers in Liuchow (Kwangsi) machine shops have a high degree of mobility. 'Going to Chungking' is the universal aim. Since industry in Chungking began to decline, however, many are coming back..."

In Chungking itself dissatisfaction was as great. Shu Hua 4/ reported that enemy agents were able to take advantage of the situation there, which he described as follows:

> "The authorities replied to all complaints by repression, and absence without leave from military plants was punished by arrest. But the worker had no way of manifesting protest except to move. Complete obedience was expected in state industries at the same time as workers were maltreated, something skilled men from the coast, with their craft pride and tradition of organization, could not tolerate. In May 1942 alone, 600 skilled workers deserted Chungking. There appeared guides who guaranteed to get them back to occupied areas for a fee of $800, or $1,500 including a puppet 'Good Citizenship Identity Card' so that they could travel there without hindrance. They went by way of Santouping (Hupeh) or Kinhwa (Chekiang). This enticement of skilled technical workers afterwards proved to be a thought-out action by the Japanese."

5. The Skilled Worker at Home

The living conditions of the workers were poor. Where the factory made itself responsible for food and housing, which was the case in many migrant plants, a constant struggle had to be put up for a minimum of quality in these services. Improvements in dormitories were difficult to win not only because of repressions preventing organization, but also because there was usually no way of getting any other place to live except by changing one's job.

Neither wages nor housing were generally sufficient to make family life possible. Shu Hwa tells us that in Chungking:

> "Married workers are in the minority. Those with families must take on subsidiary occupations after factory hours, such as peddling, to maintain them. Even then wives must take in washing, and even children must find paid employment or help the family out by spending whole days collecting waste fuel, etc. In other words, no family can live if only one member is employed.

4. Op. cit.

"The marriage rate among the younger men is very small. Lodging is the greatest problem. Wedding expenses also cannot be borne."

A typical picture of how employed immigrant skilled workers with families were compelled to live is given by Liu Wu-kou, who writes:

"On September 26, 1943, in Kweilin, I went to visit a blacksmith's mate of the Hunan-Kwangsi Railway depot who came here from Hangchow five years ago with his family of five. Because all of them could not live together in the quarters provided by the depot, and because these were too far from the town, the family has built its own bamboo hut on an empty lot in the outskirts. The hut has only one room with no window. The floor is of mud. The furniture consists of two big beds, one table, one old canvas chair, one bamboo chair and several stools.

"Two members of the family work. The man himself makes NC $1,000 a month. His 72-year old father, a carpenter who had retired before the war, has been going out for the last couple of years doing odd jobs on housing construction, which occasionally bring in as much again. The family is making great sacrifices to keep three children, a daughter of 15, a son of 12, and another daughter of 10, in school. The mother, a woman in her thirties who looks at least fifty, does all the cooking, marketing, washing and mending. She spends every minute of her spare time tramping over the surrounding area, searching for sticks and bits of coal for the earthenware stove. They cannot afford to buy fuel.

"When I came in, only the mother was at home. She poured me some boiling water in a teacup. They had no tea. She said things were getting more difficult because the old father became weaker every day and could not keep on contributing to the budget for long. Her husband was therefore doing extra jobs. He got up very early in the morning and carried water for various families living nearby. When he returned from work in the evening, he carried heavy yokes of water again. He also worked all Sunday. She herself was busy all the time. Mending of shoes and clothing was endless. They had no money to buy anything new, and the old things were so threadbare they did not hold the patches.

The elder daughter came in. Her schooling cost $50 a term, and she was in disgrace with the family because she had not passed her last examination. Then the little boy came. Although it was autumn, he wore nothing above the waist. His mother aaid he was the poorest-dressed student in his class (the fourth grade). His tuition was also $50 a term.

"A few minutes afterwards the husband himself returned, carrying two big baskets and sweating all over. In the baskets was left-over bread from the American Air Force quarters. He had bought it cheap from one of the kitchen helpers. The mother took the bread to cook for their 'meal'.

"The man said he generally worked eight hours, from 6:30
to 11 a.m. and from 1 to 4:30 p.m. When there was a night
shift the pay was four hours for every three. Besides his
wage he got 40 catties of rice. He said all the workers
were afraid to get sick. Every time they asked for sick
leave they were docked three days' pay, 'because they hold
up the job.' The depot was supposed to pay medical expenses,
but it did so only in its own clinic which handled only
slight injuries."

6. Social Oppression

Apart from economic grievances, the migrant skilled worker was made
acutely miserable by the social discrimination practiced against him.
In the eastern coastal cities the rigid feudal differentiation between
manual and intellectual labor was becoming less absolute. In the western
provinces he encountered it again in full force. This was all the more
galling because, both in his own eyes and in government preachments, he
was a volunteer in the cause of national resistance.

In the Kunming factories surveyed by Shih Kuo-heng, a constant
complaint was that chih yuan, or "staff members" (clerks, etc.) regarded
themselves as the natural superiors even of skilled men who earned more
than they did. The factories recognized this "superiority" by assigning
the "staff" better quarters, more liberal family allowances where these
were given, a higher category of medical service, and even a distinctive
identification badge. Chih yuan identified themselves with the management and addressed workers familiarly and rudely while insisting on forms
of respect for themselves and reacting violently to every real or fancied
reflection on their "dignity." Where factories were distant from the
town and provided special buses to go there, chih yuan would push ahead
of workers in the queues. Workers complained that a chih yuan would
speak to them in a friendly way if no one else was around, but would
immediately turn his back if another chih yuan appeared. The lowest
clerk saw himself as a "gentleman" and shared the Confucian idea of the
worker as a "mean man." Many conflicts resulted, and workers often
left their employment as a result of insults for which they could get
no redress.

Shu Hwa, in his Chungking study, also refers to the resentment of
workers at the "arrogance" of clerical employees and states that they
often abandoned their jobs for this reason.

7. Flight of Skilled Workers from Industry

The conditions of which we have written also explain the efforts
of many workers to leave industry altogether.

While factory employment grew more precarious and repellent, the
more adventurous were fascinated by the quick profits being made by
speculators in the wartime inflation. After 1943, the hoarder, contractor and black-market broker were the kings of interior society. Even
the smallest of these had nothing to fear from the police or the
"conscription" press gangs, because they could always pay off the
officers in charge. The medium ones were in league with provincial
executives and city mayors. The most successful had Ministers in the

National Government as patrons and partners. Every town had one or two examples of the wartime success story -- men who had been poor a few years before but had catapulted to a position in which officials and army generals were proud to attend their banquets and anxious to make themselves sufficiently useful to be invited to share in some profitable deal.

Workers, along with petty clerks, junior officers, and college professors, were drawn into the ranks of the fortune seekers by living "proofs" that nothing was impossible. All the migrant printers in Kweilin had before them the story of a man like themselves who had risen phenomenally to great wealth. According to Liu Wu-kou:

"Before the war he had worked in the Shanghai newspaper Cheng Pao. In 1937 he went directly to Kunming, where he was at first a skilled worker. After accumulating a little money, he bought machines and opened his own small print-shop. Fortunately he had acquired large quantities of imported paper, printer's ink, etc. while they were quite cheap, which he was able to dispose of on a sellers' market when the closing of Indo-China and the Burma Road sent their value up to fantastic heights. By 1942 he had half a million dollars, with which he opened a big plant called the Great China Printing Company in Kweilin."

There were instances of the same kind among mechanics, truck drivers and others. The percentage was perhaps the highest among the long-distance drivers on the international roads, where much money could be picked up on "yellow fish" (illicit) passengers and cargoes. A smart man with not too many scruples and an eye to supply and demand in the various places through which he passed could ultimately come to own one or several vehicles himself.

Shih Kuo-heng writes in his Kunming study that the trend away from factory employment was already noticeable in that city in 1940:

"A...serious matter is that some skilled laborers actual-ly change their profession. From January to July 38 out of a total of 114 skilled laborers in Sub-Factory 'O' left the plant. Five out of 26 of these are no longer connected with any factory. One became a truck driver (he had wanted to for a long time). Another became a conductor of trucks for a private company (he was not satisfied with the treat-ment of personnel in this government factory). A third decided to take on independent piece work. (He felt that there was no promotion possible for him in this factory.) The other two opened small machine shops of their own. (One of them felt that the load of work in the factory was uneven.)"

The writer is familiar from personal experience with numerous other cases. As is usual in such situations, the less bold and less lucky majority of fortune-seekers joined the procession after the circumstances that produced the early windfalls had already lapsed. Many invested their small savings in new businesses at the beginning of the wartime depression that was to wipe out practically all minor enterprises and affect large ones as well. When they tried to return to factory jobs these were no longer available.

8. The Skilled Worker at the End of the War

The surrender of Japan, instead of alleviating the conditions of the skilled workers, made them far worse. Those interior industries that had survived the inflation crisis closed down as their owners made for the coast. Shipping space back to the eastern cities was pre-empted by officials and those who had the wherewithal to bribe them, and the migrant workers, with their families, were abandoned. The monthly report of the Chinese Association of Labor for October 1945 related:

> "Since the ending of the war, many factories have either removed eastward, suspended operation or lowered production, thus resulting in the dismissal of many workers. According to investigation in Chungking city and its suburbs, about 60,000 workers have been thrown out of employment. They are seen wandering in the streets where they seek refuge, and are hungry and homeless."

CHAPTER IV.

NEW (LOCAL) WORKERS

1. Historical Data

All Chinese industry is historically new, a small retarded growth in an overwhelmingly feudal and agricultural economy. Even on the more developed coast, the factory-owner was frequently a former landlord or the son of one, almost invariably retained substantial land holdings, and often enlarged them. In periods of revolutionary ferment or other insecurity in the countryside, capital has flowed to the cities. But industrial crises have sent it back to investment in land, which with exorbitant rents assured a higher return than the rate of profit from industry.

The Chinese industrial worker is yesterday's peasant; when unable to find employment in the cities, he has sought to weather bad periods by returning to the old homestead, or to country relatives still engaged in farming. The difference between capitalist and the workers has been, however, that while the former could almost always go back to his role of landlord, an increasing number of the latter lost their roots completely and became true proletarians.

The most potent checks to the development of coastal industry in China came from foreign pressure. This took the form of restrictions of China's protective tariff, the inflow of cheap goods, or actual attack, as by Japan.

The Japanese attack, after 1937, deprived China of the urban centers where industrial capital and a true proletariat were already significantly developed. It drove the Chinese government and the industries on which it would have to depend back from areas where the break-up of traditional patterns had been considerable to areas where they were still substantially intact.

Despite the difficulty of importing plant, these latter areas were in some respects favorably situated, in wartime, for industrial growth. They were reasonably safe militarily. The factor of foreign economic and political pressure was absent. Migration could have brought in a sufficient number of technicians and skilled workers.

The chief obstacle, a still viable domestic medievalism, could have been minimized by a policy of attracting accumulated land capital to industry through the imposition of rent ceilings and progressive taxation which would make landlordism less lucrative and boost industrial profits by tax exemptions, technical assistance and, if necessary, direct subsidies. New workers would have been attracted by wages, working conditions and prospects of advancement exceeding those offered by the poverty-stricken life of the Chinese countryside -- a very modest minimum indeed. Such a policy was applied successfully in the wartime Communist-led areas, which were much worse off than the Kuomintang rear in the matter of vulnerability to enemy attack, raw materials and technical personnel. If the Kuomintang had undertaken similar measures, rear industry could have grown in wartime much more than it did. A basis could have been laid for its survival and development after the war. The previously purely rural and backward interior would have acquired factories, industrialists, and a reasonably stable working class. With suitable post-war protection, it could have begun to remedy the unbalance caused by a century of lopsided and partially parasitic industrialization on the "international" coast alone.

The overall aspects of the Kuomintang's failure to advance these objects, which it recognized theoretically during the Hankow period, are dealt with elsewhere. Here we shall show how this failure was reflected, in the recruitment of industrial labor from the villages.

2. The Unattractiveness of the Factory

One of the chief complaints of even the limited amount of industry that grew in Kuomintang China in wartime was manpower shortage and, despite a multitude of penal regulations, excessive labor mobility. The countryside produced men for roadbuilding projects and military transport when it was forced to do so by labor conscription (corvee). 1/ Many peasants did temporary out-of-season work as carriers, miners and so on. But compulsory drafts to factories were impracticable and no inducement existed to bring peasants to them voluntarily. The few who entered them had motives of a negative nature and no thought of remaining permanently.

Shu Hwa wrote: 2/

> "Workers who came because they heard that wages were higher in the city than the country were disappointed....
> State factories pay worse than private ones.... Poor peasants prefer to become roaming farm laborers, independent porters or unskilled day laborers on construction jobs, which pay better than any factory."

Shih Kuo-heng found that of a group of forty locally-recruited laborers (not including migrants from the coast) classified as "semi-skilled" in a Kunming factory only nine were peasants. Only three had come directly from village to factory, the rest having spent some time in the city in other occupations. Of 41 unskilled laborers, 19 were farmers. Only eight had had no previous urban job. Most of these, too, had come from points within five miles of the city. Wages, hours, working conditions and mobility undoubtedly explained the lack of "pulling power" of wartime interior industry.

The only large bodies of peasants voluntarily engaging in non-agricultural work in the Kuomintang rear were to be found in traditional and customary off-season manual occupations which had long existed as part of the social structure. Here the level of employment, and sometimes even of earnings, tended for a time to rise.

Stone-cutters, for instance, were much in demand for air-raid shelters in Chungking. The loss of some Yangtze steam shipping, and the

1. See Chapter VI.

2. Op. cit.

greater traffic along the upper reaches of the river incident to the important place of Szechuan in the war economy, increased the number of boatmen to 300,000. 3/ Extension of wolfram mines in Kiangsi led to the concentration of 30,000 men in the workings at Shihhwashan. Accounts of these stress that they "returned home for the harvest." The influx of officials to the cities also increased the number of ricksha men, scavengers, water-carriers and domestic servants. Aversion to factory discipline, and "new fangled" work habits among the peasantry, may have played a part in the flow to these fields. But it does not account for the failure of any appreciable number of young villagers to regard modern industry as opening new opportunities.

We are not, at this point, dealing with compulsory or semi-slave labor on public projects and in mines, where the will of the individual played no part, because he was either carrying out administrative orders or working off a debt. It must, however, be pointed out that increasing agricultural debt would, under other circumstances, have increased the number of seekers for factory jobs.

3. Refugees from Conscription

Observers of the Chinese economy have long noted that, as in Europe during the break-up of feudalism, soldiering and "banditry" have been one form of absorption of the rural unemployed. In the period between the fall of the Manchu Empire and the outbreak of war with Japan in 1937, the armies both of local warlords and of the Kuomintang Central Government had been largely built by the enlistment of mercenaries. Some displaced farmers along the coast had gone to the cities, or emigrated to the South Pacific. But for most, both along the coast and in the interior, military life was the only occupation available. This "solution" generally involved complete and permanent severance from the family -- as well as abandonment of any hope of marriage. But it was the only way to survive, and some writers have rightly classified China's soldiery, banditry and local landlord militia as part of the "coolie" population or unskilled labor reserve.

In wartime China, with her great army manpower needs, "voluntary" enlistment under economic compulsion was replaced by conscription under administrative compulsion -- or outright impressment. This, no less than the previous system, was completely conditioned by the feudal society. It was carried arbitrarily by the landlord village-head who "delivered" men for service in the army and auxiliary labor corps. The richer and more influential figures in the village, with their relatives and hangers-on, were automatically exempt. The more substantial peasants could buy freedom for their sons, or place them in exempt employment. The poorest owner-cultivators and the landless were handed over to the army roped together like cattle.

---

3. The China Information Service estimated that wooden junks with a total capacity of 250,000 tons were operating on the upper Yangtze in wartime, as compared to 100,000 tons of steam shipping on the whole river before the war.

The method by which men were impressed pre-determined their treatment when in uniform. All abuses were permissible in a force whose rank and file did not include the relatives of anybody who "mattered," and which was based on a rural manpower pool considered inexhaustible by the country's rulers. Recruits who died of hunger or disease before they heard a shot fired, or indeed before assignment to any operating unit, far outnumbered those lost in action. By the fourth year of the war the ordinary Chinese came to regard induction as an automatic death sentence, and tried to avoid it by every means.

When the Kuomintang army fronts became relatively static and defections of high-ranking officers to the enemy became a crying scandal, even the patriotic stimulus was compromised. Mass evasion of service was aggravated by mass desertions from the forces themselves. Since conscription was carried on mainly in the countryside, both evaders and deserters flocked to cities and towns, where civilian employment in "essential" categories was possible.

Refugees from conscription were of two kinds:

1. The sons of middle or well-to-do peasants, wishing to avoid heavy exemption bribes, who had the contacts to enter factories "by introduction" of personnel already employed. For these men neither wages nor continued industrial employment were an object;

2. Poor peasants and their sons who had no such contacts and who, able to get to the cities by virtue of the proximity of their villages, swelled the ranks of unskilled factory workers and contract labor employed in transport and construction. These needed their current earnings to keep alive. But they, too, looked forward to returning ultimately to their village.

The predominance of such workers, and the result in terms of efficiency, labor standards, and the struggle for improvement, are noted in every account of wartime labor in the Kuomintang rear. Shu Hwa reported from Chungking:

"Apart from the minority of skilled industrial workers who came from Shanghai and other ports, most local workers came from rural districts to escape military service and therefore do not care about the scanty wage. They say: 'To feed one's self in the rear is better than to starve in the army.'"

Dr. Yapp Chu-fay, director of the 3,000-worker National Resources Commission Electrolytic Copper Plant at Chikiang (Szechuan), which produced 80% of the copper refined in Free China, told the author in 1943:

"Many workers, even the sons of well-off people in the villages, came to this national defense plant to avoid conscription. Some came for only a few days and left after they received factory identification badges, which make their bearers exempt. Now we require a deposit equivalent to two weeks' pay before badges are issued."

Shih Kuo-heng tabulated the following reasons for entering industry, as told him by interviewed workers of the National Resources' Commission's Electric Appliances Factory in Kunming:

Table 16

REASONS WHY NEW WORKERS ENTERED INDUSTRY, KUNMING, 1941

Reason	Number	Original Occupation				
		Peasants	Students	Unemployed	Craftsmen	Others
To evade conscription	50	25	12	3	2	8
Financial reasons	18	3	2	1	5	7
Family troubles	8	-	1	-	3	4
Other reasons	10	-	6	2	1	1

Even these figures do not tell the whole story. It must be taken into account that no worker would admit evasion of army service unless he had full confidence in his interlocutor. Mr. Shih commented further:

"If all these (who are classified under other reasons) are added ... the total percentage of evaders of conscription among laborers will be even more impressive. The large number of farmers in this group also shows that only a very overwhelming social force, like conscription, can drive the tiller of the soil away from his land. One man named Wang told the author: 'Every time there is a fresh demand for conscripts in our place there are requests for introduction to the factory from my fellow villagers.'

"Another man, Chao, hired a substitute at $300 to take his name in the army and escaped Kunming himself .... A fact that came as a surprise to the author is that the majority of laborers evading conscription are from wealthy farmers' families. While in the factory some of them even had money sent from home."

Professor Chen Ta of Tsinghua University, famed authority on Chinese labor and population movements, conducted 2 census in the Kunming area during the war. He too, told the author that the evasion motive was bound to be understated in all figures. He said peasants and workers were keenly aware of the menace of conscription and very suspicious of questions. For instance, his census-takers had found a number of villages which reported no men of military age at all, though these were everywhere visible. Professor Chen remarked further that "labor that comes to factories for such reasons cannot be expected to stay in industry after the war."

A March 1943 report to the Chungking Hsin Hua Jih Pao from the main tungsten mining area in Kiangsi, where thousands of men were employed directly and through contractors by the National Resources Commission, contained the following passage:

"The miners are underground for ten hours a day. Wages have not risen with the market price of wolfram, but the worker's cost of living has. Some say that the only reason there are still any miners here is that the job offers protection from conscription."

Miss Liu Wu-kou reported of the building of airfield roads by contractors for the U.S. Army in Kweilin (from April to December 1943):

"Of the 1,500 men employed, 130 to 170 were stonemasons and the rest unskilled 'earth workers' and wagon pullers. Most of them were farmers from Hunan who left their native villages in order to evade military service. In Hunan conscription is not only very strict but very unfair. It is repeated every year, and persons who have been exempted once may be taken the next time. Even only sons are taken. When they got here and found the conditions, some wanted to leave, but it was too late because they were under contract."

The "conditions" referred to by Miss Liu are described elsewhere in her paper as a form of semi-slavery, with incidence of disease as great, and life-expectancy as poor, as in the Kuomintang army.

CHAPTER V.

WOMEN AND CHILDREN IN INDUSTRY

1. The Pre-war Background

Women and child workers outnumbered men in China's pre-war factories. The causes included the low price at which such labor could be obtained and the predominance of the textile industry, where it could be most profitably employed. The low wages paid to male working-class heads of families also made it essential for their wives and children to enter the factories.

Both Chinese and foreign entrepreneurs filled their plants with women and children who worked under conditions that outdid the oft-recounted horrors of the early English industrialization. Chinese-owned factories were worse than the others, partly because Chinese industrialists had to compete with imports under onerous tariff restrictions and with the better-mechanized and better-capitalized foreign enterprises. But the difference was not great. Female and child workers were so plentiful that they were considered cheaper to "expend" than to feed and train into a stable and efficient labor force.

Pre-war statistics vary, the lowest figure given for women in factory industry throughout China being 45% [1]/ and the highest 56%. [2]/ For Shanghai, the estimates in various years ran from 53.7% [3]/to 58.7%. [4]/

The greatest concentration of female labor was,as we have noted, in textiles. A 1937 China-wide survey states that 62% of workers in this industry were women. [5]/ In Shanghai, the greatest center, the proportion once reached as high as 89%, [6]/ and in the Shanghai-Wusih textile area as a whole, 78%. [7]/

Where the proportion of women was smaller, that of child workers was invariably higher, as for instance, in Tientsin, where they comprised 20.5% of the working force of all industries, [8]/ as compared with all-China estimates varying from 6 to 8%. Although the statistics for various years are not sufficiently uniform or complete to permit accurate comparisons, there seems to have been a slight decrease in the proportion

---

1. Ministry of Industry survey for 28 cities (1930), as analysed by the Nankai Institute of Economics, quoted by Nym Wales in The Chinese Labor Movement, N. Y., 1945.
2. Chinese Labor Yearbook, 1933, quoted by Hsu Sheng-tze in Study of Chinese Industrial Labor, Kweilin, 1942.
3. Dr. Franklin L. Ho, quoted by Nym Wales, op. cit. Figure for 1931.
4. Shanghai Public Safety Bureau Survey, 1928, quoted by Nym Wales, op. cit.
5. Ministry of Industry, 1930.
6. Miss Cora Deng of the Y.W.C.A. Industrial Section (Nym Wales, op. cit.)
7. Mrs. Dorothy Orchard, figures for 1931-32 (Nym Wales, op. cit.)
8. Dr. Franklin L. Ho, quoted by Nym Wales, op. cit.

of women in all industries between 1928 and 1937, and a slight increase in industries other than textiles.

According to Miss Cora Deng, the average woman worker in pre-war Shanghai was nineteen years old, and few stayed in industry beyond their 25th year. The median wage for women in Shanghai factories was Chinese $14.50 for a working month of from 25 to 30 twelve-hour days. All sources agree that the average wages of women in both skilled and unskilled categories were 60-80% of those paid to men doing similar work. The wages of children were given as half, or less, those paid to adult males.

Many children in industry, however, worked as apprentices, receiving nothing but food and board. Because the Chinese government was sensitive on this point and anxious to make a good impression on such bodies as the International Labor Office, the figures on child labor are far from reliable. No official estimate for the whole country placed the number of children in industry at above 10 per cent, a figure that will certainly be doubted by anyone who had the opportunity of visiting pre-war factories and seeing for himself.

Both female and child labor were the objects of the worst abuses of the contract system, under which a large part even of the meager wages paid found its way into the pockets of recruiting agents and contractor-foremen.

2. Women and Children in Wartime Industry

The available evidence on wartime interior industry indicates both an absolute and a relative decline in the number of women workers. The proportion of women in factories was slashed in half -- from a pre-war national average of over 40 per cent to an average of just over 20 per cent in "Free China." The proportion of child workers did not change greatly from that previously reported.

Textile mills were still the largest single employers of women, but not as predominant as formerly. Women represented 55 per cent of all of workers in textile mills in 1943 -- as compared with between 60 and 80 per cent in the 1930's. Of all women working in industry, 64.3 per cent were in textiles -- also lower than the pre-war proportion.

There were several reasons for these changes. The migration of skilled workers included very few women (the only considerable body came in with the equipment of Hankow cotton in which they had previously been employed.) Married male workers who came from the occupied cities seldom brought their families. Custom made it more difficult to recruit local women workers in the backward western provinces than in the coastal areas. Most women who entered industry early in the war came from the families of non-proletarian migrants and refugees, such as small merchants and petty government employees.

It appears, however, that the old tendencies later reasserted themselves. Shu Hwa, in his Conditions of Employees and Workers in Chungking, noted late in 1943:

"The ratio of female and juvenile workers is greatly increasing. Men workers are already very few in cotton mills, and women workers are used even for heavy packing. Nearly all silk workers are women. Some printing houses now also employ women workers. Little girls are employed in cotton and silk and little boys in other occupations and in the coal mines."

The table below recapitulates official figures on women and children in wartime factories:

Table 17.

Women and Child Workers in Wartime Interior Factories, by Industries, 1943

Industry	Total Workers	Women Workers	Child Workers
Textiles	77,184	34,494	8,034
Chemicals	56,866	7,383	4,703
Machine tools	36,772	301	3,620
Smelting	21,435	1,452	336
Food	14,557	4,528	1,116
Metal Mfrs.	12,286	240	650
Clothing	9,180	5,432	507
Electric supplies	8,818	614	465
Paper & printing	6,232	598	648
Miscellaneous	5,737	600	311
TOTAL	249,067	53,642	20,390

Compiled from statistics of the Ministry of Economics, Chungking, December, 1943.

Breaking these figures down into approximate percentages, we obtain the following picture:

Table 18.

Percentages of Women and Children in Interior Industries, 1943

Industries	% of Women	% of Children	% of Women & Child Workers Combined	
All Industries	21.6	8.1	29.7	
Textiles	44.7	10.4	55.1	
Clothing	37.3	5.5	42.8	Above general
Food processing	31.1	7.6	38.7	average
Chemical	12.9	8.3	21.2	
Paper & Printing	9.5	10.4	20.0	Below general
Electric supplies	6.9	5.2	12.1	average
Machine tools	0.8	9.8	10.6	
Smelting	6.7	1.5	8.2	
Metal Mfrs.	1.9	5.4	7.3	
Miscellaneous	10.6	5.4	16.0	

The territorial analysis that follows tends to show that the proportion of women workers was highest in areas which had a previous industrial history (Kwangtung, Fukien, Hunan), while the proportion of child workers in relation to women appears to have been greater where the traditional economy was least touched prior to the war (Shensi, Kansu, Sikang). As distinct from pre-war centers like Shanghai, where child labor was mainly female, the children in wartime factories were mostly boys.

Table 19.

Women and Child Workers in Wartime Interior Factories, by Provinces, 1943
(Ministry of Economics, Chungking, December 1943)

Province	No. of Factories	Total Workers	Women Workers	Child Workers
Szechuan	1,822	105,649	21,721	6,790
Hunan	786	45,904	10,071	3,828
Shensi	261	23,166	2,576	3,641
Kwangsi	316	16,487	2,520	1,001
Yunnan	124	16,088	6,243	1,117
Kansu	158	7,836	1,369	974
Kiangsi	90	6,083	1,518	406
Kweichow	170	5,962	417	381
Fukien	36	5,136	1,800	537
Kwangtung	63	2,971	900	488
Hupeh	23	1,590	107	140
Sikang	7	533	57	93
Others	155	11,662	4,447	994
TOTAL	4,011	249,067	53,746	20,390

Based on the above, we find the following proportions of female and child labor in the various industrial areas:

Table 20

Percentage of Women and Child Labor by Provinces, 1943

Province	% of Women	% of Children	% of Women & Child Workers Combined	
Kwangtung	30.3	16.4	46.7	
Yunnan	38.8	6.9	45.7	
Fukien	35.0	10.4	45.4	Above
Hunan	34.1	8.3	32.4	general
Kiangsi	24.9	6.6	31.5	average
Kansu	17.5	12.0	29.5	
Sikang	10.7	17.4	28.1	
Szechuan	20.5	6.4	26.9	Below
Shensi	11.1	15.5	26.6	general
Kwangsi	15.3	6.0	21.3	average
Hupeh	6.7	8.6	15.3	
Kweichow	7.3	6.9	14.2	
Others	38.0	8.5	46.5	
TOTAL	21.6	8.7	30.3	

- 38 -

A census of the Kunming lake area (Yunnan) taken in 1942 by the Department of Sociology of Tsinghua University, under Dr. Chen Ta, indicated a somewhat greater number of industrial workers in that area, and a greater number of women workers, than appeared in the Ministry of Economics survey. The discrepancies do not, however, contradict the general picture. Of more interest are the remarks of the census-takers on the participation of women in industries other than textiles, clothing and food-processing, indicating that they were employed in many of these as office help, cleaning women, etc. rather than as productive workers.

These facts probably applied to the whole industry of wartime China. We tabulate them below.

Table 21

Nature of Employment of 3,232 Women Workers in Kunming, 1942
(Tsinghua University census, 1942)

Industry	Total Workers	Women Employed	Of whom: Clerical	Coolies	Productive Workers
Textiles	5,359	3,232	132	-	3,100
Clothing	3,809	1,545	-	-	1,545
Food	2,410	398	-	-	398
Machine tool	2,014	118	26	55	37
Chemical	671	84	19	56	9
Cement	458	96	6	25	65
Furniture	1,037	241	12	55	174
Leather	966	117	16	56	45
Printing	1,398	192	-	-	192

The conclusion is that the spread of wartime women workers from their pre-war specialization in a few light industries was more apparent than real.

Finally, the Kunming figures provide valuable clues to the origins of women who entered factories in wartime. The following table shows the relative number of men and women workers from provinces other than Yunnan in the same Kunming (Yunnan) industries. The great majority of these may be taken to be wartime migrants, as few people from outside had immigrated in normal times. How few women came, even in wartime, is clearly seen.

Table 22

Male and Female Workers from Provinces Other Than Yunnan in Some Kunming Industries, 1942   (Compiled from Tsinghua University Census, 1942)

Industry	Total Workers Male	Female	From Other Provinces Male	Female
Textiles	2,127	3,232	409	184
Clothing	2,264	1,545	614	199
Machine tool	1,885	128	708	27
Chemical	587	84	Total 114	
Furniture	796	241	114	20
Leather	966	107	34	6
Printing	1,398	182	254	34

Ju-kang Tien, in a brief study of 634 female workers in a Kunming factory 9/ found that 90 per cent of them were young unmarried girls. The great majority came from families whose menfolk were in military service, small trade and government jobs. Less than 10 per cent came from the families of manual craftsmen and less than 5 per cent from peasant homes. The number from the families of industrial workers is not even given in Mr. Tien's table. A report from a second Kunming mill, however, says that 23.68% of the women there were of peasant origin and 16.75% from the homes of workers.

Most of the women studied by Mr. Tien entered the factories by personal introduction. He records no evidence of the old contract practices prevalent in Shanghai. Flight from oppression in old-fashioned families, such as beating by husbands and tyranny by mothers-in-law, seems to have been as potent a force in driving women into industry as evasion of conscription was in the case of male local workers. Mr. Tien concludes from his studies that the desire for freedom was a greater motive than financial need. He states that he did not find a single family of several interviewed, that wanted its daughters to do factory work to help its budget. But this view of the matter is flatly contradicted by another survey, 10/, conducted by Miss Chang Shao-mei and Miss Shen Yao-hua of the Southwest Associated University under the supervision of Professor Chen Ta. This study tabulates the reasons given by 114 women workers for entering the factory as follows:

Table 23

Reasons for Entering Factory Given by 114 Women Textile Workers in Kunming

Reason	Number	Percent
Economic need	67	58.78
Attraction of factory work	25	21.93
Family troubles	13	11.40
Students whose schools moved away	4	3.50
Don't know	5	4.39
Total workers questioned	114	100.00%

The answers the same women gave on how they spent their wages appear to clinch the argument.

---

9. Female Labor in a Kunming Factory, by Ju-kang Tien (B.A., South-west United University), Yenching-Yunnan Station of Sociological Research, Kunming, January 1943 (mimeographed). Edited version published as appendix to China Enters the Machine Age (Harvard University Press, 1944) as "Female Labor in a Cotton Mill".

10. "A Kunming Weaving Factory & Its Labor", by Chang Shao-mei and Shen Yao-hua, supervised by Dr. Chen Ta, a manuscript thesis in Chinese, Kunming, 1943.

Table 24

How 114 Women Textile Workers in Kunming Spent Their Earnings

	Number	Percent
Contributed to family expenses	82	71.92
Individual expenses only	18	15.78
Divided between family and self	13	11.40
No answer	1	0.90
Total workers questioned	**114**	**100.00%**

A point on which the two surveys agreed, however, was the inability of factories to retain their women workers. Mr. Tien reported the duration of employment of the 634 women workes he studied as follows:

Table 25.

Duration of Employment of 634 Women Workers in a Kunming Cotton Mill

	Number	Per cent
Over three years	22	3.5
Over two years	66	10.4
Over one year	143	22.5
Under one year	403	63.6
	634	100.0%

Miss Chang and Miss Shen found the reasons for such extraordinary mobility in the factory itself, where women expressed greater dissatis-faction with conditions than did their male fellow-workers.

Table 26

Opinions of Factory Conditions Held by 114 Female and 49 Male
Textile Workers in Kunming

Opinion	Women Workers		Men Workers	
	Number	Per cent	Number	Per cent
Bad	56	49.12	15	30.61
Tolerable	21	18.42	16	32.6
Good	35	30.70	18	36.73
Don't Know	2	1.75	-	-
Individuals asked	114	100.00%	49	100.00%

The men seem to have been less dissatisfied because they were generally in the better jobs. They were also more reconciled to rough treatment than the women who, in many cases, had never worked before. Sample complaints by women reported by Miss Chang and Miss Shen include over-intensity of work, resentment toward factory officials, and insufficient freedom. Male workers were more liable to complain of low wages, night work, etc. Significantly, migrant workers from the coast, who had experience of factories elsewhere, held the most grievances.

The two studies agree that women who left the factories did not generally wish to return to industrial employment. Mr. Tien reports that what many women wanted from their jobs was not professional training and permanent independence, but enough temporary financial independence to enable them to exercise a choice, free of family pressure, with regard to their future. Their goal was still marriage and home life. Only 9 per cent of the women workers he studied had been married. A number of these were widows, wives of soldiers or fugitives from bad husbands. Those who stayed in the factory after satisfactory marriage were very few indeed.

The potential emancipatory influence of industry for the women of the feudal interior was clearly manifested. But, as with locally recruited male workers, factories actually existing in the wartime interior did not offer sufficient inducement to hold and develop their labor. Although the plant Mr. Tien surveyed was a comparatively "progressive" one, he records as many complaints as Misses Chang and Shen do. Some of these grievances stemmed from the incompatibility of industrial practices with older, traditional habits in work and human relations (some of the women expressed dislike of the "impersonal" factory atmosphere). But the main cause was the depressed economic position of the Chinese working class in general and of its women members in particular.

That Mr. Tien himself did not state this conclusion reflected not only the caution which Chinese scholars who want to keep out of trouble must exercise but also the shortcomings of the "social anthropology" techniques in which he was trained. The factual observations he made were careful and valuable. But they did not, unbelievably enough, include a single reference to the earnings of his subjects -- much less the necessary information on how these compared with the income of male workers in the same industry, and of women in non-industrial employment. The Misses Chang and Shen, however, stated that low wages were the chief reason why factories could not retain their workers -- and the main problem of the workers themselves.

3. Wartime Wages of Women and Children

We have already seen that the pre-war wages of women industrial workers in China averaged from 60 to 80% of those paid to men engaged in the same work, and that the wages of children were half or less those of men.

The general decline of wages during the war affected women and children most sharply, as can be seen from the following table and the succeeding paragraphs.

Table 27
Comparative Daily Wage of Men and Women in Szechuan Cities and Industries, 1937 and 1943

City	Industry	Average Daily Wage, 1937			Av. Daily Wage, Mar.1943		
		Men	Women	Women as % of Men	Men	Women	Women as % of Men
Chungking	Textile	$0.48	$0.37	77.1	$7.80	$6.50	83.3
	Printing	0.33	0.25	76.8	14.29	7.01	49.0
Loshan	Textiles	-	(Not given)	-	9.50	3.33	35.0
Wanhsien	Textiles	-	"	-	4.34	1.94	44.7

Source: "Wage Indices in Important Cities", Ministry of Social Affairs
Bulletin, Chungking, 1943. Figures in Chinese currency.

We find above only one case in which the wages of women as compared to men increased, and only one case in which women's wages averaged more than half those paid to men in 1943.

A survey carried out in Kweilin by students of the Kwangsi Commercial College, with the cooperation of statisticians from the Kwangsi Provincial Government, showed that women's earnings in 1943 in small weaving workshops in that city averaged 40% of those of men. Among 699 workers in the cigarette industry, the average earnings of women were 80% of those of men, and those of children were 33%.

The real wages of all workers had declined, by the end of 1943, to about 50 per cent of pre-war (51.1% in textiles in Chungking). On this basis we can say that the real wages of women at that time were little more, and in some cases even less, than one-third of those they had received before the war.

4. Women Workers in a Wartime Munitions Plant

The life of women workers in the pre-war and wartime textile factories of China has been amply described. The following information on women workers in a Kweilin armament plant operated by the government was obtained by Liu Wu-kou. The interview with a girl employed in assembling detonators for hand-grenades is of especial interest both because the wartime munitions industry was inacessible to independent investigators and because the field was new to Chinese women.

In the plant in which the informant worked, women comprised 100 out of a total of 700 workers. Few were of local origin or had come straight from farms. Most were young girl refugees who had come with their families from Kwangtung, Hupeh, Hunan, Kiangsu or Chekiang and had previously done domestic work only. The informant herself was the daughter of a warehouse keeper who had been employed in the same arms factory for many years and had moved with it from its old location in Nanking.

The working day in the plant was ten hours -- from 6 to 11 a.m. and from noon to 5 p.m. Workers received Sundays and six national holidays a year off. The monthly earnings in the informant's department and grade of skill averaged $400 a month plus the equivalent of 40 catties of rice, or the average consumption of one person. They were based on the pre-war wage scale, supplemented by inflation allowances. The minimum basic wage was 80 cents a day, rising to $1, $1.70 and $1.80 in succeeding classes of skill and seniority. Women who remained on the job continuously for a year were advanced two grades at the end of it, but they were apparently not many in number. The allowances for different grades did not vary very greatly; this fact tended to equalize the actual earnings more than the basic wage spread might indicate. Here too, however, seniority played a part. While no wages were paid to any worker during periods of enforced absence due to illness of injury, those who had been in the factory a year or more continued to received their monthly rice allowances. Those who had worked less than a year received nothing.

Dormitory space was available for all who wished to live on the premises. Workers who ate in the factory mess surrendered their entire 40 catties of rice and paid $20 a month extra as their share for supplementary foods, value $600 in cash for the whole service. Since the average expenditure of a worker at this time, apart from food and board was $300-400 a month, it was impossible for anyone in the informant's grade (medium) to accumulate savings, contribute actual cash for family expenses, beyond their own upkeep, or make provision for disability. The family budget of the informant, who lived at home, indicated this clearly. The old worker father was in the same position as his daughter, who had entered industry recently. His total earnings, including rice allowance, amounted to $1,300 a month. The minimum monthly budget of the whole family, which consisted of the father, the mother (who had no outside job) and the girl, was $1,800 (120 catties of rice worth $800, fuel worth $70 bought from the factory canteen, and $900 for vegetables, soy bean curd and sauce, and oil). Housing was provided. Meat was practically never seen in this home. If the daughter had not gone to the factory, the family could not have fed itself. Even with two members of the family working, other miscellaneous expenditures, as for clothes, could not be met without borrowing.

This can be seen from prices at the factory canteen, which was called a "cooperative" but allowed the worker-customers neither a voice in its management nor access to its accounts. While its charges were below those on the outside market, and thus provided another factor discouraging any change of employment, they were still very high in relation to wages. Coal could be bought at the canteen for $38 per 100 kilograms, which was the ration per worker per month. A pair of cloth shoes could be bought for $40 every three months, and 12 feet of narrow cotton cloth, at less than the outside commercial rate, every six months. Some food items also were sold.

In the absence of sick pay, the factory maintained a clinic that was equipped to handle relatively simple ailments. Workers were not charged cash for treatment but surrendered 22 ounces of their rice allowance for each day in hospital.

Occasional compulsory deductions from wages included "gifts" to the army. The workers in this plant, who had fled before the Japanese, were consciously patriotic and not against contributing. But they resented such involuntary donations, of which they often learned only on pay-day.

The main wage complaint was that the factory refused to pay rice allowances in kind instead of at an arbitrary cash valuation, which was considerably below the actual price outside. The greatest source of dissatisfaction, however, was lack of any insurance of injury compensation. Work in the informant's shop was extremely dangerous, involving not only the manufacture of new grenades but also the taking apart of Chinese and enemy "duds" collected on the battlefields. Ten workers had been killed when one such grenade exploded and detonated other materials. The factory had given only $200 (a week's wage) to the family of each victim and had provided a poor coffin worth another $200. Burial expenses had been collected among the surviving workers. The plant never consented to assume them.

It was still worse when workers perished from other causes. A few weeks before the interview, more than ten had died in a cholera epidemic. The factory had provided coffins only, and giving not a cent to the families. It had collected $1 from each worker remaining on the job to pay for the funerals.

The workers had no union to negotiate these or any other grievances.

CHAPTER VI.

"COOLIE" LABOR: CONSCRIPT, CONTRACT AND SLAVE

1. Workers Outside Industry

Outside the factories, which accounted for only a small part of the production of the wartime interior, much of the work incidental to the war was performed by involuntary labor. The bulk of such labor was conscripted directly by government organs or "delivered" to the government by contractors to whom the workers were indentured for various periods to pay off a debt or a lump money advance. These practices followed, under somewhat different circumstances, the patterns established in imperial times with regard to public works construction, and those used by the building and manufacturing contractors of China before the advent of machine industry. While they had been modified by modern capitalistic development along the coast, their history in the western provinces had been unbroken. The arrival of coastal influence with the wartime Kuomintang government did not modify them, as might have been expected, because the government found them most useful.

As will be shown, the war also brought with it a revival of bond servitude and chattel slavery in parts of China where it had been extinct for many decades as an institution but had always tended to reappear when large-scale military or natural upheavals deprived the peasant masses of their livelihood.

2. Labor Conscription (corvee) in National Defence Construction

Administrative conscription or requisition of labor was the means of accomplishing such wartime construction feats as the Hunan-Kwangsi and Hunan-Kweichow railways, the Burma and Great Northwest roads to the outside world, and some of the great airfields built for the U. S. Army Air Force. It was also used by commanders of armies in the field to tear up communications in the path of the enemy, transport military supplies, etc. As in the conscription of soldiers, laboring man power (and woman power) was requisitioned by means of orders to district and village authorities, who then collected it in any way they saw fit. But while a soldier was taken for an indefinite period, the worker was retained for a definite number of days or the duration of the job. Machinery to trace or check abuses being totally absent, the system was turned to private gain. Recruiting organs and agents consequently made huge profits at the expense of labor conscripted for "national service."

Railway Building: How provincial governments enriched themselves by "investing" the labor of their peasants in national defence enterprises, and the conditions under which these peasants had to toil, has been authoritatively described by Dr. Chang Kia-ngau, Chinese Minister of Communications. Dr. Chang's account of the building of the Hunan-Kwangsi railway in 1938-39, 1/ is both a clear picture of methods used and an unconscious revelation of official Kuomintang psychology. Dr. Chang wrote:

---

1. Chang Kia-ngau, China's Struggle for Railway Development.

"In Hunan, 40,000 laborers were conscripted from districts within ten miles on either side of the railroad, people from the age of 16 to 45 being called to work for a period of 30 days. In Kwangsi, 100,000 laborers were conscripted.... The wage scale was based on the minimum subsistence requirement... When the work was completed the laborers turned over to the railway all implements and returned to their village under the escort of their unit sergeant or company captain.

"Payment of wages and management of labor were under the direction of the provincial authorities .... All expenses incurred by the provincial authorities in conscripting labor, buying (read "requisitioning" -- I.E.) land and acquiring local materials were accepted as capital investments made by the provincial governments.

"Selection (of laborers) was made by drawings, and anyone whose name had been drawn, but who was unable to leave his own employment was required to pay to the local labor office a corresponding sum to employ a substitute....

"Rewards were given for work completed before schedule. On the other hand, when the work dragged behind schedule, or when the village and borough elders failed to produce the scheduled number of laborers they were punished.

"The volume of earthwork done on the Hunan-Kwangsi railway was approximately 20,000,000 cubic yards, involving the mobilization of over half a million conscript laborers."

In another place, Dr. Chang wrote:

"The sum of 20 cents Chinese money (equivalent to six cents in U.S. currency at that time) was given for every cubic meter of earthwork when construction was carried on on a level not higher than three yards from the ground.... Each laborer was assigned to do 42 cubic yards of earthwork in 45 days (note the contradiction with the previous statement that only 30 days of service were required from every person. -I.E.)"

A simple calculation will show that the building of the Hunan-Kwangsi railway alone used about 25,000,000 man days of work. The cost was six cents U.S. currency per man-day to the provincial authorities, who reimbursed themselves by a share in the road and its future revenues.

Kuomintang officials did not regard railway building by corvée as something undesirable or justifiable only by urgent wartime need. On the contrary, Dr. Chang was careful to explain in his book that the system reduced construction costs in China to such an extent that even the most unsettled conditions could not prevent an adequate return on capital. This was the chief argument he presented to attract foreign investment in Chinese railways after the war.

- 47 -

Highway Construction: The two great international roads completed by China during World War II ran through very thinly settled country. Conscription of the necessary labor was a correspondingly greater weight on neighboring communities.

Dr. Fei Hsiao-tung has reported 2/the effect on the village of Luts'un in Yunnan Province, which he investigated:

" A form of tax is the conscription of labor for public works. The construction of the Burma Road, which was accomplished entirely by workers so obtained, had, according to the estimate given by the villagers, required 800 man-days from each household, in the period from 1929, when the work was begun, to 1938. (Since the major part of the work was accomplished in 1937-38, we may take it that most of the burden fell on those years, - I.E.) After the road was completed, each household had to provide 25 man-days a year for maintenance. It was only after the central government took over the road that wages were paid. ... The villagers have been left with a deep-rooted resentment. It may well be true that the heavy burden placed on the people by the construction has deeply affected the economy of the villagers."

The writers of several literary and rather romanticised accounts of the building of the Burma Road during the war also testified to this situation. They described the procurement of national minority labor in the non-Chinese sections of the country through which the road passed, through the medium of the Sawbwas or local lords. Here not only the economic base but the institutions were purely feudal -- or even tribal and pre-feudal.

As regards the Northwest Road, all eyewitness reports told of the widespread employment of women and children as well as of men, and of a callous lack of concern for the concurrent needs of local economy. As happened elsewhere, officials in the Northwest gained a taste for the use of conscript workers and tried to keep up the level of compulsory labor service for their own purposes, even after the road itself was completed. Excessive requisitions of labor, carts and farm animals were the main grievances leading to a widespread revolt of Moslem peasants in Kansu in 1942-43.

3. Contract (Peon) Labor on Wartime Projects

On Airfields: During 1942-44, more than a score of major airfields were built or enlarged for the U.S. army in the provinces of Szechuan, Yunnan, Kwangsi, Kwangtung, Hupeh, Kiangsi, Chekiang, and Shensi. While some were constructed by pure conscript labor, others were entrusted to private contractors who were generally identical with provincial officials or who split fees with the latter. Financing arrangements were different from those employed on land communications. Since no revenues could be expected, there was no question of "investing" conscript labor against part ownership or a share in income from operation. The cost of earthwork was generally shouldered by the Central Government as a form of reverse

---

2. Earthbound China, Chicago, 1945.

lend-lease. Additional construction was usually paid for by the U.S. Army in cash to the local authorities or private contractors. Americans had ample opportunity to convince themselves of the disparity between these payments and the compensation given to displaced farmers and the workers who built the fields.

A study of laborers under private contract on the advanced medium-bomber and fighter base at Kweilin was made by Liu Wu-kou 3/ for the present work. We have already quoted from it (in Chapter IV.)to show that many men took up such labor voluntarily to avoid military conscription. Here we are concerned with another group, of whom Miss Liu writes:

> "(They) came because they were in debt. They owed money to the contractors from a time when they had worked for them on other jobs and had to continue to work to pay off such debts. They too were farmers in origin."

How were such enslaving obligations incurred, particularly those described as dating from previous employment? Miss Liu's account of conditions on the airfield gives an exhaustive answer.

> "Recruitment: First the company sent representatives to the countryside. They contacted go-betweens who introduced them to sub-contractors each of whom was to collect a working gang. For this the go-between received a fee. From then on the company dealt with the sub-contractors who were paid a bonus of $100 for each worker. The worker himself, before he left home was supposed to get $200 'to settle his family'. But since this payment was made through the sub-contractor, the latter pocketed part or all of it by charging the worker a fee for 'recommending him to the job.' Often the sub-contractor used the 'family settling' fees he thus accumulated to lend out to the workers, and other poor peasants, at high interest, or to buy rice and hoard it. The worker's traveling expenses to the job were covered by the company.

> "On the Job: When workers arrived at the field they were still under the control of the sub-contractor, who became their foreman. Wages were paid to the foreman for his whole gang, with which he lived in the same hut. They were paid not by time but for piece work, calculated at $12.50 for every cubic meter of earth excavated for earth workers, $70 for each cubic meter of work removed for stone workers, and $100 to wagon pullers for each cubic meter of materials moved one kilometer.

> "When it rained, work stopped but the laborers still had to eat. If the earth was hard or difficult to dig because of the depth at which work proceeded, no allow-

---

3. "Account of Work by a Private Company on the Runway of the Li Family Village Airfield, Kweilin", from "Materials on Kwangsi Labor", by Liu Wu-kou, MS., 1944.

ance was made. Then there was the so-called 'extra transport'. The excavator himself had to move the material he dug from the airfield area, whether he worked near the edge of the field or in the middle, several hundred yards away from it. There was no extra pay for this.

"The average a worker could earn in a month of fine weather was $900 a month. The foreman retained 10-20% of this as his commission, in addition to which he was paid a retainer equal to 10% of the payroll of the group by the company. Really this too came out of the wages. The more the work done, the greater the foreman's share. So he drove the men hard.

"The Foreman: Food and fuel were provided by the company and its cost deducted from the wage by the sub-contractor-foreman who was supposed to give the workers the balance. The foreman 'ate on the workers'. They were charged for his food as well as their own. Another deduction was for the wages of a cook, whom the foreman hired.

"In fact, little cash found its way to the workers. I did not find a single one who had been able to save $1,000 to send to his family in six months of labor. Most of the workers were not able to cover their own expenses and had to borrow from the foreman to pay for cigarettes, drinks, etc. The workers were unable to dispute the foreman's monthly accounts of all debts and charges. These generally showed that they were not entitled to anything more, but on the contrary owed him money. Only a small percentage of them received anything at the month's end.

"A further deduction was made by the foreman for the rent of implements (shovels, etc.), and for ropes, which the workers had to buy themselves because they were perishable.

"Life and Liberty: During the eight months of work, sixty workers (out of a total of 1,500) died on the job. Many of these were not even provided with coffins for decent burial. Workers with stronger characters expressed great hatred for their foremen (they did not see beyond the foremen to the company with which they had no direct relations). The weaker ones simply bemoaned their fate. To run away was difficult. Workers visiting the town had to get a special permit from the foreman or the company to pass the airfield guards.

"As this is written, the work is approaching its end. Only four hundred workers remain. It is getting cold. The workers have no cotton padded quilts. The company provides only a coarse cloth sack for each worker to sleep in. The huts provide no real shelter from the weather. They are built of bamboo with thatched roofs with bunks, also of bamboo

and so rough that men sitting or sleeping on them often
tear their clothes. The huts have no windows, only a
door, and no benches, stools or tables. Just three
tiers of bamboo bunks.

"Who Profited?: The cost of building the airfield
was $80,000,000 Chinese currency which was advanced by
the Aeronautical Commission. The company that built the
runway received $30,000,000 for its part. When the work
began it had 27 staff members on the job, but now it is
nearly over only eleven are left.

"The salary of the manager was nominally only $2,600
a month but in fact he alone drew $7,000,000 from February
to December 1945 (for himself alone!) His expense sheet
for "entertainment" was $2,000,000. This included gifts
of as much as $10,000 at a time to inspectors coming to
check on the work.

"The total payroll for the workers and foremen
(including food) was $10,000,000, so $20,000,000 went to
the company and its officials.

"The manager referred to has a very bad record, he
absconded from a factory in Shanghai with a large sum of
company money to come to the interior. He was appointed
to 'manage' this job because of his official connections."

At about the same time, the author learned of events surrounding
the contract building of an airfield, in the town of Kanhsien (Kanchow),
South Kiangsi. The local administrative prefect (chuan yuan) was Chiang
Ching-kuo, elder son of Generalissimo Chiang Kai-shek. His government
was reputedly progressive and certainly unusually "clean." Young Chiang
did not accept bribes and sometimes punished officials who did so.

Here the contractors failed to pay sums owing to the workers when
construction was finished. The workers appealed to the authorities.
After lengthy examination, Chiang found the charges justified. He
sentenced the contractors to pay a fine of several million dollars to
the national war fund. The workers, however, received nothing. Perhaps
this was because the investigation took so long that most of them went
home before it was completed.

In the Chungking Coal Mines: Contract labor was the rule in China's
wartime mines. Shu Hwa wrote: 4/

"Coal mines in Chungking are divided into two areas,
the South Bank (of the Yangtze) field, with 240 enterprises and 1,455 workers, and the Kialing River field,
with 80 pits from Chungking to Peipei. Few are large.
Except for the Tien Fu mine (connected with the Anglo-
Chinese Peking Syndicate) most of them employ manual
power. The biggest pits have over 500 workers each,

---

4. Op. cit.

the others not more than 20 to 30. The total number of colliers along the Kialing does not exceed 5,000.

"The contractor system is generally employed. Let us take the Lungmenhao coalfield on the South Bank as an example. It has about 300 workers. Each foreman or sub-contractor controls twenty or thirty. The contractor receives a sum from the company out of which he pays for implements, food and wages. The workers have no direct relation with the company. There are night and day shifts. Many child workers are employed. They are war-stricken juveniles. They are not allowed to leave the field. Besides food and clothing they are given a dollar a day as wage."

The present writer visited mines in Chungking but company offi-cials were always careful to accompany him. The workers, who were invariably bedraggled and half-starved looking, would not answer any but the most innocuous questions. They waited for the escort to reply to the rest. The officials themselves, while pretending paternal solicitude for the miners, made no bones about admitting that many of them were working off their own or their parents' debts.

A young student of Futan University whom the writer asked to conduct an investigation encountered the same obstacles. He was able to speak to a maimed former child worker in the neighborhood of one mine. This boy of twelve said that he had become a coal carrier at ten for the contractor in whose employment his father had previously been crippled and an uncle had gone blind. No compensation was paid for the injuries to the elder men, or to the child himself who had been run over by a truck.

The boy said that before the accident he had carried 30 catties (about 40 lbs.) of coal a distance of 30 li (10 miles) every day. He had been paid a small money wage, varying from week to week with the rocketing inflation, plus an allowance of coal for cooking purposes. The whole family was permitted to live in a company hut. This was in a primitive "native" mine. But the management of the Tien Fu (Peking Syndicate) field also declined to allow students near their workers, even refusing a formal request by a group from the Futan Journalism Department to visit the enterprise.

The Kochiu Tin Mines: The great Kochiu tin mines, which employ 55,000 workers in Yunnan provinces, are an old example of contract debt slavery. An eye-witness pamphlet on conditions there, written by Su Er-kiang in late 1938, was summarized in an admittedly "softened" English version by the China branch of the International Labor Office in February 1943. The I.L.O. paper contained the following observa-tions:

Of the population of 95,000 persons in Kochiu district only five percent were unconnected with tin production. Workers were recruited from the villages by company agents who advanced "family allowances" and traveling expenses, both deducted from future wages. The custom-ary term of work was one year, but bad conditions plus the worker's realization that he had been lied to when recruited resulted in many

- 52 -

premature escapes. Half of the workers were under 16 years of age. Small children were used in shafts which were less than 4 feet high.

There was no definite working time. Each worker had to mine 500 catties of ore daily, which he could not do in less than ten hours underground. The work week was seven days, with no rest periods or paid holidays whatsoever. The average monthly pay in 1938 was $7.00 Chinese currency. Food, valued at $5 monthly, was supplied. But the worker had to buy his own clothes, a mat to sit on while in the shaft, oil for lamps used while working, etc.

The paper stated that "annual mortality in the Yunnan Tin Company mines, which were the best, was 25.2%. In other mines it was even higher." Most of the casualties were traced to "perpetual darkness and water which, mixed with the minerals, produced poisoning." The mines had wooden props but cave-ins were common. Poor ventilation was credited with causing many deaths by suffocation. Because there were no paved paths , crippling or fatal injuries frequently resulted from collisions and falls of workers carrying heavy loads. Living quarters were "of flimsy construction, made of broken stones and mud, dirty and without windows."

Miners were expected to bear their own medical expenses, regardless of the cause of illness or injury. Since they had little or no money, this meant that they went without treatment. In 1938 the books of the Yunnan Tin Corporation, with 3,000 workers, showed a total of $840 spent for medical care to staff and workers. Listed under burial expenses paid by the company in the same period was a sum of $230. The paper notes that the contractors ran gambling and opium dens where workers squandered what cash they had and ran into new debts.

The mines were taken over by the National Resources Commission at the end of 1938. It was stated that conditions then improved. The writer has seen no independent account of the subsequent situation.

4. Chattel Slavery

Walter Chen, Southeast China regional director of the Chinese Industrial Cooperatives, told the writer early in 1944 that chattel slavery had reappeared as a result of the great famines in Kwangtung in 1942-43.

Early in 1943, a flood of starving refugees swept north from Kwangtung toward Kiangsi. Alarmed, the Kiangsi provincial government turned them back with machine-guns. This left tens of thousands stranded and desperate in the tobacco-growing Nanhsiung (Namyung) area on the inter-provincial border. They began to sell their women -- the time-honored last resort of the famine-stricken in China. Traditionally, women and girl children have been sold individually for concubinage and domestic service. The Nanhsiung tobacco growers, however, bought whole groups for field labor. Regular markets were established, and young women picked for health and strength were purchased at so much a pound. Mr. Chen saw both the sales, and the slaves at work.

The writer heard rumors of similar developments in the Kuomintang-held Northwest after the Honan famine, which also occurred in 1942-43, but was not able to substantiate them.

CHAPTER VII

KUOMINTANG LABOR LAWS AND DECREES

1. History and the War Emergency

The labor laws issued by the Kuomintang Central Government of China during the war with Japan stemmed directly from those of the preceding decade of civil war, which had been marked by fear and suppression of both labor and peasant organizations.

The repressive Labor Union Law of 1929, passed to prevent the resurgence of the great trade union movement that had been repressed in 1927, was not amended, during the war years, till 1945. And the amended law not only failed to reverse the "police" character of its predecessor but was in certain respects even more stringent.

This was both anomalous and significant, in view of the radically changed political alignment in the country. Different stages of the civil-war period of 1927-37 had been accompanied by violent class clashes of capital vs. labor, landlords vs. peasants, and workers and peasants vs. the government -- passing into armed terror on the one hand and armed insurrection on the other. In the war against Japan, on the contrary, workers and peasants supported the Central Government in national defence. Notably, the policy of the Communist Party, political and military spearhead of their former protest and revolt, changed to one of cooperation with the Kuomintang and social peace within the country. The Communists in 1937-1945 opposed strikes as detrimental to the war effort and undertook no independent organization of labor (and the peasantry) in Kuomintang-administered areas.

What was hoped for in the cooperation of various classes for war purposes was a more equitable distribution of burdens expressed in a popular slogan of 1937-39: "Those with money must give money; those with strength must give their strength." Sacrifice of "money" by the owning groups implied not only appropriate contributions to the war chest in taxes and gifts but also lower rent charges by landlords, more moderate profits for commerce from articles of mass consumption, and better wages paid to labor by industrialists. How these aims were to be achieved through voluntary organization and economic regulation by governmental organs truly solicitous of the war effort as a whole was widely discussed throughout the nation in the earlier period of the war.

Nonetheless, an analysis of Kuomintang writings, and of official wartime documents having the force of law or policy reveals no single concrete project for the re-distribution of income and burdens so long overdue in Chinese society, and so essential to the mobilization of energies for resistance. Those issued during the united-front "honeymoon" of 1937-38 confined themselves to paying rather qualified lip-service to the principle. Administrative enactments from 1939 on, while pretending to implement these statements, actually marked a retreat even from such lip-service.

The pronouncements of the Emergency National Congress of the Kuomintang, held in Hankow in April 1938, and marking the highest point of the party's wartime "progressiveness", were supported by all other groups -- including the Communists -- as a charter for the national war effort. The Manifesto of the Congress stated that "the producing elements of the population cheerfully contribute the fruit of their sweat and toil" and that "the patriotism of the peasants and laborers is particularly praiseworthy." But in the sphere of social and economic reform it had no recommendation other than "elevation of moral standards" and "advancement of scientific studies."

The Program of Armed Resistance and Reconstruction passed at the Congress pledged measures against hoarding and excessive prices. Its chapter on "The Mass Movement," declared: 1/

"The people throughout the country shall be aroused and organized into occupational groups such as unions of farmers, laborers, merchants and students. The rich shall be asked to contribute in money and the able-bodied shall contribute in labor service. All classes... shall be mobilized for war." (Art. 25).

"Freedom of speech, press and assembly are to be fully protected by law during the war, if they do not contravene the Three People's Principles and provided they come within the scope of laws and ordinances." (Art. 26).

The section on "Economic Affairs" merely stressed the need for more war industries, mine production, agricultural output and attraction (not mobilization) of private investment. It failed to advance any specific measures for preserving, much less improving, the level of livelihood. Labor, as such, was not mentioned. Never implemented at any time, the promises in the "Mass Movement" Section of the Program of Armed Resistance and Reconstruction were explicitly revoked in the National General Mobilization Act of May 5, 1943, 2/ This was actually no more than a collection into one enactment of numerous separate decrees issued from 1939 on.

Article 22 of the National General Mobilization Act specifically empowered the government, "whenever necessary" and with no other qualification, to "restrict freedom of speech, publication, writing, correspondence, assembly and organization."

Article 28 made it clear that "occupational groups", such as were spoken of in the Program of Armed Resistance and reconstruction, would not be permitted to arise by "arousing the people", but would be organized only by orders from above and used as instruments of control. It laid

---

1. All quotations are from the official translations of the Chinese Ministry of Information, Hankow and Chungking. The same texts are to be found in Chapter II, China Handbook, 1937-43, compiled by the Ministry and published in the United States by Macmillan, New York. All italics inserted for stress by the present author.

2. See Chapter I.

down that persons concerned with national defence production could be "ordered to form guilds or professional associations or join existing ones", which the government would "supervise, readjust and improve."

Article 14, dealing specifically with industrial relations, read:

"... The government, whenever necessary, may issue ordinances to prevent or settle labor disputes and may strictly prohibit lockouts, strikes, go-slow strikes or other activities hampering production...."

A supplementary measure entitled Fundamentals of Government Enforcement of the National General Mobilization Act, promulgated by the Executive Yuan on June 22, 1942, permitted trial by court martial and the application of penalties under military law for violation of the above provisions. Where they concerned war production plants, the enforcement agency was the Ministry of War.

In considering the development of Kuomintang attitudes to labor in 1937-45, one fact must always be kept in mind. The economic and financial policies of the Chungking government during the war years raised the Central and provincial administrations to the position of main owners of industry throughout the country and direct employers of the majority of workers in factories, mines and mechanical transport. The remaining "private sector" of economic enterprise was also largely monopolized by "bureaucratic capitalists" -- who were themselves government officials at the highest policy-making level. 2/

This situation placed a government in which labor had no share, and the leading members of that government in their personal capacities, in the position of benefitting in the most direct way from low wages and the lack of free labor organization. 3/ A government of this kind cannot allow independent trade unionism. It can be expected either to suppress all unions or to insist on all workers joining a state Labor Front, i.e., a glorified "company union" organized and dominated by its agents. These were precisely the features that marked Kuomintang labor legislation in the ten years before the war, and were exacerbated in the wartime period. The same factors prevented development of the democratic promises of the 1938 Program of Armed Resistance and Reconstruction, which were historically rooted in a still earlier trend, that of 1924-27.

2. The 1924 Pattern: Freedom to Organize

The present author heard from a Hankow textile worker who had gone through both periods that what labor expected from the reconstitution of the Kuomintang-Communist united front in 1937-8 was "to go back to the days of the Northern Expedition." 4/ It seemed logical to this worker that a return would be made to the labor policies of the Kuomintang during 1924-27, when the two parties together had challenged the power

---

2. See Chapter I.
3. For good descriptions of bureaucratic monopolies in Chinese trade and industry immediately after the war, see "Monopoly and Civil War in China," by Chen Han-seng, in No. 20 (1946), and "Business and Politics in China", by Harley Stevens, in No. 19 (1946), Far Eastern Survey, New York.
4. See Introduction, above.

of foreign imperialism and the northern warlords, and cooperation among all classes engaged in that revolutionary effort had been the watchword.

At that time, Sun Yat-sen had written in his Fundamentals of National Reconstruction (1924): "The primary task of reconstruction is the people's livelihood..." 5/

Paragraph 11 of the Declaration of the First National Congress of the Kuomintang (January 1924) had stated:

"Labor laws shall be enacted to improve the workmen's living conditions, to protect labor organizations and foster their development." 6/

The Trade Union Regulations subsequently proclaimed by Sun Yat-sen in November 1924 provided that:

(1) ...Trade unions and employers' associations be placed on an equal footing; (2) Trade unions have freedom of speech; (3) Trade unions have the right to conclude collective agreements with employers; (4) Unions have the right to ask administrative authorities to inquire into, or arbitrate, disputes; (5) Unions have the right to strike; (6) Unions have the right to participate with employers in regulating hours, working conditions and factory hygiene; (7) In disputes in private industry government authorities could investigate or arbitrate but could not enforce decisions by compulsion; (8) Security of trade union property be guaranteed; (9) Previous legal provisions limiting the right of meeting, association and strike should not be applied to trade unions; (10) The principle of industrial organization be encouraged. 7/

The labor policy outlined in these documents led to the organization of more than 2 million Chinese workers prior to the 1927 split. In conjunction with Sun Yat-sen's Three Great Policies in the National Revolution, which called for "alliance with the workers and peasants", it made the labor movement a pillar of support for the contemporary Kuomintang and a major factor in bringing it military victory.

In the war against Japan, however, the expectations of the Hankow worker quoted above did not come to fruition. There was no return either to the general principles or to any of the separate provisions of the enlightened Kuomintang labor legislation of 1924.

3. The 1929 Pattern: Control of Labor

Instead, wartime Kuomintang labor laws were elaborations and extensions of the Labor Union Law of October 21, 1929 (amended in 1931 and 1933), the first attempt of the right-wing Kuomintang to introduce legality into its labor relations after the sanguinary suppression of the trade unions in 1927.

---

5. China Handbook, 1937-43, Chapter II.

6. Ibid.

7. Summarized from Lowe Chuan-hua, Facing Labor Issues in China. Shanghai, 1933.

Chao Pan-fu, an official of the Ministry of Social Affairs, dealing with labor matters, has characterized the concepts thus inaugurated as a transition from "the system of free development of the labor movement to the principle of regulated development." 8/ Lowe Chuan-hua wrote that the Kuomintang, after 1927, "commenced to enforce its policy ... of party government. It claims that since the masses are ignorant and are apt fundamentally to become the victims of vicious propaganda the Nationalist Party should perform the duty of organizing and training all the mass movements in China." 9/ Shih Wei-huan, writing as late as the middle of the war, is similarly clear on the contrast between the labor policies of the early Kuomintang and those of its post-1927 successor. He says:

> "The 1924 regulations of the Canton Military Government under Sun Yat-sen ... were the widest labor union law of our history. They not only fixed the right of association but gave labor many conveniences ....

> "After the 'party purge' (the 1927 split -I.E.) the government, because of the low level of the intelligence of labor, decided that if workers were allowed to organize freely it would not only disturb social peace but would at the same time fail to promote the happiness of the workers themselves.

> "Therefore the Labor Union Law passed in 1929, although it recognized the right of association, limited it very strictly. It gave the government power to control labor organization by practical methods ...." 10/

The distinction between "freedom" and "control", recognized so frankly by Kuomintang as well as independent writers, was indeed the watershed between the liberal Labor Union Regulations of 1924 and the master Labor Union Law of 1929-33, which was diametrically opposed to them in conception.

Analyzing the latter law, which has formed the foundation of all subsequent labor legislation by the Kuomintang, we find that:

1. Freedom of organization had been surrendered:

Article 3 of the Labor Union Law of 1929 prohibited altogether the organization of "workers, office staff and office employees of military institutions and military industrial establishments", as well as civil "government office staff and office employees", including teachers in the schools but not including "workers" -- meaning servants, messengers and persons performing other tasks regarded as menial in such enterprises.

---

8. Economic Bulletin of the Central Bank of China, June 1942.

9. Facing Labor Issues in China, quoted by Nym Wales in The Chinese Labor Movement, John Day Co., 1945.

10. "The Question of the Right of Free Organization for Labor After The War", by Shih Wei-huan, in Chungshan Wenhua, April 1943, quarterly published by the Sun Yat-sen Cultural and Educational Institute, Peipei, Chungking municipality, Szechuan.

Article 5 permitted the organization of unions in private industry, but only after approval, by "competent government authority", of a petition signed by at least fifty workers in the case of a craft union and 100 workers in the case of an industrial union. The petition, along with a copy of the draft constitution of the union, was to be handed in by a delegation of five to nine workers' representatives, each of whom was also required to provide two copies of his life history.

Article 6 forbade the establishment of more than one union in a given industry or craft in the same locality. It has the effect of making it impossible for a new, competing organization to arise where the one already authorized was company-dominated or in other respects did not satisfy the needs of its membership.

2. <u>Unions, once organized, enjoyed no autonomy</u>:

Article 15 provided that the government could appoint officers to "assist" a union in carrying out activities which the government deemed necessary.

Article 20 abolished the right of unions to determine who should be admitted to membership. It made it compulsory for them to admit workers "qualified by law and the union's constitution" and to deny membership to workers disqualified by law or the union's constitution. "Law" was not defined or limited to the provisions of the Labor Union Law itself.

Article 26 required the union to supply to "the competent government authority" twice a year, and by special order at any other time, the following documents:

(a) Names and biographies of all officers; (b) Membership rolls; (c) Reports on activities; (d) Reports on disputes and settlements.

This requirement was reinforced by penal provisions (Arts. 47 and 50) laying down fines of up to $200 for officers and members guilty of violations; and specifically fixing a fine of $100 for failure to submit full reports semi-annually or as ordered.

Article 27 empowered "competent government authorities" to annul union decisions (including elections) which they deemed contrary to the provisions of government decrees and laws, or of the union constitution as officially approved.

Article 37 gave the government power to dissolve any union. It outlined no procedure for appeals against such dissolution.

Article 38 deprived members themselves of the right to dissolve unions. It made approval by "competent government authority" necessary before any general members' meeting decision to dissolve could take effect. This provision of course, made it impossible to remove an unsatisfactory authorized union from the field to make way for the legal establishment of one more in accord with the members' desires, which would otherwise be prohibited under the anti-dual unionism clause of Article 6.

3. Not all unions had the right to bargain collectively:

Article 16 denied the right to bargain collectively to authorized unions of workers employed by the government or by institutions which the government owned or controlled (a large part of Chinese labor in industry and transport fell into this category, including all those employed in railways, posts, telegraphs, etc.)

Article 15 required government sanction of all collective agreements concluded even by these unions (in private enterprises) entitled to participate. Unapproved contracts could be voided under Article 26 and those responsible punished under Articles 47 and 50 (see above).

4. The right to strike was annulled or limited:

Article 23 prohibited strikes in government service or in government-controlled enterprises. The same article provided that no union anywhere could strike for wages higher than the "standard rate" determined by government authority.

5. The open shop was mandatory:

Article 27 provided that no union or union member could require an employer to hire only such workers as were recommended by the said union or union member.

6. Freedom of federation, affiliation and international contact was denied:

Article 45 required approval by "competent government authority" before unions could federate industrially, regionally or nationally.

Article 38 required similar approval before unions could affiliate with any foreign or international union or federation. 11/

7. Legal protection of unions and members was severely conditional:

Government protection was extended only to unions formed under, and complying with, the above provisions of the law. As outlined in Articles 31-36, it provided:

(a) Exemption of authorized unions from income, business and registration taxes; (b) Exemption of authorized unions from confiscation of dues funds, labor insurance funds, headquarters, schools, educational and welfare institutions; (c) Guarantees of non-discrimination by employers, in the fields of hiring and treatment, for members of authorized unions; also specific guarantees against dismissal during government arbitration of disputes (but not before or after submission to arbitration.) These provisions were buttressed by Articles 48 and 49, which provided fines up to $300 for proved instances of discrimination by employers, and fines of from $10 to

11. Summarized from A Complete Collection of Laws, Rules and Regulations of the Republic of China, Shanghai, 1936.

to $100 for illegal dismissal as described.

4. Wartime Theory and Enactments

During the war, the government increased its control of labor without any contemporary extension of rights or benefits, or any recognition of the changed social and political atmosphere.

Startling frank was a passage in an article by Chin Fen, Vice-Minister of Economic Affairs, telling what the Kuomintang expected of labor in the war. Writing a very few months after his own party had adopted the resounding "Program of National Resistance and Reconstruction" Mr. Chin said: 12/

> "Patriotism would urge the workers to contribute their utmost and prevent them from giving any more trouble to their fellow-countrymen. They also know that business in general is uncertain and if once they lose their job they will find it difficult to get another one ...."

> "The government in the meantime has promulgated ... wartime control of agricultural, mining, industrial and commercial enterprises. Strikes, sabotage, lockouts, etc. are all prohibited ..."

What really happened was that the government utilized the war emergency to launch a one-sided class struggle, a new offensive against the already miserable standards of Chinese workers. This was unconsciously confirmed by Mr. Chin in a later paragraph, in which he stated:

> "In some of China's war industries the employees have worked 10 to 12 hours every day without complaint or demand of any kind .... During the first three months of 1938, disputes related mainly to the dismissal of workers as necessitated by the war .... Industrial conflicts are surprisingly few, considering the fact that the cost of living has increased .... The real wage, therefore, has dropped sharply. Worse than that, the workers have had to be content with a reduction of the nominal wage as well."

Their meaning of all wartime labor decrees from 1938 on was further elucidated by Mr. Chao Pan-fu, who had noted the transition from "free development" of unions before 1927 to "regulated development" during the next ten years. Under wartime powers, he stated:

> "The government ... has passed from the policy of partial control which characterized the second period to a policy of active control." 13/

12. Chinese Year Book, 1938-39. (Emphasis mine. I.E.)

13. Chao Pan-fu, op. cit.

- 61 -

Shih Wei-han wrote:

"After the outbreak of the war of resistance, the
government, in order to enable people's organizations to
do their duty in wartime, proclaimed in July 1940 the
Draft Law on People's Organizations in Wartime ... Then,
on October 11, 1940, it promulgated the Wartime Law for
Compulsory Joining of Professional Organizations and the
Limitation of the Right of Withdrawal From Them, with
the purpose of forcing workers to join unions and cur-
tailing their right to leave.

"On February 10, 1942 it passed the Wartime People's
Organization Law, to which labor unions were made subject.
On March 2, 1942, the Ministry of Social Affairs announced
the People's Organization Adjustment Law and its Guidance
for the Reform of People's Organizations. After this
reform the workers' right of association was subjected to
very severe checks ...." 14/

Labor relations by government decree and compulsory incorporation
into government-run unions were thus the two main features on which the
wartime labor policy of the Kuomintang government was based. The second,
compulsory unionization without the right of withdrawal, was new. It
paralleled the institution of Fascist Corporations in Italy and the Nazi
Labor Front in Germany, but had no resemblance to the legislation either
of Britain and the United States or of the U.S.S.R. Once announced, this
principle was built into all subsequent labor laws passed by the National
Government of China, although, as we shall see later, it was never
effectively applied.

During 1941, the National Government incorporated it in the new
Regulations Governing the Organization of Public Bodies in Time of
Emergency and Provisional Regulations Governing the Control of Labor
Unions in Time of Emergency (August 21).

In October 1942, what was heralded as a new and progressive labor
policy was adopted by the First National Social Administration Conference,
convened by the Ministry of Social Affairs in Chungking. It consisted of
two documents: A Draft Outline of Labor Policy and Draft Regulations
Covering the Enforcement of Labor Policy in Time of Emergency. 15/
Described by official spokesmen as "the first complete program for the
realization of Dr. Sun Yat-sen's labor policy", 16/ the drafts were
forwarded to the Supreme National Defence Council for promulgation.

All the above documents, and certain provisions of the General
National Mobilization Act of May 5, 1942 were made the basis of the
Amended Labor Union of November 20, 1943, which was to remain in force
without further changes until almost two years after the end of the war --
June 14, 1947. The word "amended" refers to the labor Union Law of 1929,
which still remained the foundation of the country's labor legislation.

---

14. Shih Wei-han, op. cit.
15. Translation supplied by Chinese Ministry of Information, Chungking.
16. China Handbook.

Analysing the Amended Law of 1943, and the relevant emergency
decrees that continued to have the force of supreme law, overruling
this and all other civil legislation in wartime, we find the following picture. The headings below are roughly the same as those
under which the provisions of the basic law of 1929 are grouped on
pp. 58-61 above.

1. Freedom of Organization

The Draft Outline of Labor Policy of October 1942 stated that
"Workers in military industries do not possess the right of organizing
unions" (Chapter III., Art. 3). In apparent contradiction to this,
the Draft Regulations Governing the Enforcement of Labor Policy in Time
of Emergency, published by the same authority on the same day, said that
"All workers shall join labor unions" (Chap. I, Art. 2). The Amended
Labor Union Law of November 20, 1943, clarified the inconsistency. Its
Article 12 reaffirmed the principle of compulsory membership but
limited it to "areas where trade unions are organized." Article 6, in
terms even more rigorous than those of the 1929 law, defined areas in
which no organization would be permitted as follows:

> "Officials and workers 17/ in organs of national
> executive and educational establishments, and workers in
> military factories, may not organize labor unions." 18/

The 1929 procedures for establishing unions were substantially
retained. Article 7 laid down the minimum number of workers entitled
to petition for permission to organize at 30 in any craft or 50 in any
industry. Under Article 9 they were required, after permission was
granted, to "elect preparatory officers and form a preparatory committee,
notifying the competent official organ thereof for purposes of record."
Article 9 further stated that:

> "Before the labor union convenes its foundation meeting,
> they must report to the competent official organ the
> proceedings of the preparatory committee and submit the
> draft of the regulations. They should also request the
> competent official organ to appoint an officer to supervise
> at the election of the union's officials. When the union
> has been completed, two copies of the list of members, and
> of a list showing details of the careers of the union's
> officials, should be forwarded to the competent official
> organ for record."

Article 10 laid down the required content of trade union regulations. From these provisions we see that official permission or con-
firmation was required, and would be withheld for reasons which were
neither specified nor limited in the law, at three distinct stages in
the formation of any union -- in response to the original petition,

_____

17. The 1929 law applied this restriction to "officials" only,
     specifically exempting "workers."

18. Translation prepared by the U.S. Embassy, Chungking. All further
     citations of the Amended Labor Union Law of 1943 are made from
     this English version.

after the election of preparatory officers but before the foundation meeting, and after completion of organization. Even if permitted, organization could not be completed by election of officers unless a government official was present to supervise. The government assumed no obligation to depute such an official, nor did it undertake to do so within any specified time limit. Since his "supervision" was not defined, the official, even when present, could delay organization or annul elections by refusing approval.

Article 8 repeated the restrictions of the 1929 law against more than one union in the same industry or trade in the same place, and limited the area of jurisdiction of any union to the physical boundaries of the county or municipality in which it was situated. Exemption from these limitations could be obtained only "in special circumstances and if the competent official organ approves."

Article 5 stated:

> "The competent official organ in the Central Government is the Ministry of Social Affairs, in the province the Provincial Government, in the Hsien (county) the Hsien Government, and in the Municipality the Municipal Government, but particular matters which come under particular authorities should be subject to the control of those authorities as the law requires."

The result of these restrictions and of the multiplicity of hurdles and authorities placed in the way of union organization has been that, for many years, legal unions have not been established in Kuomintang China on the initiative of their prospective members at all. The only unions that have come into being have been those set up by the authorities themselves for purposes of "labor control." In most such cases, the necessary procedures have been purely symbolic -- being limited to the drafting of documents which state that all steps have been complied with. In other instances there has been no procedure at all. The practical rule has been simple. "Unions" organized by official organs exist and are recognized. No other workers' organizations are considered as legal, or have any chance of achieving legality.

2. Autonomy

The autonomy of legally organized unions, already so whittled down by the 1929 law, was further reduced by wartime enactments.

The Provisional Regulations Governing Control of Labor in Time of Emergency of August 21, 1941, provided for:

> "Dispatch of government officials to direct and supervise the work of unions" (Art. 2, Section D); and

> "Readjustment of work and personnel of trade unions whenever necessary" (Art. 2, Section E).

The General National Mobilization Act of May 5, 1942 defined people's organizations as convenient vehicles for government control rather than as carriers of popular initiative. It affirmed the right of the government to appoint the officers of such bodies, including unions. The Draft Regulations Governing the Enforcement of Labor Policy in Time of Emergency (October 1942) stated:

"Competent authorities shall appoint qualified persons to be secretaries of labor unions" (Part I, Art. 3).

In practice the appointment of labor union secretaries had long been a prerogative of the Ministry of Social Affairs, which had previously been a department of the Kuomintang party but during the war was transferred to the government. The Ministry operated special classes to train candidates for this position. The Draft Regulations further stipulated that:

"Concerning the control of labor, provisions in the National General Mobilization Act shall be applicable" (Chap. 14).

The Amended Labor Union Law of November 20, 1943, provided:

"If there are any changes in the regulations (articles of association) of a union or in the directors or other officers, they must be reported immediately to the competent official organ and published by the latter within fifteen days" Art. 32).

"Changes in the regulations (or articles of association) may not become effective until they have been approved by the competent official organ" (Art. 33).

"The elections or decisions of labor unions may be cancelled by the competent official organ if they contravene the law or the regulations of the union concerned." (Art. 35)

With regard to membership the law repeated (in Art. 28) the limitations imposed by the 1929 law on admissions of "unqualified" persons to membership and refusal to admit "qualified" applicants. Closely linked with this provision was Article 13: "Officials ... employed by an industry or trade shall be qualified to be members of the union of their respective industry or trade, except when they are representing the employer in carrying out control functions."

Union officers were not free to call members' meetings at will. Article 21 stated that all meetings other than the annual general meeting of members to elect new officers, at which a government official had to be present under Article 9, could be convened only on "notice being given fifteen days beforehand to the competent official organ."

The freedom of unions to collect and apply funds was also severely limited. Under Article 24, initiation fees could not exceed one day's pay in the given industry or trade, and current dues were held down to 2% or less of the member's income. No special funds could be created, and no assessments of any kind levied, "without permission first obtained from the competent official organ." Article 34 forbade unions "illegally to extort subscriptions." Article 59 provided for fines and criminal liability for such "extortion."

As in 1929, union officers were obliged, on pain of fines and penalties (Article 62), to conform to the following provisions:

"When the formation of a union had been authorized, it shall prepare a list of members and account books in duplicate ... (and) ... one copy ... shall be deposited with the competent official organ. The membership list must indicate ... about the members: their names, number, date of joining, place of occupation ..." (Article 30).

"Unions should send to the competent official organ every year 19/... (1) a list of names of union officials and particulars of their careers; (2) list of members and those who have withdrawn (3) account books; (4) a statement of the conditions of trade in the particular industry ..." (Article 31).

The "competent official organ" was given power to dissolve any union for the following reasons:

"(1) If it does not comply with any of the basic conditions of foundation; (2) If there is any serious contravention of the law; (3) if it is guilty of interfering with public law and order or damaging public welfare" (Article 45).

Appeal against such dissolution could be made within thirty days of the official order, but there was no mention in the law of where the appeal should be lodged or how it should be handled.

Unions themselves were empowered to dissolve in case of bankruptcy, insufficient membership or amalgamation or division into other unions (Article 46). Reasons for dissolution were to be notified to the authorities. Immediately after dissolution by official order, or as a result of bankruptcy, the union was to be "referred in accordance with the laws" (Article 50). As for any amalgamation or division, "permission therefore must be obtained from the competent official organ" (Article 48).

The membership of a union dissolving itself was not allowed to decide freely on the disposition of its assets. The law ruled (Article 51) that these should be transferred to the "reconstituted union", or in its absence to any federation of which the dissolved union was a member, or, if the union had not been so affiliated, "to the self-governing body in the place where the union was situated."

3. The right to bargain collectively and to strike

The author does not know of a single case, during the war, in which a collective contract on internationally-accepted lines was signed between management and any labor union in Kuomintang China. Throughout the war, strikes were illegal.

In Kuomintang labor legislation, the right to bargain collectively and to strike was limited to "Ordinary Labor Unions", as distinct from "Special Labor Unions" in enterprises which were publicly owned or had the character of a public utility. The distinction was first drawn in

19. Twice a year in the 1929 law.

the Regulations for the Organization of Labor Unions and the Regulations Concerning the Organization of Special Labor Unions promulgated by the Standing Committee of the Central Executive Committee of the Kuomintang on July 9 and July 26, 1928, respectively. [20]/ It was incorporated into the Labor Union Law of 1929 and all subsequent amendments to it.

A striking wartime reaffirmation of the principle was to be found in the Draft Outline of Labor Policy of October 1942. It contained the following interesting collection of provisions.

"Labor unions possess the right of collective bargaining".
"Labor unions possess the right of striking."
"Special and ordinary labor organizations shall be separately formed."

"Workers in military industries do not possess the right of organizing unions. Special unions of public enterprises do not possess the right of striking and collective bargaining. Special unions of privately-owned public utility and communication enterprises possess the right of collective bargaining but not the right of striking."

The sense of all previous wartime decrees was summarized in the National General Mobilization Act, which prohibited strikes of every kind. The Draft Regulations Governing the Enforcement of Labor Policy in Time of Emergency (October 1942) stated: "Members of both ordinary and special labor unions may not declare strikes."

The Amended Labor Union Law of November 20, 1943, prohibited organization of certain categories of workers in Article 6. In Article 63, it declared that "Provisions regarding special labor unions shall be enacted separately."

Article 20 of the law, applying to ordinary unions alone, read:

"No strike may be declared over disputes between employers and laborers until the dispute has been submitted for conciliation or arbitration, and more than 50 per cent of all the members of the union have agreed to it by secret ballot at a general meeting .... Strikes are also not permitted in the case of disputes which have been submitted to arbitration or which are required by law to be so submitted.

"In times of strikes unions may not take action harmful to public peace and order or likely to endanger the lives and property of employers and third parties.

"Unions may not declare a strike resulting from demands for the payment of wages above the standard level.

"Nor may unions declare strikes for any reason whatsoever during an emergency period."

---

20. *China's Labor Laws*, Ministry of Industries, Nanking, 1934, cited in The Chinese Labor Movement by Nym Wales.

"Go slow" strikes were forbidden at all times under Article 34, Section 7, of the same law, and were punishable by a moderate fine, with or without criminal prosecution, under Article 59. Under Article 5 of the Fundamentals Governing Enforcement of the National General Mobilization Act (June 1942), however, strikes of all kinds could result in trial by court martial and offenders could be punished by a fine of $100,000 and imprisonment up to seven years.

4. Picketing

. Peaceful picketing was made illegal under Article 34, Section 1, which forbade union officials or members to "seal (or blockade) a shop or factory", on pain of fines and/or criminal prosecution (Article 59). Also relevant here was Article 20, making the union responsible for compensating any loss "if the director of the union or his representatives inflicts damage on third parties in carrying out his duties."

5. Open Shop

The 1943 law followed that of 1929 in establishing the open shop through prohibiting any action that would "interfere with the use by an employer of workers recommended to him" (Article 34, Section 4). The penal provisions for violation were those of Article 59, which were also applicable to "go slow" strikes, picketing, sabotage and "extortion" of assessments.

6. Freedom to Federate or Affiliate

No National federation of labor existed in wartime Kuomintang China. The substitute was the Chinese Association of Labor, an outside "service" organization and not a federation in any sense. An examination of the 1943 law reveals numerous obstacles which made it impossible to organize such an organ.

Article 4, Section 1, listed "formation, alteration or annulment of instruments of affiliation with other bodies" as a function of labor unions but immediately followed this with the proviso: "But the above shall not be valid unless approval of the competent official organization has been obtained."

Article 22 permitted general meetings of unions to discuss or pass resolutions on "the organization of a General Labor Union or a Federation of Labor Unions" (Section G) and "amalgamation or division of the union" (Section H), but not to take action in this regard.

Article 53 stated that a group of different industrial or craft unions could form a Hsien (county) or Municipal General Labor Union with official permission, but the activities of such a joint body were specifically limited to "increasing production capacity and facilitating the application of government regulations." This suggests the real nature of General Labor Unions as organs of control In practice they have invariably served this purpose, as instruments of the Ministry of Social Affairs and its local counterparts (bureaus).

Article 56 laid down regulations for provincial "federations." On the provincial level, however, the "Federation" could not embrace all trades but only local unions in one particular industry or craft. The purpose of such "federations" was "to increase the knowledge and skill of workers ... and manage mutually advantageous enterprises." They could be formed by five or more unions, i. given official permission.

In view of the limitations on local and provincial organizations, it is not surprising to find that a nationwide federation was nowhere legally defined. Nor did the law permit the establishment of <u>national</u> unions in separate trades. (National <u>special</u> labor unions have existed for some time but are actually operated by the government in all but name and cannot bargain collectively or strike.) Conferences of provincial "federations" of particular trades could be convened only by the Ministry of Social Affairs "when the Ministry of Social Affairs or the competent authorities of the trade or industry concerned consider it necessary." The term "competent authorities of the trade or industry" was not explained, but could presumably mean the employers. The Ministry could also convene such a conference "if the federation of labor unions in five provinces or more request it."

7. <u>Freedom of International Contact</u>

The All-China Labor Federation that existed legally from 1925 to 1926 and was driven underground in the latter year to lead a limited existence until 1931, had been affiliated to the Red Trade Union International (Profintern) and the Pan-Pacific Trade Union Secretariat. It has exchanged delegations with, and received aid from, a number of foreign unions both within and outside these bodies. After the Federation was outlawed, the Kuomintang acted vigorously to isolate the Chinese labor movement from contact with its counterparts abroad.

From 1927 until the International Trade Union Conference held in London in February 1945, which set up the World Federation of Trade Unions, the International Labor Office of the League of Nations was the only body to which Chinese "workers' representatives" were sent. Chinese delegations to the I.L.O., like those of other states, were composed of spokesmen for employers, labor and the government respectively. Their "labor member" was invariably an officially appointed and approved member of the Kuomintang. Following the inauguration of the Chinese Association of Labor under official auspices, in 1935, this function was discharged by the C.A.L.'s President, Chu Hsueh-fan, an officer of the Postal Employees' "Special" Trade Union.

In 1946, Mr. Chu, who had also become chief Chinese delegate to the newly-formed W.F.T.U., asserted the independence of his organization. He was forthwith deposed from the presidency of the C.A.L. by "the competent official authorities", forced to flee China, and replaced on the governing body of the I.L.O. by a more tractable designee. Chu and other long-standing C.A.L. officials then set up a new headquarters in Hong Kong and established closer relations than ever before with rank-and-file groups within Kuomintang China, as well as with the unions of the Communist-led Liberated Areas. The W.F.T.U. threw its support to the Hong Kong group and continued to recognize its delegation. A detailed consideration of the events outlined above will be found in the next chapter. The above facts form a framework for the consideration of wartime measures of the Kuomintang government in the sphere of international labor contacts.

The Outline of Labor Policy of October 1942 illustrated very graphically the official view of the scope and desired objectives in this field. Under the heading of "Strengthening International Labor Cooperation" (Chapter 11), it listed the following functions:

"A. The Three People's Principles (official Kuomintang ideology - I.E.) shall be publicized among international workers to enable them to understand the spirit of our national reconstruction.

"B. Participation in meetings convened by the I.L.O.

"C. Rectification of international labor conventions fitting our national conditions.

"D. Assistance in matters engaged in and promoted by the I.L.O."

The simultaneously-issued Draft Regulations Governing the Enforcement of Labor Policy in Time of Emergency (Chapter VIII.) had a more liberal sound.

"Concerning international labor cooperation, workers, with the permission of competent authorities, may set up an organization in order to participate in the international labor movement prior to the formation of a national labor union, and to make necessary association with labor organizations in the democratic countries such as Great Britain, the United States and the U.S.S.R."

Analyzing this recommendation, we note that the proposed organization was to have "labor diplomacy", under government auspices, as its main function. It was to occupy the place rightly belonging to a Chinese national labor federation, towards the establishment of which no concrete measures were being taken within the country, in any United Nations trade union body to which a purely government-composed delegation, such as that sent to the I.L.O. would not be acceptable. Its presence would exclude any other body claiming to speak for Chinese labor. Its function, as may be seen from the heading of the Draft Regulations, was to apply the Labor Policy (see above) under existing wartime circumstances.

In actual fact, no such "organization" was set up, the C.A.L. continuing to represent Chinese labor internationally, and on the government's behalf, in both the I.L.O. and the W.F.T.U. formed later. Events toward the end of the war and in the following years did indeed lead the C.A.L. to a position of "participation in the international labor movement prior to the formation of a national labor union", but under circumstances the government had not anticipated, and in opposition to its policies.

Returning to wartime legislation, we find in the Amended Labor Union Law of November 20, 1943, the following provision (Article 39):

"A union may not establish any connection with a foreign
union unless the government allows it."

For its own reasons, the government did permit the C.A.L., which
was not a union in the sense of the law, to participate in the W.F.T.U.
On the other hand, early in 1945, it rejected the petition of a strong
group of the strictly-controlled Chinese Seamen's Union, several thousand
of whose members, employed on foreign ships, were based in Liverpool
during the war, to affiliate with the International Transport Federation.

8. Legal Protection of Unions

The Amended Trade Union Law of 1943 extended protection to unions
formed under its strict provisions.

It prohibited employer discrimination against members of such unions
(Article 40), making abstention from holding union office a condition of
employment (Article 41), and dismissals of workers while a wage dispute
was under process of conciliation or arbitration (Article 42). Penalties
were provided against contraventions (Articles 60 and 61). On the other
hand the law afforded no security against dismissal subsequent to such a
dispute, in connection with disputes on questions other than wages, or
for strike activity.

Unions were "entitled to claim priority" over other creditors of
their bankrupt debtors (Article 43). Union funds, workers' insurance
funds and the real or movable property of unions, including libraries,
schools, clubs, hospitals, cooperative societies, etc. were secured
against confiscation (Article 44).

Unions not licensed and controlled by government authorities under
the Act did not fall within the scope of its protective provisions, but
on the contrary were liable to prosecution under various laws and wartime
decrees as illegal associations.

5. Conciliation and Arbitration

Kuomintang labor legislation subsequent to 1927 made it illegal to
call strikes until disputes had been submitted for conciliation and/or
arbitration. The procedures employed were not defined in the Labor
Union Law, but were established under the Act Governing the Settlement of
Disputes Between Employers and Employees of June 9, 1928, with its
subsequent amendments.

This act provided for arbitration boards of five members, one each
from the "designated government authority", the local Kuomintang party
organization, the local law court, and from among "employers and workers
not directly involved in the dispute, chosen from panels registered with
the Ministry of Industries." Under a 1933 amendment, municipal Bureau
of Social Affairs were designated as the "competent administrative
authority", in place of direct representatives of the local governments
as before. The Ministry of Social Affairs and corresponding local organs,
which already exercised supreme authority over the formation and functioning of trade unions and soon came to appoint their secretaries from
among their own officials, thus came to have a decisive voice in conciliation and arbitration procedure as well.

In pre-war practice this conciliation and arbitration scheme was extensively employed only in Shanghai outside the International Settlement. Even there it was often a mere formality which masked the reality of administrative compulsion or "compromises" and "labor fixing" through the medium of the gangs. Similar machinery existed in Peiping, Tientsin and other "special municipalities" but was less used.

In basic form, the regulations on conciliation and arbitration boards remained unchanged throughout the war. The work of these boards was, however, largely taken over by administrative officials of the Ministry of Social Affairs as well as other agencies with arbitrary powers created under the National General Mobilization Act and other decrees. In 1943 a Labor Disputes Arbitration Board was functioning in Kweilin. It was made up of representatives of the Kuomintang party headquarters, the city government, the district court, capital and labor. During that year it handled only five disputes, all concerning wages. Despite the existence of 110 "modern" factories in the city (munitions, radio, machine-building, flour, textiles, soap, cement) only one of the grievances submitted involved industrial workers (printers). Of the others three involved craftsmen in small workshops (carpenters, pen-makers and tailors) and one the coolies' union. Other industrial centers presented the same picture.

This checks with data from other places showing clearly that conciliation and arbitration machinery played a purely subsidiary role in wartime labor relations. The chapter on "Industry and Labor" in the official China Handbook fails even to note its continued existence.

6. Labor Mobility and Wage-Fixing

Other fields that were the subject of many decrees and regulations issued during the war were labor "poaching" by factories in the Kuomintang rear, mobility of labor, particularly among skilled workers, and control of wages. These are considered together because the first wartime wage-control measures grew precisely out of the problem of mobility, though subsequent ones were perhaps more connected with the general inflationary crisis. What interests us here is not so much the relation of these measures to the immediate economic situations they were devised to meet as their political and social character -- which was inevitably fascist or "corporative".

This feature appears very early in the war, in an anti-poaching enactment by the Industrial and Mining Adjustment Administration of the National Ministry of Economics in September 1938. The measure was directed mainly against mutual raids on one another's labor force by the mushrooming factories of the interior -- which were desperately short of skilled workers. Its stated aim was to control the employer rather than the worker. Yet the text, according to the China Handbook 21/ "ordered employers not to poach and workers not to change employment without the consent of the employers" (italics mine - I.E.). Factories were required to submit copies of workers' registration cards, with their photographs, to the controlling authorities. Workers leaving without employers' permission could be forcibly sent back to their original

---

21. Chapter XI, "Industry & Labor".

factories. The main weight of administrative sanctions was directed at the worker, not the "poaching" owner. While the aggrieved employer could appeal to the authorities, the worker was entirely under his control and had no such recourse, individually or through his union, if he could not produce evidence of employer consent. Similar inequality was the essence of German, Italian and Japanese labor legislation, which made the employer the "leader" of labor in his enterprise, though the wording and forms were different.

The "corporative" character of Kuomintang control of labor poaching was further evident in the self-regulatory scheme devised by the Association of Factories Moved to Szechuan with the approval of the Industrial and Mining Adjustment Administration. This provided that a fine of $500 be paid by "poaching" employers for each worker so recruited. Investigation was undertaken by the Association, but fines were to be levied by local governments at its request. Here again, the interests of the worker himself received no protection.

As more skilled workers arrived from the occupied cities, and industry in the rear failed to develop to the extent expected, labor poaching ceased to be the main problem. Workers themselves began to move from enterprise to enterprise or to set up their own workshops, privately or cooperatively owned. In the labor-poaching days of 1938 the real wage index for machinists (base: January-June 1937=100) had been 166.7 By 1940 it had dropped to 77.1, by 1941 to 53.1 and by March 1942 to a low of 41.1. In other words, these skilled workers in the spring of 1942 were receiving one quarter, in terms of purchasing powers, of their pay four years earlier, 22/ The same thing occurred in other trades. Consequently, as the China Handbook admits, earlier regulations lost all meaning and effect -- because they were not linked to any guarantee with regard to wages, or any official action to deal with great wage variations between different localities and between different factories in the same place.

The result of this realization by the government was the passage of the Regulations Governing the Stabilization of Wages (Executive Yuan, January 15, 1941). The regulations, which were to be applied first to Chungking and then to other industrial cities, empowered the Ministry (and local bureaux) of Social Affairs to fix wages on the basis of cost-of-living indices. They served as the basis for a nation-wide wage-fixing enactment under the Regulations Governing the Strengthening of Price Control January 15, 1943).

The Ministry of Social Affairs then ordered that wages be stabilized at the level of November 30, 1942 (about 50% in real value of those of 1937) in all areas, "where price control measures were in effect". The order was applicable to the main industries (machinery, textiles, printing, flour, etc.) and to occupational workers (carpenters, builders, boatmen, rickshaw pullers, etc.) Committees to decide wage rates were to be composed of representatives of local Kuomintang headquarters, the

---

22. From the monthly reports of the Ministry of Social Affairs, Chungking.

local government, the San Min Chu I Youth Corps, the Chamber of Commerce, and labor. 23/ But the final authority was to lie, as always, with the Bureaux of Social Affairs as well as, in this case, with the Reconstruction (Economic) Departments of country and provincial governments. Wage Regulation Committees were specifically given powers "to organize and control labor unions" and were thus added to the multifarious official organizations already possessing jurisdiction in this field.

During the same period restrictions on job-changes by workers were greatly intensified. The Regulations for Government Control of Skilled Labor in Time of Emergency (Ministry of Economics, April 9, 1942) were put into effect in metal, machine, electrical, chemical, textile, food, printing and stationery industries in the main factory centers of the country. They instituted certificates of registration without which no worker under their jurisdiction could be hired by any enterprise, or conduct one of his own, with penalties for violation applicable to both employer and employee. The certificates were to be issued by local Committees for the Control of Skilled Workers, headed by mayors or country magistrates, the other members being the police commissioner and delegates of the Ministry of Social Affairs, Industrial and Mining Adjustment Administration and National Resources Commission in each place. The last two organizations in reality represented government-owned and operated industries, which the National Resources Commission of the Ministry of Economics managed directly. Not only Labor, but private employers as well, had no representation or voice. The shift was from control of skilled workers for the benefit of all employers to control for the benefit of "bureaucratic industry" exclusively.

Even after this, Kuomintang "labor theoreticians" pressed for still more stringent controls. Particularly interesting in this regard is an article entitled "My Opinion on the Prevention of Labor Mobility", by Chen Pu, in the Chungyang-Saotang Pao, combined organ of the military and political wings of the party. 24/ The author cited figures to show how wage differentials between different plants had given rise to a 10 per cent monthly turnover of the labor force in some individual cases. The remedy he advocated was a government-supervised training program for new workers, their indoctrination in Kuomintang principles, "unification of wages" through further all-round reduction, labor espionage to forestall workers' protests and regulation on the models adopted in Germany and Italy, with which China was then at war. We quote:

----

23. Liu Wu-kou, in her survey of Kwangsi labor prepared for this study, reports that the "Wage Regulation Council" in Kweilin in 1943 consisted of representatives of (1) the gendarmerie, (2) the provincial Kuomintang headquarters, (3) the municipal police, (4) the municipal chamber of commerce, (5) the provincial government, (6) the Kweilin district court, (7) employers' organizations, (8) labor unions, with the Mayor as Chairman and two functionaries of the Bureau of Social Affairs always present ex officio.

24. February 24, 1943, The Chungyang Jih Pao (Central Daily News) and Sao Tang Pao had been combined after the Chungking bombings because of shortage of technical facilities. They afterwards resumed separate publication.

"Wages and similar rewards are one ... reason for high
mobility. We cannot allow such great differences as have
hitherto existed.... According to output standards, we
can create a uniform standard of wages (and overtime).
Thus the worker will have no basis for thinking that
another factory is more advantageous than the one he is
in.... When unification of wages and other conditions
is considered ... we must think of the difficulties of
smaller factories. Big factories have a lot of capital
and can meet every wage and welfare requirement. But
small factories have not enough....

"After unification of wages there is the possibility of
labor slowdowns and black markets in labor. In this
connection we must supervise factory federations and labor
unions and strengthen the reporting system.... encourage
the good and punish the bad.

"The factory law ... regulates in detail employment
and dismissal. But this means that both sides are controlled by agreement. Lacking is the organ with power to
enforce compliance .... So hereafter we hope that the
government will regulate employment and dismissal by
adaptation of the Italian and German labor regulations in
issuing work-books.... After they have acquired such a
book workers should be allowed to take up employment, not
otherwise.... When the factory wishes to dismiss a worker
or a worker asks to leave, they should ... ask government
permission. The worker can leave only after his work book
has been stamped with official authorization..."

While "work books" of this kind, and the tying of workers to jobs,
existed in Allied countries at war as well, the insistence on German and
Italian models correctly reflected Kuomintang concepts of basic labor
policy. This can be proved by reference to the whole body of wartime
and pre-war social legislation.

7. Post-War Tendencies

It is not our purpose here to deal with post-war labor policies in
detail. Suffice it to say that large-scale class conflicts broke out
after V-J Day both in the industries of the wartime rear, which
experienced mass flight of capital and bankruptcy, and those of the
liberated cities, where workers tried to smash the pattern of Japanese
and quisling exploitation. The Kuomintang government resorted to
armed action against workers in both areas, and maintained almost without
change the structure of labor control established by the enemy in
Shanghai, Tientsin, etc. There was some relaxation of wartime restrictions during the first months of the Kuomintang-Communist talks for a
coalition government, refereed by General Marshall.

On May 30, 1946, Ku Cheng-kang, Minister of Social Affairs,
announced "workers must abide by factory discipline and should not stage
strikes of any kind. If they did so, they would be heavily punished by
law." He added that most strikes were the work of political agitators,

and anyone inciting them would be severely dealt with. 25/

On August 6, 1946, police confiscated the headquarters of the Chinese Association of Labor in Chungking and an order was issued for the arrest of its President, Chu Hsueh-fan.

In the summer of 1947 all Kuomintang China was once more placed on a military footing and a new Mobilization Act, for the purpose of prosecuting the civil war, imposed more stringent regulations on labor than those which had been in effect during the war with Japan.

Apart from these "emergency" actions, the Labor Union Law of 1929 was once again refurbished -- in the Amended Labor Union Law of June 13, 1947. The law was to apply only to "normal times", so that unions never actually enjoyed its benefits. It was of particular interest as representing the most the Kuomintang was willing to offer the workers in return for their docile support in the civil war.

There were no changes, as compared with previous amendments, in the provisions of this law requiring the permission of "competent authorities" at each successive step in initiating the organization of a union, drafting a constitution, etc. As before, the presence and approval of government officials were necessary at meetings and elections. Membership rolls, accounts, reports on activities, and biographies of officers had to be submitted at stated intervals and "whenever required." Changes of union rules were still not valid without official approval (Articles 9, 30, 31)

Workers in government-operated enterprises were still not permitted to form unions, bargain collectively, or strike.

In private industry, on the other hand, the right to strike was granted. This now included public utilities which were privately owned. Provisions were made, for the first time, for payment of wages during strikes.

A National Federation of Trade Unions, previously prohibited, was now permitted, but only if officially approved.

Legalization of the strike in private industry, as distinct from complete prohibition of all organization and strikes in "bureaucratic industry", must be viewed in the light of the bitter post-war conflict between these two types of enterprises. Even more than in the war years, bureaucratic monopoly in 1946-47 employed the vast majority of Chinese workers, and utilized every possible form of government pressure to extend its grip. A bulletin of the China Branch of the International Labor Organization reported, understandably enough, that private employers in Shanghai thought that "workers employed by government-operated enterprises should also organize and have the right to strike." Workers in Shanghai, it said, made the same demand.

The right to form a National Federation of Trade Unions, with official approval, was granted to forestall the strong post-war trend toward the organization of a Federation outside, and in opposition to,

---

25. Summarized in C.A.L. Faces a Crisis, by P. E. Lee, Chinese Association of Labor, Shanghai, November 15, 1946.

the shackles of existing "labor control." "Liberalization" of the law
in this regard came after the persecution of the Chinese Association of
Labor under Chu Hsueh-fan, which became the main vehicle for a new
federation, under rank-and-file pressure, soon after V-J Day.

the obstacle of existing "liberalization" of the law
in this regard came after the persecution of the Chinese Association of
Labor under Chu for a new
Federation, under

CHAPTER VIII.

LABOR ORGANIZATIONS AND THE LABOR MOVEMENT

1. Labor in the Shanghai Battle

The three-month battle of Shanghai raged in the streets, among the homes and work-places of its wage earners. Its outbreak had been preceded by several months of anti-Japanese agitation and organization on the political level. Immediately the fighting broke out, the National Salvation Association (N.S.A.) which had been chiefly responsible, became the most active element of a much broader body, the Shanghai Anti-Enemy Rear Auxiliary Association (also known as the General War Work Committee.) The network of branch NSAs, which already had over 100,000 members in educational institutions, professional circles and among white-collar employees and industrial workers, was integrated into the new organization. Because of the closing down and destruction of factories, and their own pre-war weakness caused by the limitations of Kuomintang law, it was not the trade unions but sections of the War Work Committee which served as media for the patriotic mobilization of the working class.

Consultation was instituted among underground organizers like the Communist Pan Han-nien, officials of legal unions like Chu Hsueh-fan, government labor functionaries, liberal intellectuals interested in workers' education, and Tu Yueh-sen's "Green Ring" labor-gang chiefs. Discussion and common action centered on work at the "front," which ran through the city, and on organizing support from the "rear," lying a few blocks away in the untouched International Settlement. Under the urgent stress of the time, these widely differing groups cooperated much more effectively than might have been expected. The organizational principle of cooperation was mutual non-encroachment. Each group was left to carry out the general plan in areas which it had dominated before the war.

In education and propaganda, National Salvationist intellectuals manifested the most activity. They inaugurated classes, sent out speakers and dramatic groups, and published specially created newspapers such as the National Salvation Daily News, edited by Kuo Mo-jo and Hsia Yen, and Resistance, edited by Chao Tao-fen. Many older publications also shifted entirely to war mobilization tasks. There was an out-pouring of handbooks on political and technical subjects. A four-volume set of "Wartime Texts", for illiterates and semi-literates, sold at three cents per booklet. For the first time in many years, books by Chinese Communist leaders on partisan warfare, and such works as Edgar Snow's Red Star Over China and R. Palme Dutt's World Politics were sold openly. All were produced in shortened form and simplified language, for broad accessibility.

The General War Work Committee developed considerable efficiency. Provincial guilds and employers' organizations like the Chamber of Commerce provided money and essential supplies. Thousands of middle-class women worked as nurses in hospitals improvised from dance-halls and theatres. Workers driven from their factories by shellfire produced many wartime necessities in improvised shops. Appeals for services were made by placard, telephone, radio and propaganda truck. A number of sectional, street and block units were set up, and each was provided with a new work plan every week. When the weather turned cold, for instance, a call went out for warm uniforms and padded vests for the soldiers. The more well-to-do inhabitants of each block were taxed for materials and money to hire sewing machines, and the working women made up the suits.

Military commanders at first kept aloof from this work, regarding any contact with it as the job of their quartermasters. Soon, however, they began to go directly to committees in their sectors. This was the quickest way to get stretcher bearers, motor transport and drivers, and even new supplies of rough hand-grenades, which were produced by unemployed mechanics from tin cans collected by Boy Scouts. Once, when sandbags were urgently needed, the War Work Committee managed to round up and fill 8,000 in three hours. Thousands of unemployed mill operatives of the Yangtzepoo gave their services as trench diggers. In the wrecked sections of Hongkew former workers in Japanese factories proved invaluable as guides through the mass of ruins and cellars.

On the other hand, there was no attempt to arm workers, or to utilize the 1925-27 tradition of military organization. The only approximation was the creation, by Tai Li's blueshirt secret police and Tu Yueh-sen's "Green Ring," of a sharpshooters' corps whose core was Tu's pre-war private "army" of gunmen and labor spies. The quarters of this group were shelled, and many of its members killed, before it had fired a shot. Because what weapons were left in Chinese hands in Shanghai were entrusted to police and gangster elements instead of to popular bodies, early post-occupation armed resistance in the city assumed an "underworld" rather than "underground" character, with much corruption, intrigue and betrayal. A new, more genuinely popular, underground was to be created later, in connection with the New Fourth Army guerillas operating near Shanghai.

Work of a different kind was to continue for some time in the International Settlement, where great numbers of workers, students and intellectuals took shelter after the Japanese moved into control in the former Chinese-administered parts of the city. It concentrated on mass education concerning the objects of the war, monetary and material collections for the Chinese army, and local clandestine resistance. Whole industries were set up in 1938-41 to serve the war effort. They sent their products to the Kuomintang rear by sea through Hongkong and to the Communist-led New Fourth Army along the smuggling routes.

Agitation was carried on among skilled workers to go to the interior. Necessary papers were provided, and regional guilds made themselves responsible for passage money. In 1938, special agents of the Chinese Ministry of Economics began to function in this field (see Chapter III). The Shanghai activities of the Chinese Association of Labor, under Chu Hsueh-fan, were also concerned more with procurement of skilled hands for interior industries than with local organization. Here left-wing elements were far more active. The latter also carried on labor recruiting for New Fourth Army plants.

2. Workers' Activities in the Wuhan Period (1938)
Wuhan

After the retreat from Shanghai, Wuhan (the triple city of Wuchang, Hankow and Hanyang) became the greatest industrial center of unoccupied China.

Its equipment included the Hanyang iron works and arsenal, a number of textile mills, tobacco factories and egg-drying plants (owned by Anglo-American interests) and a large number of minor enterprises. Electric power, coal, iron and cotton were readily available from nearby sources. The Yangtze River and north-south railways provided connections with many free provinces, and with the outside world through Canton and Hongkong. Wuhan's industries were largely Chinese-owned. Their 200,000 workers, by contrast with Shanghai, were mainly adult males with a comparatively high degree of literacy. In 1938, the industrial population was augmented by refugee workers who came from Shanghai and other lower Yangtze cities by water, and from Shantung, North Kiangsu and Honan by rail.

There had been modern factories in Wuhan since the 1880's. Its history of large-scale and militant labor activity went back to the Peking-Hankow railway strike of 1925. In 1927, at the zenith of the first united front and the political labor movement, Wuhan had been the capital of the National Government. The ranks of the 1927 working class were decimated by the subsequent suppression, but clandestine rank and file unions continued to exist for many years afterwards. Communists worked both in these and within the "legal" organizations which were dominated by the police and the "Red Ring" secret society (as distinct from the "Green Ring" in Shanghai).

When the writer was in the city in 1938, textile workers told him that the unions of 1925-27 (which they called "Northern Expedition unions") were well remembered. The memory was not merely political. Wages in the mills had risen, at that time, from 30 cents to 70 cents a day. After the suppression they had returned to the old level, never to recover.

Anti-Japanese feeling had been present since some time before the war. Hankow's Japanese Concession (the British had been retroceded in 1927) was a constant local reminder of imperialism. As recently as 1935-36 several factories had been put out of business by Japanese dumping of cloth and yarn. Labor had participated in several anti-Japanese boycott movements after 1931. Though it had not been allowed to interfere with the "better classes," vigilante squads had been formed to prevent purchase or use of Japanese goods by workers themselves. These activities had been encouraged by students. Some students had themselves been driven into factory work by the 1935-36 economic crisis.

With this background, the Wuhan workers took the reconstituted united front very seriously. They expected the return of the "old" unions, with improved livelihood and scope for activity. When popular pamphlets on the exploits of the Red Army (which had become the Eighth Route Army) began to appear in the bookstores, they were read eagerly. The Eighth Route Army office in Hankow was always full of trade unionists who came to ask for help in returning to the status of 1927. 1/ The Communist delegates, one of whom was the old Wuhan revolutionary Tung Pi-wu, explained the different circumstances. Many were disappointed and asked to go to North Shensi, which the Eighth Route controlled. Several hundred did so.

The Political Department of the National Military Council had festooned Hankow with posters urging all citizens to band together for patriotic work. But the authorities soon became alarmed by the number of organizations, including labor, which quickly sprang up. They were fearful of every form of activity not initiated directly by officials, and soon began to suppress them. Especially great was the effort to confine workers to the framework of the moribund legal unions and the new officially-sponsored "labor service corps."

At the Chinese New Year, the traditional commercial debt-settlement date and season for labor disputes and re-negotiation of contracts, the Wuhan Garrison Headquarters re-issued the special anti-strike proclamation made annually since 1927. On February 24, 1938, General Chen Cheng, as head of the Political Department, promulgated an order forbidding all demonstrations and requiring mass organizations to register. The effect of this order was to outlaw any group to which registration was refused. Most of the new groups were eliminated in this way. 2/

A typical instance was related to the writer by a group of workers. Displaced employees of the Tientsin-Pukow Railway and other enterprises seized by the enemy organized the "Unemployed Workers' Anti-Japanese National Salvation Association." A registration official asked whether they proposed "to start for the front immediately." When told that they had not been asked to but planned to work in Hankow, he declined to license the organization because it was "unnecessary." The workers argued that the employed had unions to work through, but the jobless had no such medium. The official asked: "How many of you are Kuomintang members?" Not satisfied with the answer, he closed the conversation by saying: "This is all a pretense. You are probably up to something quite different. You hang out a sheep's head, but are selling dog meat inside.' The organization was never authorized.

April 1938 was the high month of the united front, the month of the Taierhchuang victory and the Emergency Congress, with its promises of freedom of assembly and association. It found Wuhan workers enthusiastic over plans for a large-scale celebration of the hitherto proscribed May Day and for the reconstitution of an All-China Trade Union Federation.

---

1. The Hein Hua Jih Pao, first legal Communist daily to be issued in Kuomintang China in a decade, appeared in Hankow in January 1938. Because of its simple style and the attention it devoted to their problems, it was a favorite with workers. One of them told the writer, however, that they were afraid to be seen with it because of the police and the fact that other workers had been dismissed from their jobs when observed reading the paper.

2. Simultaneously the Ministry of Education issued statements condemning "inviting people freely to give talks in schools," and bookshops were ordered to cease selling works on guerilla warfare. There were rumors of negotiated peace.

- 81 -

The Kuomintang Mass Movement Committee (under Chen Li-fu) and the Political Department thereupon decided to organize the demonstration themselves. In place of the Federation, they advanced the Chinese Association of Labor, a nebulous body established in 1935. The C.A.L. did not spring from the unions themselves, and its functions were never properly defined. Chu Hsueh-fan, its appointed head, was an official of the Postal Workers' (Special) Union. He had been in the 1925-27 movement till the Kuomintang jailed him in the latter year. But unlike the scores of union leaders executed at the time, he had been released under the "protection" of Tu Yueh-sen, head of the "Green gang." Afterwards Chu had gone as "Chinese workers' delegate" to I.L.O. conferences and other international labor gatherings. Considered a safe man by the Kuomintang, he was at the same time not too odious to the workers. Despite his involvement in official unions, he had never been directly identified with suppressions, arrests, and shootings.

The May Day Parade of over 100,000 was duly held. It passed through the streets of Hankow and wound up in a mass meeting in the municipal park, where Kuomintang officials, Chu Hsueh-fan, representing the C.A.L., and Wang Ming, representing the Communist Party, addressed it as a symbol of unity. Wang Ming appealed only for support of the government and the war effort, for patriotic activity and increased production.

The careful attitude of the Communist party at this time was exemplified in the following answers given by Wang Ming to the questions of two United Press correspondents and the present writer.

Q. Do you want posts in the government?

A. We wish to share the burden of the national crisis with Kuomintang. We have not demanded anything. If it agrees or permits us to enter the Cabinet on terms that will enable us to contribute effectively to its work, we are willing to come in.

Q. It is rumored that the Communist Party will be given the Mass Movement Committee, as in 1924-27, and that a Communist will replace Chen Li-fu as its head.

A. This is untrue. Chen has not even asked our help. But he should join hands with us in mass work.

Q. Would you work under his direction?

A. In the political and military field, the Kuomintang is the main power. Mass work is different. Here the united front should mean equal opportunity and cooperation. Democracy should be the main principle in the mass movement. It is too early to talk of leadership because neither party can yet boast of great successes in this field. Leadership can be discussed only when good, successful work has been done. Now it is only beginning.

Q. Have you asked for removal of all restrictions on mass organizations?

A. We have made no such concrete demand. All we ask is
   that the Kuomintang carry out Chiang-Kai-shek's
   slogan' 'Fight on to the end.' But we have pointed
   out that this includes improving cooperation
   between the army and people, etc.

Beginning its wartime work, the Chinese Association of Labor
announced that it would serve as a preparatory body for the ultimate
establishment of a Federation. The renovated C.A.L. was formally
representative of all groups, and a Communist was invited to join its
committee on behalf of unions in the Shensi Kansu-Winghsia Border
Region (Yenan area.) Encouraged by the May meeting, Chu Hsueh-fan
wished to make field organizing trips, to establish new unions and
integrate existing ones with the C.A.L. But the Kuomintang Mass Movement Committee, staffed almost exclusively by the reactionary C. C.
clique, refused to permit this. It made it clear that Chu was not to
interfere with the complete control exercised over separate unions by
the social affairs bureaus of local party headquarters.

June 1938 brought a resurgence of police activity. A number of
mass organizations, notably in the youth field, were dissolved. Bookstores were cleared of "Left" literature. The Communist daily was
repeatedly suspended and thirteen of its editorial staff were arrested.
As a counter-movement to the leftward swing, the Kuomintang energetically developed the San Min Chu I Youth Corps. 3/

The final phase of the mass movement in Hankow was connected with
preparations for evacuation. Communist representatives, supported by
liberal and left-of-center groups, called for a stand that would make
the city "the Madrid of China." They drew up and popularized a
detailed plan of defense in which labor unions occupied an important
place. The government favored a policy of retreat.

There was general agreement, however, that the city must be
cleared of non-essential population and industries. Labor was active
in the "Factory Evacuation Movement," in which a good deal of machinery
was shipped up-river to Chungking and by rail to Paochi, in Shensi.
There was resistance to moving on the part of many factory owners, who
did not budge even in the face of Chiang Kai-shek's threat to blow up
all factories ignoring the evacuation order (some explosives were
actually placed, but nothing came of it). Many workers were mobilized
to agitate for removal and to carry it out. They formed squads to
dismount and pack machinery, guard it en route, etc. Before Wuhan fell,
a fair portion of its industrial workers had left, either with their
factories or without them.

Changsha 4/

---

3. The corps employed organized intimidation, as in the attack on the
   Hsin Hua Jih Pao and the "anti-Communist demonstration" of March 23,
   1938.

4. The sources of this information are personal interviews in Changsha,
   visited in April 1938.

The second industrial town of free China in 1938 was Changsha, capital of Hunan province. Here 3,000 workers were employed in the First (Hunan Provincial Government) Cotton Mill and smaller textile enterprises, 2,500 in the provincial arsenal, and hundreds in the railway depot. There were between four and five thousand stevedores, 10,000 ricksha pullers and 10,000 workers in nearby antimony mines. Crafts were highly developed, with great numbers engaged in hand-weaving, embroidery, etc. As in Hankow, labor in Changsha had made many gains in 1924-27 but had lost them in the "great purge". Afterwards, under the pressure of the purely landlord administration of Governor Ho Chien, and of the great influx of poverty-stricken refugees from a countryside torn by civil war, backward practices returned to the labor field.

Dock-workers in Changsha and nearby Hsiangtan in 1937-38 had to pay a $200 initiation fee (about nine months' earning, in constant employment) to join a "union" that was really a mixture of guild and gangster protection racket. The daily nominal wage of a stevedore was Chinese $1.00 (then about 29 cents U.S. currency). This was not low in comparison with other local rates, but the worker had to pay up to half of it over to a gang-appointed "lord of the wharf," who controlled hiring. The rise in commodity prices in 1938 was not accompanied by a rise in wages.

Ricksha pullers, who also had a "union," were exploited in much the same way. They rented their vehicles, and had to pay police license fees and current repairs out of their own earnings. Because the total of licenses issued was strictly limited, a new worker had first of all to buy the "number" of a retiring one, generally paying about Chinese $100 for the transfer. In one respect, however, the Changsha pullers were better off than those elsewhere. Ricksha men in Shanghai, Peiping and Hankow, quickly ran themselves to exhaustion. In Changsha they did not run but walked. A puller urged to speed up would invariably dump his shafts and invite his fare to get out, saying, "if you want to run, run by yourself." This highly-prized privilege must have been won, as it was maintained, by the action of the workers themselves. Its importance to the length of the puller's working life, and physical life-span, may be seen from Shanghai statistics and from such books as Lau Shaw's Ricksha Boy.

Changsha cotton mill workers sold their places to newcomers for $30 to $40. Hiring was by personal introduction by an old worker to the foreman, who had to be bribed with part of this sale price, and sometimes with a part of the new worker's wage.

In practice such initiation and transfer fees meant that the new worker, who seldom had the required sum in cash, started with a heavy debt to a moneylender (often the foreman, ricksha renter or "lord of the wharf" himself) on which he had to pay both principal instalments and interest. The transfer fee received by the old workers from their successors generally went to cover their own unsettled debts. Workers sometimes sold their jobs to meet the expense attendant on family illnesses, funerals and other emergencies. In such cases they were left not only without employment but with debts still outstanding.

The experiences of 1924-27 and the civil war had had a traumatic
effect on the provincial bureaucrats. Ever since, they had been prompt
to spy out and smash any working class organization, even of the most
modest economic type. The result, as one informant put it, was that
"everyone in Changsha became either a feudalist or a determined revolutionary. There was no room in the middle." Early in 1938 the Communists
sent a legal delegation to Changsha. It was headed by Hsu Teh-li, a
Hunan educationalist who had been identified with every progressive
movement since Manchu times. The local gentry were frightened, and
organized to prevent any "dangerous" consequences. Although in Hunan,
as elsewhere, Chiang Kai-shek had taken advantage of the war to instal
his own governor and provincial party chief, district and municipal
administration had remained in local hands. This included direct
supervision of mass movements.

As in Hankow, the war raised workers' memories of the first united
front. Official labor bodies had been extremely sketchy in Hunan.
Parallel secret rank-and-file unions never ceased to exist, notably
among the railway depot workers. But large sectors of industry, such as
the cotton mills, had no organization when hostilities broke out. In
1938 the textile workers petitioned to be allowed to form a union for
the purpose of:

   (1) increasing productivity, so that hours could be reduced
      without prejudice to output; (2) improving the life of
      the workers; (3) Educating and mobilizing the workers
      for patriotic activity.

The Changsha Kuomintang headquarters refused its consent. No new unions
of any kind were formed.

The contemporary Communist gauging of the situation is interesting.
According to Hsu Teh-li, Communist delegate, Changsha was less "liberal"
than Wuhan, where an effort was made to preserve at least the outward
forms of national unity and popular participation. Interviewed by the
writer on April 24, 1938, Hsu said that he had been warned, immediately
on arrival, to speak publicly on nothing but "abstract and spiritual
topics." He thought that an inter-party May Day celebration on the lines
of the one in Hankow could not be held in Changsha. "Even if the Central
Government orders it," he remarked, "the local tangpu (Kuomintang office)
may refuse. For instance, the Kuomintang Congress announced freedom of
assembly. But the local tangpu says, 'submit the nature of your meeting
and the names of those attending' and even then does not give permission."

Hsu Teh-li also said that great efforts were being made to keep
National Salvationist students from contact with the peasants and workers.
More educated industrial workers, as in textiles and the railways, were
prevented from getting into touch with craft workers and coolies.
"Generally," he concluded "the power of the masses is suppressed. I
imagine it can show itself only when the enemy is near and danger is
imminent. The landlords, merchants and government fear the Japanese and
the people equally. When the enemy is advancing, fear of Japan prevails.
But now the enemy is still far. So fear of people is greater."

Facts proved this statement to err on the moderate side. When the
enemy movement was resumed, the Hunan Highway Commissioner organized road

workers into semi-military formations to defend communications and
destroy them when necessary. Although he was an old provincial
official, the higher authorities held that he had neglected "proper
precautions" in dealing with such dangerous matters. They therefore
arrested and tortured him as a "Communist." (A Communist had
previously told the writer that the man was "a lackey of Ho Chien" --
the former governor.)

As the military danger increased, the provincial government was
occupying itself with a conference to which General Feng T'i, a
Whampoa secret service officer, and Pan Kung-chan, its C.C. clique
secretary, reported on "reactionary groups" (the term used by the
Kuomintang, which considered itself the guardian of Sun Yat-sen's
revolutionary heritage, to describe all opposition). One of the
serious questions discussed was the popularity of the Communists, 5/
who were supporters of the war and, at the time, studiously avoided
public criticism of the government. Another was the fact that their
Hankow Hsin Hua Jih Pao had 5,000 readers in the city. Among the
"dangerous groups" to which major attention was given was the War
Service Corps of the Changsha Y.M.C.A.!

When the enemy threat increased, the Kuomintang authorities
did not call on the people but instead burned Changsha over their
heads without warning. The city's industries were destroyed, and an
uncounted number of residents perished. The fires were set most
thickly around the office of the Communist delegation. Chou En-lai,
then in the city, narrowly escaped incineration.

The panic turned out to be premature. With the exception of
interludes lasting several days in all, Changsha was to remain in
Chinese hands for five and a half more years. But neither its gutted
industries nor its labor were of any further importance during the
war period.

3. The Rear Areas, 1939-45; Organization from Above

The main industrial centers of Kuomintang China between 1939 and
the end of World War II were Chungking and its suburbs (Szechuan
province), Kunming (Yunnan), Kweilin and Liuchow (Kwangsi), Kweiyang
(Kweichow), Sian and Paochi (Shensi) and Lanchow and Tienshui (Kansu).
The minuscule proportions of post-1939 rear industry may be seen
from the fact that the total of factory workers in all these places
together never exceeded 250,000. 6/ only a small proportion of

---

5. This popularity dated from civil war days but began to express
itself openly in the united front period. Hsu Teh-li told the
writer that peasants had come to him to ask whether they could
set up a branch of the Eighth Route Army to fight the Japanese
by guerilla methods, a request comparable to those made by the
Hankow workers, and, like them, refused in line with the party's
policy of non-infringement of the Kuomintang rights in its own
territory.

6. A Ministry of Economics tabulation for 1943, supplied to the
writer by Minister Wong Wen-hao, gave the total in registered
factories as 249,067.

whom had previous factory or union experience. 7/ This was less than
half the number of such workers in pre-war Shanghai alone. In Chungking,
largest industrial city of "Free China" in wartime, there were less
than 80,000 workers in national defense arsenals, heavy industries,
mining, factory production of consumers' goods, printing, municipal
utilities and mechanical transport combined. 8/

The rear areas also had over a million craft workers, (builders,
carpenters, stone cutters, etc.) and coolie laborers in old-style
transport (boatmen, carriers, wheelbarrowmen, stevedores, ricksha
coolies, etc.) engaged on large-scale projects or grouped together in
significant numbers in the cities. Few, if any, of these had been
unionized before the war.

As has already been made clear in Chapter II, and in the account of
unionization efforts in the early war period, wartime Kuomintang labor
laws and official practices made the growth of autonomous unions impossible. Opposition parties had given up organizing "unauthorized" unions
in the rear. In the war years, as never before, what "unions" existed
were purely and simply organs of government control. All hopes of a
united labor federation embracing workers in both Kuomintang and
Communist-led areas faded, along with the United Front "honeymoon," in
early 1939. Cultural work by "National Salvationist" intellectuals in
labor's ranks was suppressed at the same time.

Workers in munitions production, the largest single industry, were
forbidden by law to organize unions or associations of any kind whatsoever. They were jealously guarded from contact even with officially-
sponsored unions in industries where these were permitted. Nor were
they permitted to utilize in any way the government-recognized outside
"service" organization theoretically concerned with all workers, the
Chinese Association of Labor. Chu Hsueh-fan, President of the CAL,
complained to the writer in early 1944 that even his petitions for
housing and other forms of relief on behalf of arsenal employees already
discharged from their jobs had been menacingly dismissed by the authorities on the ground that "military labor was none of his business." It
was only in the few months immediately preceding and following V-J Day
that the CAL was allowed to help mediate some disputes in which such
workers were individually involved. 9/

Another major category of workers, those engaged in public utilities, whether government or private-operated, were permitted to unite
only in "Special Labor Unions", which even under peace-time law had no

---

7. Figures for worker migrants from pre-war industrial cities varied
   between 12,000 and 15,000. To these must be added the labor force
   on railways still in Chinese hands.

8. Shu Hwa, op. cit.

9. The Report on Progress of Work (Vol. I, No. 2, June 1945), issued
   by the International Department of the CAL, mentioned a case
   involving ten dismissed workers in an oil refinery subsidiary to
   the Nan-An Arsenal which the CAL helped to settle. Similar cases
   listed in subsequent reports included a demand for better treatment
   by military machine-shop workers (July) and one or two in the following months. Most pertained to the liquidation of wartime enterprises at the end of hostilities.

right either to bargain collectively or to strike. These included the Railway Workers' Union, the Seamen's Union, the River Boatmen's Union and the Postal Employees' Union, with a membership at the end of 1942 of 158,140, of whom 692 were women and 335 were minors (606 of the women and 326 of the minors were in the postal service.) 10/

"Ordinary Labor Unions" were permitted by law to bargain collectively and to strike only in peacetime, but even then only after the failure of compulsory conciliation and arbitration and the satisfaction of other legal requirements. In 1942 such unions claimed 138,583 members. They took in workers in mines, industrial power plants, chemical industry, civilian machine shops, printing, textiles, food, furniture and other consumers' goods production. Among their members in that year were 24,210 women and 5,328 children. 11/

"Occupational" or "Trade" unions with 125,929 members in 1942, included fishermen, tailors and food industry workers in small handicraft shops, construction workers, transport coolies, etc. They, too, contained a small percentage of women and children, who numbered 1,708 and 1,489 respectively. 12/

The last-mentioned form of "union" was not uniform in structure. Often it was only a new name for the old-fashioned guild, in which both masters and journeymen were represented. 13/ The Kuomintang Ministry of Social Affairs organized several "model unions" to set the standard for this type of organization, notably among the sedan-chair carriers and ricksha pullers of Chungking, who were not wage-workers at all but rented (or in a very few cases owned) their vehicle. 14/

Even among craft and coolie workers, certain categories were singled out for particularly close administrative supervision. Of the 17 "ordinary" and "Occupational" unions in Kweilin at the end of 1943, six were designated "Controlled Unions" because, in the words of the head of the city's Bureau of Social Affairs, they were "greatly concerned with wartime life." They included printers, journeymen tailors, carpenters, barbers, coolies and ricksha pullers, accounting together for 6,000 workers, or more than 80 per cent of all union members in the city at the time. According to a local survey:

10,11,12. Third Annual Report of the Chinese Association of Labor presented to the Fourth Annual Convention of the C.A.L. in Chungking, January 1943, and published in pamphlet form.

13. This point was repeatedly stressed to the writer by Prof. Chen Ta of Tsinghua University and was amply documented in A Study of Sixteen Trade Unions in Kunming, a thesis prepared in 1942-43 by Mr. Chu Hang-yuan, a Tsinghua student, under the direction of Prof. Francis Ching-han Lee (unpublished).

14. Shu Hwa, op. cit.

"These Controlled Unions are strictly supervised by the municipal government. Every month they hold a meeting with representatives of the government present to decide the month's work, how to promote welfare, how to carry out work according to government regulations."

Coolies' and ricksha pullers' unions (with 4,000 members between them) were further required to register all persons in their trades, each one being required to supply two photographs at his own expense (the cost of the photos at wartime prices was equivalent to several days' wages). Although this regulation was passed in 1943, the resistance was so great that the local government had to keep advancing the deadline through 1944. 15/

It is worth noting, in connection with the figures given above, that relatively few genuine industrial workers were incorporated into government-sponsored unions, despite the fact that all administrative decrees after 1941 made membership in them compulsory, and that this provision appeared prominently in the National General Mobilization Act of May 5, 1942, the highest wartime law in the land. 16/

Chungking statistics compiled late in 1943, 17/ a year and a half after the act was passed, showed that only 53,336 workers in both industries and "occupations" were organized, out of 96,000 listed as coming within the sphere of compulsory unionization (exclusive of those in military plants). Moreover, those officially claimed to have been organized were predominantly handicraftsmen and coolies. The late Wendell Willkie unearthed some interesting facts by informal questioning during his visit to China some months earlier. Talking to workers in the show-places of Chungking's industry, the largest steel, textile and paper factories, he was told in every case that no union existed. 18/ This may well have been because some workers carried on official union rolls literally did not know they "belonged," since the union had no activities and dues-payments were among the many arbitrary deductions from wages which were never even explained to those affected. (Shu Hwa listed ten of the 79 unions in Chungking as "industrial", embracing workers in the China Enterprise Corporation Machine-Tool Plant, the Yu Hsin Steel Works, Ho Tso Metal Company, city power plant, city waterworks, Yu Hwa Cotton Mill, Jui Hwa Glass Factory and Szechuan Sericulture Co.)

15. Liu Wu-kou.
16. This seems to have been an unalterable feature of government-sponsored labor organization, remaining constant after V-J Day and the reincorporation of Japanese occupied industrial regions. Thus, the Ministry of Social Affairs was to claim on June 30, 1946, that the 218 "Special Unions" throughout Kuomintang China had 610,796 members and that 4,423 ordinary unions had 1,001,171 members, of whom only 60,646 were industrial workers, as compared with 718,938 handicraftsmen and coolies and over 200,000 otherwise classified. Miners numbering 267,630, railwaymen (65,623), salt workers (103,503) and workers in privately owned communications and transport were all listed, at this time, under the figure for "special unions" -- i.e., those having no legal right to strike under any circumstances whatsoever.
17. Shu Hwa, op. cit.
18. The writer accompanied Mr. Willkie on his factory visits, and reported the questions and answers in an Allied Labor News dispatch.

The same picture was observable in late 1943 in Kweilin. Of seven
factories answering a questionnaire prepared by Miss Liu Wu-kou for
this study only two reported the existence of unions. One of these,
moreover, explained that "a union has just been organized according to
government regulations." The two factories thus "unionized" employed
196 workers between them. The five reporting "no union" had 2,844
workers. A list of Kweilin unions compiled by Miss Liu at the same
time showed 17 organizations of which one was a "special union" and ten
were "occupational." Among the remainder only the printers', cement
workers', cigarette and tobacco workers' unions could be classed as
industrial, while the other two consisted of newsboys and shoe-shine
boys. Members of craft and coolie unions totalled 5,521, those of
industrial unions, 1,684. The country's largest radio works
(782 workers), a steel works, several machine shops, textile and oil-
pressing factories were located in the city, but none of these industries was unionized.

In Kweiyang, in 1943, there were no unions at all. The sixteen
"labor unions" studied by Mr. Chu Kung-yuan of Tsinghua University in
Kunming, wartime China's second largest industrial city, were listed
by him under highly instructive headings. 19/ He called three of
them "guilds in disguise" (transport, seal-carvers' and furniture
makers); five "professional associations" (builders, glaziers, hand
cigarette makers, weavers & dyers and bathhouse employees), and
the rest "quasi-unions" (these included truck drivers, mechanics,
ricksha coolies, newsboys, tailors and the Kunming General Labor Union).
20/

The "General Labor Unions" existing in the main cities served as
channels for the orders of local governments, party headquarters, and
municipal bureaus of social affairs. County "federations", which
existed in some places, were the rural equivalent of these General
Unions. None was in any sense a result of rank-and-file initiative
or rank-and-file operated. All were officered by government-appointed
bureaucrats who in most cases had no labor background.

A Chinese analyst described the channels of labor control from
Chungking as follows: 21/

---

19. Op. cit.
20. China Labor Memo. No. 2, prepared for the International Secretariat
    of the Institute of Pacific Relations in 1941, analyzed a Chinese
    Ministry of Economics recapitulation of "unions" registered in
    October 1940-May 1941. The total membership reported for 207
    organizations was 25,593. Only two "unions", with a membership
    of 361 workers, were described as industrial. Of all union
    members only 4 per cent (1,150) were women.
21. Shu Hwa, op. cit.

"The leadership of the workers' movement belongs to the Ministry of Social Affairs, while the party headquarters is in a position of assistance and guidance.   Organization is as follows:

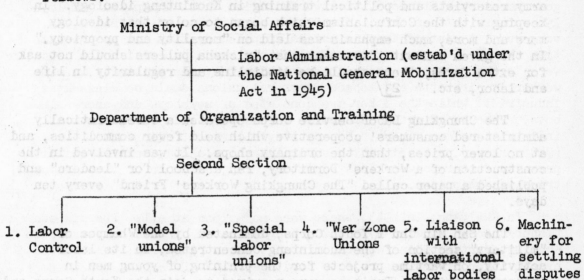

Ministry of Social Affairs

Labor Administration (estab'd under the National General Mobilization Act in 1945)

Department of Organization and Training

Second Section

1. Labor Control   2. "Model unions"   3. "Special labor unions"   4. "War Zone Unions"   5. Liaison with international labor bodies   6. Machinery for settling disputes

"Local Government Control: In each province there is a Workers' Movement Section of the provincial Social Affairs Administration. In municipalities there is either a Mass Movement section or a Workers' Movement Section of the Bureau of Social Affairs. In counties there is a Social Affairs Section.

"Kuomintang Party Control: In the Central Kuomintang Headquarters (national) there is a Mass Movement Department. Each provincial party headquarters has a Mass Movement Section which is also in charge of labor. In the Central Headquarters of the San Min Chu I Youth Corps the Departments of Organization and Training are concurrently in charge of labor affairs. Each branch Youth Corps headquarters is organized on similar lines."

"The Ministry of Social Affairs trains and appoints union secretaries. It also has a Social Welfare Department, under which is a Workers' Welfare Department.

"The main spirit of wartime labor policy is: 1. Workers must join unions in their respective localities and not withdraw; 2. Workers are not allowed to shift from one factory to another without good reason; 3. Strikes are strictly prohibited; 4. Workers should work at the stabilized wage fixed by the price-control authorities."

Apart from the "unions" and their superstructure of official control, bodies known as Labor Service Corps were established in Chungking and various other places to facilitate mobilization of workers for various wartime public projects. These were supervised by the Ministry of Social Affairs through a special headquarters but later passed to the

Labor Administration (see chart). 22/ The basic organization was a group of 10 to 15 persons. Three such groups formed a squad, two to five squads a unit, and three to five units a detachment. Corps members were supposed to receive the military training laid down for army reservists and political training in Kuomintang ideology. In keeping with the Confucianism which began to color that ideology more and more, much emphasis was laid on "morality and propriety." In the given context this meant that "ricksha pullers should not ask for extra fares, there should be discipline and regularity in life and labor, etc." 23/

The Chungking Labor Service Corps operated a bureaucratically administered consumers' cooperative which sold fewer commodities, and at no lower prices, than the ordinary shops. It was involved in the construction of a Workers' Dormitory, ran a school for "leaders" and published a paper called "The Chungking Workers' Friend" every ten days.

The San Min Chu I Youth Corps, dominated by the Whampoa or "military" section of the Kuomintang concentrated, in its labor activity, on wartime projects for the training of young men in industrial skills. Trainees were required to join the Youth Corps and be active in its work. Much time in the courses themselves was consumed in indoctrination. Graduates placed in factories, like Youth Corps members in the universities, were in duty bound to recruit among their fellow-workers and to report on them, as well as on other factory affairs and personnel. The Youth Corps hoped in this way to keep its hand in industry and provide itself with a "labor base." Articles in its publications outlined a more grandiose ambition -- to create a "new Chinese working class" with the requisite loyalties in place of the "selfish and ignorant" Chinese labor of the past.

In addition to the above bodies there was a Workers' Air Raid Precautions Organization under the Chungking garrison headquarters, and workers were supposed to register for militia service under the National Military Council. The internal espionage systems of all Kuomintang groups were active in labor's ranks. Shu Hwa sums up the picture of control as follows:

"The Central Organization Board of the Kuomintang demands that employees and workers join the party. The Ministry of Social Affairs demands of them that they join its unions. The San Min Chu I Youth Corps fights to get all young workers under its control. The Labor Administration holds the Workers' Service Corps firmly in its hands..."

---

22. The significance of this was that the Ministry of Social Affairs under Ku Cheng-kang (as well as the Mass Movement Department of the Party under Chen Li-fu) was in the hands of the "CC" clique while the Labor Administration (under General Ho Chung-han) was affiliated to the Whampoa group.
23. Shu Hwa. op. cit.

Chu Kung-yuan's account of Kunming trade unions ended with some remarks as to why rear area unions as a whole did not develop, despite government effort. In his conclusion, he wrote:

"The unions studied reflect the nature of society and social relationships. In the first place they reflect the first period of mercantile capitalism. Their members are not workers in big industry but small shopkeepers, artisans, and coolies. So there is no high standard of social solidarity or collective action. The workers, in the majority of cases, pay no attention to them because they are not adapted to new developments in industrialization. The government power sets them up automatically, and appoints their officers.

"Secondly, the union can play no part in society because they cannot carry out their functions. Their membership is small and unrepresentative. No real leaders can be created under such conditions.

"Thirdly these unions are unstable in nature. As society changes further, they must disappear. As industrialization progresses, relations between employers and workers will become acute. Unions which are really guilds or professional associations will give place to organizations of the workers themselves, which the law will be compelled to recognize. They will be pushed up by labor's own power and will demand social justice and political representation...

"It is suggested that (even now) trade unions may grow and suit the situation if the government adopts a policy of non-interference..."

It took some courage, at the time, to put down common-sense thoughts of this kind, even for a student in the relative privacy of a mimeographed college thesis.

4. Other Forms of Organization: Gangs, Cliques, etc.

Gangs: One feature of the 1939-45 period was a diminution of the role of traditional secret societies or gangs in the labor field. The well-known activities of Tu Yueh-sen's "Green Ring: as an instrument of Kuomintang labor control in the lower Yangtze valley after 1927 were not duplicated in the wartime rear.

Not that the secret societies were not strong in the middle and upper Yangtze. Here the influence of the allied "Red Ring" or Ko Lao Hui (Elder Brothers' Society) was well established, particularly in the rural areas and among stevedores, boatmen and river sailors. The "Red Ring", like the "Green" had largely lost its original character as a nationalist and peasant organization, becoming instead an instrument of the rich and powerful. But the ruling class interests it came to represent were those of local merchants and landlords, who were jealous of encroachments by the central power. This made it difficult to reduce it to a coordinated arm of the Kuomintang secret police, as had been done in Shanghai.

A Hankow worker told the writer of how the "Red Ring" had worked in that city just before the war: 24/

> "The gang actually controlled many legal unions, which
> even leftists joined to keep close to the workers and get
> the protection they offered against abuse by 'outsiders.'
> Union members, who at the same time enlisted in the 'Red
> Ring', enjoyed the privilege of free entrance into theatres,
> feeding on credit in the teahouses and financial assistance
> when married or buried. The gang collected no dues but
> 'presents' had to be made to Elder Brothers everytime they
> sent out a circular such as, 'I am about to celebrate a
> birthday.' Those who did not carry out the orders of Elder
> Brothers were beaten. Members had to kowtow to superiors.
> Initiation was by blood oath, in which the novice and the
> Elder Brother drank cock's blood out of the same cup.

> "In one election to the city Kuomintang, a member of
> the party Executive Committee was not sure of getting
> sufficient votes and tried to guarantee those of workers by
> bribing a very famous Elder Brother, Jen Han-cheng. The
> bribe was a big one and Jen bought a house and a big car.
> He threw a huge banquet to which hundreds of factory workers
> were summoned and the Kuomintang candidate was invited. The
> latter, impressed by Jen's 'mass following' advanced money
> for more entertainments. But when the elections came, Jen
> ordered us to vote for him, not for his patron. The
> municipal party was loosely organized at the time. No
> one dared question the credentials of gang members. Jen
> was elected, did very well out of it, and afterwards
> repeatedly told, with great relish, about how he had out-
> witted the other fellow...."

In parts of Hupeh, Hunan and Szechuan affected by pre-war rural unrest some local "Elder Brothers" groups had reverted to their peasant beginnings. Members well up in the hierarchy took part in anti-landlord uprisings, and even became Communists. The famous Red general Ho Lung, for instance, belonged to the top grade. In the Soviet districts, of 1931-36 all feudal societies were dissolved, giving place to peasant associations. But the connections of such men were successfully utilized for work in the Kuomintang areas.

All these factors led the wartime Central Government to discard the practice of labor control through gangster intermediaries in favor of increased direct administrative intervention.

Another difficulty in the way of using gangs on the Shanghai pattern was the mixed regional origin of the labor force in plants of the wartime rear. While refugee workers from "down river" might be under Green Ring influence, those locally recruited came within the Red Ring jurisdiction. Under the arrangements of the secret societies themselves, Green Ring leaders were only "guests" in Red Ring terri- tory, entitled to deference according to their lodge standing but limited as to rights of independent activity.

---

24. From notes taken in 1938.

Of more than ninety independently written accounts of 1939-45 labor relations in the possession of the writer, only three or four make specific mention of the gangs. One dealing with industries in Liuchow (Kwangsi) mentions that there were members of both "Rings" among the workers, but does not suggest any results flowing from this. Another, an account of labor in the Kuomintang Northwest, notes that truck drivers, who came from the coastal provinces, belonged to the "Green Ring" while employees of the Lunghai Railway were "Red." The "Green Ring" did exercise some of its old influences in highway transport throughout the country. But truck drivers were the aristocrats of wartime labor and, by the nature of their occupation, separated from local affairs. Gang connections were mainly useful to them in the promotion of rackets, such as smuggling, and in keeping interlopers out of the profession. (The "anti-smuggling" guard and "highway inspection" bureaus under secret service chief Tai Li conveniently contained many "Green Ring" police agents from Shanghai, etc.) In the case of the Lunghai Railwaymen the characteristic independence of the "Red gang" seems to have asserted itself. One report records cases of slowdown as well as expressed resentment against the government practice of running luxurious special trains, under difficult frontline conditions, for high officials, foreigners and visiting dignitaries.

As the war came to an end, the government thought once more of using the "Green Ring" to manipulate the workers of liberated Shanghai, who had organized their own factory police to prevent last-minute Japanese sabotage. Tu Yueh-sen was flown to the city by a U.S. Army transport plane immediately after Japan's surrender. 25/ But by this time there were too many other claimants to labor guidance. The ramified official machinery of direct control asserted its own interests. Many of the workers themselves would follow only the leadership developed by the Communist-organized anti-Japanese underground, which now began to play a part in economic conflicts. The umbilical cord that had once linked Chu Hsueh-fan and the Chinese Association of Labor with the "Green Gang" and Tu Yueh-sen appeared to have withered. Late in 1946 Tu Yueh-sen himself left Shanghai, after quarreling with the government, which now wished to monopolize too many of his pre-war fields of endeavor.

One may say, in consequence, that the wartime development of Chinese labor, and of the situation as a whole, left no major place for the secret societies that had been such a feature of the pre-war industrial scene. While they persist in their commercial racketeering and mutual-insurance aspects, they are no longer a shaping factor. Their decline is good for Chinese labor.

Territorial Cliques: Territorial cliques, combining workers with common places of origin, were another remnant of the past. In pre-war Shanghai, for instance, workers were grouped into Kiangsu, Chekiang, Hupeh, Anhwei and Kwangtung cliques. The Kiangsu men were further sub-divided into Shanghai-Wusih and Kiangpei (North of the Yangtze) regional cliques. The Chekiangese were split along similar lines. Members of the respective cliques helped each other with introductions to jobs, loans, lodging, organized social gatherings, and generally consorted together as much as possible to the exclusion of others. When a factory employed a majority of workers from one place, these tended to push out

25. Reported in a Shanghai dispatch by Tillman Durdin in the New York Times, Sept. 9, 1945.

everyone but their fellow provincials, to make room for "their own" people. Along with the gangs, the territorial cliques were a reactionary obstacle to modern industrial organization.

In wartime industries, too, cliques flourished, formally or informally. The lines of division, however, tended to be fewer -- running between local and immigrant labor as a whole. Among the wartime immigrants Kiangsu-Chekiang, North China and Cantonese workers grouped themselves separately, along language lines. In factories in Sian there were Hopei and Honan cliques besides the local Shensi workers.

Increased national feeling and wide and frequent travel acted to erase regional prejudices. But the impossibility of organizing for broad class objectives, and the constant search for a better place of work caused by the decline of real wages, made competition for the better jobs intense. This had the opposite effect of inflaming sectionalism.

The more reactionary the atmosphere in the rear, the more the bright promise of the early war period was forgotten and the more such cliques became rooted in industrial life. In the Communist-led areas, however, they disappeared almost entirely.

Factory Clubs: Clubs for workers existed in some enterprises, notably those of the National Resources Commission. They did not achieve any great popularity because of the invariable inability of factory administrators to keep their hands off and let workers run them for themselves. Shih Kuo-heng 26/ relates that despite the provision of all sorts of organized activities the workers objected to everything and "preferred the dirty teahouses," where they felt free and at home.

5. The Chinese Association of Labor Assumes a New Role

Throughout the previous account the Chinese Association of Labor, under Chu Hsueh-fan, has hardly been mentioned. In fact it was not very much in evidence in rear-area labor relations during the period considered. As already explained, the C.A.L. was not a federation of unions or an active element in the structure of "labor control." Rather it was a service body, which had among its stated objectives the formation of such a federation in the future. Despite its officially favored position at the time, the C.A.L.'s only effort to take concrete steps in this direction had been squelched very quickly in 1938. It preserved from this experience the formal affiliation of unions in the Communist-led Shensi-Kansu-Ninghsia Border Region, as well as of many in Kuomintang-administered "Free China." Although both these links stayed on paper for several years to come, they were to acquire great significance later.

In 1939 the government recognized the C.A.L. as "an organization preliminary to the formation of a National Labor Union." This, too, was purely on paper so far as any tangible results within China were concerned. Recognition was accorded for the purpose of enabling Chu

26. *Op. cit.*

Hsueh-fan and other Association emissaries to appear, with credentials drawn up in due form, at international conferences affecting labor which called for union as well as government delegates. The C.A.L. was thenceforth permitted to list all legal unions in China, including many with which it actually had little or no contact, as coming within its jurisdiction. As a representative of these unions Mr. Chu took up a seat on the I.L.O. executive, attended wartime maritime parleys to press for better treatment of Chinese seamen on foreign ships, and made contacts with American and other national labor organizations. In the same capacity he accepted, on behalf of China, the invitation of the British Trade Union Congress to the international labor congress which set up World Federation of Trade Unions in London early in 1945. All this was done with official consent.

After the United States and Britain entered the war against Japan, the C.A.L. by virtue of its foreign contacts, became the recipient of U.S. labor donations for welfare projects for Chinese workers. Those contributed by the A.F.L. and C.I.O. through the President's War Relief Fund and United China Relief from 1943 to 1945 amounted to over US$600,000. They were used to build a clinic, several hostels, nurseries, a meeting hall and other projects at Chungking, Chengtu, Kweiyang, Sian and Paochi. Some money was expended for repatriation of workers from occupied areas, and for direct relief during the retreat of industries and workers from Kweilin before the Japanese campaigns of 1944-45. Reports to donors for a typical month listed 8,891 cups of tea, 7,275 meals and 7,275 haircuts provided at cut-rate prices; 1,742 visitors to reading rooms; 3,104 treatments and 4,600 cholera inoculations given at clinics, 588 letters written for illiterates; 25 persons lodged in hostels, 22 registrants for employment, etc. 27/

The workers so served do not appear to have had any part in running the projects. Nonetheless their existence, and the fact that the C.A.L. was handling substantial sums of foreign money for their maintenance, aroused the acute jealousy of the Ministry of Social Affairs and other official labor control agencies. Despite its superior power, the Ministry could not become the direct recipient of such funds because the C.I.O. and A.F.L. would give them only to another labor organization -- if only one in name. The Kuomintang government treasury benefitted substantially from the donations (they were paid into the Central Bank in American dollars against payments of Chinese dollars to the C.A.L. in China). This probably militated, for a long time, against its countenancing any move that might stop the remittances.

While the C.A.L. thus acquired a certain financial independence, economic and political conditions in the rear and on the international scene pressed it toward a more independent stand in other respects. Chu Hsueh-fan had long been restive under a situation which condemned him purely to the role of the government's "labor stooge" abroad. Honorific titles at home, such as membership in the Legislative Yuan, did not render any less his desire to incorporate workers into the C.A.L., in fact as well as in theory, if only to give himself some sort of base apart from the fickle one of official favor. Foreign labor questioning of his role made the same thing necessary. At home, the C.A.L. had never

27. Report on Progress of Work by the International Department of the Chinese Association of Labor, June, 1945.

openly opposed any wartime Kuomintang policy, labor law or enactment. It had even endorsed the grotesquely unfair wage-fixing regulations of November 1942 which pegged wages at a money level that represented about 50 per cent of the pre-war real wage and was slipping even lower as the inflation progressed. Chu seemed to be willing to be a government-sponsored labor "guide", subject to all the restrictions of the Labor Union Code, but he still wanted to lead labor and not be separated from it. To do that he had, in some degree at least, to listen to workers' grievances and take some action to mitigate them. This was the original mildly reformist role mapped out for him by the Kuomintang itself, but it had never been put into effect. The nature of the party's dilemma had been pointed out at the very beginning of the war by Ho Han-wen, a pro-Kuomintang commentator, who wrote:

"Dangers are evident in the present labor movement in China.

"1. The unions led by the Kuomintang have been Yamens [the name of government offices under the Empire] without close ties with rank-and-file workers....They are organized on a local basis without systematic mutual liaison, which is neither sound nor conducive to unity...

"2. Since the party purge [Kuomintang name for the suppression of left-wingers in 1927] the Kuomintang has been fearful of the labor movement. Meanwhile, it belittles the strength of the workers. The result is that it merely 'plays' with unions and thereby affords Communists and other counter-revolutionaries [in relation to the Kuomintang as "revolutionary" party] many opportunities to form illegal labor organizations which the Kuomintang is powerless to suppress...." 28/

The industrial deterioration after 1943, and the number of unemployed relief cases coming to the American-financed C.A.L. labor centers, made the Association a recipient of many workers' complaints which it forwarded to the government. We have told how cavalierly these were treated in the case of discharged war industry machinists. The C.A.L. also had to pass on workers' demands with regard to wages and conditions encountered in the course of labor mobilization activity with which it was charged by the authorities (in 1943, for instance, it helped recruit a "worker's battalion" for service with Chinese troops in India and Burma). If it had not done even this, as Ho Han-wen pointed out in the passage quoted above, some sort of underground labor organization would inevitably have arisen, even without the intervention of the "counter-revolutionaries" whom Mr. Ho so wanted to guard against.

But even in such modest tasks the C.A.L. ran into a completely inflexible official attitude with which it found itself increasingly in conflict. The Kuomintang ruling group had moved so far to the die-hard Right in the later war years that even the C.A.L., which had not itself undergone any change of personnel, became more and more "Left" by comparison. The same tendencies in the government were

28. Ho Han-wen, Workers in the Extraordinary Era, Shanghai, August 1947.

simultaneously creating a sizeable non-Communist body of protest on the national political scene (the Democratic League, etc.). Even the United States, in the person of General Stilwell, was pressing for reform in the interests of more efficient war against Japan. By imperceptible degrees Chu Hsueh-fan and most of the C.A.L. leadership took a course parallel to the very broad general movement whose slogans were more democracy in government, renewed inter-party unity instead of civil war, and a lightening of the people's burdens.

These were also the primary necessities without which Chinese workers as a class could not look forward to any national economic progress (more jobs) or any opportunity for forming the free organizations they lacked (defense of their own interests). Thus once again, as briefly in 1938, the Association began to reflect the true requirements of Chinese labor. The reflection was pale and not characterized by any undue boldness of spirit. But it was real and therefore widened the rift between the C.A.L. and the official machinery of labor "control."

The first overt indication of this process came in the spring of 1944 when the "Chinese Laborers' Welfare Association" was launched in Chungking under government sponsorship. Its board of directors included officials, industrialists, Kuomintang social workers and functionaries of approved unions -- Chu Hsueh-fan's name was conspicuously absent. The C.A.L. and union officers close to it took up the challenge by boycotting the public inauguration meeting of the parallel organization, held on May 1, 1945. The Ministry of Social Affairs retaliated in turn by summoning Chu Hsueh-fan and demanding (1) that the C.A.L. obey all instructions issued by the Ministry; and (2) that Chu himself sign a "letter of repentance" as a member of the Kuomintang. Chu refused. 29/

The wedge was driven deeper later in 1945, when the economic crisis in the rear and flight of industry back to the recovered coast paralyzed most of industry and reduced wages in the rest to worthlessness. The summer and fall brought a wave of spontaneous strikes and demonstrations, in military as well as private enterprises, which neither wartime laws nor police action could any longer cope with. The C.A.L. gave these strikes no leadership, but occasionally lent its "good offices" as a third party in settlement. Cases in Chungking alone are listed below: 30/

1945

June   Strike of Upper Yangtze shipping pilots, against failure
       of employers to pay wages partly in rice, coal, cooking
       oil and salt (to offset inflation), as laid down by the
       government Pilotage Control Committee.

---

29.   "Battle for the Chinese Association of Labor", Hsin Min Wan Pao,
      Shanghai, September 5, 1946. Tracing the history of disagreements between the C.A.L. and the government, this liberal
      newspaper commented: "Observers who are now familiar with the
      inside story began to see that there are two different labor
      organizations in China."
30.   Report on Progress of Work by International Dept. of C.A.L. for
      months cited.

July	Strike of Yu Hwa cotton mill workers against an unfair dismissal.
	Strike in the Fu Hsing (government) Company Bristle Factory for higher wages. Increase of 100-120% in money wage granted.
	Demand for severance pay and bonus by discharged workers of Weh Sun Electric Co.
	Demand for better treatment by War Ministry machine shop workers.
August	Protest by workers against arbitrary dismissal due to removal in Ming Ya Machine Shop and Ta Sun Iron Works and due to lowered production in Ya Sun Iron Works. Demand for more pay at Government Cotton Control Administration.
September	29 strikes and conflicts, of which 28 involved dismissals and non-payment of severance, of which six were in factories that failed or closed down, three in plants where "production was cut", and the rest unexplained. The remaining case involved a demand for shorter hours and guaranteed work. Factories affected were 18 metallurgical and machine works, 2 textile plants, 2 cement works, a rubber factory and several unspecified, many of which were government-owned. Number of workers affected not given.
October	60,000 workers in Chungking thrown out of employment. 27 strikes and conflicts, fourteen of which were for dismissal and eight for better wages and treatment.

Wholesale abandonment by the government of workers who had obeyed its call to come to the interior was confirmed by the C.A.L.'s report that Chungking's 60,000 industrial unemployed were completely destitute. The powerlessness and lack of initiative of the C.A.L. itself in this connection could be seen from the pitiful section of the same report dealing with its Employment Registry which recorded that "during the month 37 unemployed workers were registered of whom six got jobs." The Association stated under "Emergency Relief" that:

"In sympathy with the workers we have advocated aid to the unemployed by the employed. A contribution campaign among the Association staff was started, which required each of the staff members to contribute 50 per cent of his salary or wage...."

and further that:

"The American Labor Hall [donated by the A.F.L. and C.I.O] is now used as a cinema theater for regular showing of American pictures. In each show 20 seats will be reserved for workers free of charge. Sunday morning shows admit workers free. The association has appropriated Chinese $15 million [about U.S.$15,000 at the time] for emergency relief and this sum is to be covered by the proceeds of the cinema shows...."

As for government participation in allaying the catastrophe, the report said only:

> "The Association, in an attempt to solicit contributions from other sources is negotiating with the Ministry of Social Affairs on this problem." 31/

The U.S. $15,000 appropriated during the month amounted, of course, to only 25 cents per starving, unemployed worker. The Ministry of Social Affairs, to which the C.A.L. was subject, and with which it was compelled to negotiate for "contributions", was the government organ which had arrogated to itself full authority over labor organization and responsibility for workers' welfare -- the organ which was responsible for the absence of real unions in Kuomintang China.

6. Toward a United Labor Federation

The C.A.L. faced a choice in these months. It could oppose the new wave of strikes and revert to the position of an additional, and very minor, cog in the structure of Kuomintang labor control. In this case whatever prestige it had gained in the eyes of the workers would automatically disappear. Or it could orient itself to the demand of workers, including those in the liberated cities, for a better post-war deal, and to the general movement for peaceful post war unity.

By August 1945 the C.A.L. leadership appears to have embarked on the latter course. When the American-owned Chungking (wartime) edition of the Shanghai Evening Post & Mercury was forced to close by censorship because of liberal criticism of the Kuomintang, Chu Hseuh-fan wrote a letter of sympathy to the editors which contained two significant statements:

> "Chinese workers ... now that they begin to know their strength of organization, can demand more easily better working conditions, better hours and higher pay through their unions. Strikes have become familiar in Chungking recently, which means that the workers are awakening.
> (Italics mine - I.E.)

> "I am sorry to hear that your paper ... has been suspended because of present censorship, but I trust it will always be remembered by your Chinese readers who have liked its point of view ..." 32/

The direction taken by the C.A.L. seems also to have influenced the trade unions of the Communist-led Liberated Areas, and the Communist Party in the whole country, in their view of post-war organizational forms for labor.

Unions in the Shensi-Kansu-Ninghsia Border Region, the original pre-1937 Administrative enclave of the Communists, had brought their

---

31. Ibid. for October 1945.

32. Printed in the temporary American (New York) edition of the Shanghai Evening Post & Mercury, August 3, 1945.

registered 53,000 members into formal affiliation with the Association in 1938, in the boom period of the wartime United Front. Real contact had been lost shortly afterwards, owing to newly-developing nation-wide political rifts.

Unions of the eighteen new Liberated Areas established under Communist auspices in 1939-45, with a total of over 800,000 members, did not follow the example of those in the Border Region. Late in 1944, federations already existing in the individual areas set up a Preparatory Committee for the China Liberated Areas Federation of Labor. Its chairman was Teng Fa, a seaman and Communist party leader whose trade union experience dated back to activity in the pre-1927 All China Labor Federation. The Vice-Chairman was Tsui Tien-fu, originally a North Shensi agricultural laborer and peasant partisan concurrently heading the Border Region Federation. The tendency was then to seek separate representation in the projected W.F.T.U. Unrepresented at the February 1945 London Conference which set up the international body, the Liberated Area Unions planned to send their own delegates to apply for admission at the Paris conference in September.

Two things occurring at the time, however, radically altered the situation. One was the wave of strikes and labor activity in newly-recovered Shanghai, where workers took over factories from Japanese owners, preserved them from sabotage until Chinese government representatives arrived to take over, made demands on the government thereafter for rapid resumption of production under improved conditions, and were to a great extent backed in these demands by the C.A.L. Late August and September alone brought 276 disputes, involving 65,000 workers in 344 enterprises. The five months following witnessed 615 conflicts (121 of them strikes), with 446,420 workers from 6,693 enterprises participating. 33/ Isolated actions gave way to city-wide ones. No fewer than 75 unions, for instance, participated in a committee to support a walkout in the American-owned Shanghai Power Company. It is not necessary here to go further into Shanghai's post-war labor history, but a mere comparison of the above figures with those with which we had occasion to deal in considering conditions in the wartime interior will show that the C.A.L., in moving toward a position representative of workers' interests, had access to a base of a totally different order of magnitude from that previously at its disposal. Moreover, the Shanghai workers had not been the subject of Kuomintang control efforts for a number of years. After shaking off the Japanese-devised tyranny by which they had been governed during the war years, they were not at all disposed to accept the imposition of similar restrictions from their own government.

The second development was the beginning of new Kuomintang-Communist negotiations for a general national settlement, which went on for many months simultaneously with recurring civil war clashes. Contact between the two areas became briefly easier. Conversations began between their labor spokesmen. As a result, the Liberated Areas Federation also affiliated to the C.A.L. and a joint delegation was sent to Paris, with Chu Hsueh-fan as its head and Teng Fa as chief Liberated Area representative. Another Liberated Areas delegate

33. Figures of the Bureau of Social Affairs, Shanghai Municipal Government.

was Liu Ning-yi, a Communist trade-unionist from the Kailan Mines, China's largest collieries, who had spent several years in Kuomintang prisons before the war.

In Paris, on October 4, 1945, closer organizational agreement was reached on the basis of a document entitled "Important Demands of the Chinese Labor Movement." This followed closely proposals submitted by the Liberated Areas Federation as its program for labor unity, and contained eight points as follows:

1. Establishment of a peaceful, unified and democratic China;

2. Punishment of traitors and confiscation of their property. Disbandment of all quisling troops and labor unions. (This demand referred to the situation in Shanghai and other recovered cities, where none of these things had been done but ex-quislings, on the contrary, continued to be used to control the population. - I.E.)

3. Freedom of association, speech and press for all the people. Freedom for workers to organize their own unions.

4. A maximum work-week of 48 hours for the period of national reconstruction;

5. Social insurance measures to guarantee workers' livelihood, employment and medical care;

6. Abolition of the prevailing system of apprenticeship;

7. A voice for workers in political affairs of the state;

8. Effective enforcement of free education. 34/

A further step in the consolidation of the entire labor movement on a more independent basis and progressive political program was taken during the Political Consultative Conference of January-February 1946, at the time of General Marshall's mediation. At one point in the discussion, right-wing Kuomintang leaders "mobilized" 170 organizations to press Chiang Kai-shek and the conference not to revise the old undemocratic list of delegates to the forthcoming National Assembly, against which all opposition groups had protested. The method was simple -- the names of these organizations were affixed to a "petition" without the

_____

34. Supplied by Chinese Association of Labor, Chungking. Chu Hsueh-fan, writing in the China Weekly Review, Shanghai, gives the original eight points of the Liberated Area delegate which differ from the above only in the following particulars:
Point 4. A maximum work-week of 44 (not 48) hours.
Point 5. Does not mention social insurance. Incorporates abolition of old apprenticeship system, as in Point 6 above, adding: "An apprentice should be paid according to his ability" and "equal pay for equal work without sex discrimination."
Points 6 and 7 parallel Points 7 and 8, as above.
Point 8 reads: "In order to develop industry and restore normal economic life in post-war China, the proficiency of workers should be increased."

formality of asking their consent. The C.A.L., finding itself listed, exposed the fraud in letters to newspapers. 35/ In defiance of official instructions to the contrary, Chu Hsueh-fan and other officers took part in mass meetings, jointly with the Democratic League and similar bodies, which advocated an immediate and effective political settlement. Soon reactionary Kuomintang groups began to smash up such mass meetings. Chu Hsueh-fan and I Li-yung, C.A.L. Secretary-General, were badly beaten, with democratic leaders, in an attack on a gathering to celebrate the signing of new unity agreements held at Chouchiangkow, Chungking, on February 10, 1946. The right-wing terrorist acts were referred to by General Marshall, in his famous mediation report, as "the quite evidently inspired mob actions of last February and March, some within a few blocks of where I was then engaged in completing negotiations."

It was at this point that the C.A.L. issued another key document, quoted below: Sub-headings (in italics) have been inserted by the present author for facility in reference:

URGENT REQUEST AND MINIMUM DEMANDS OF THE CHINESE ASSOCIATION OF LABOR ON THE CHINESE POLITICAL SITUATION AND LABOR MOVEMENT 36/

After the victorious ending of the war, both the domestic and international situations have altered. But the common demand for world democracy is undeniable. Standing on behalf of the Chinese workers, we deem it necessary to make the following requests and demands.

National Unity and Democracy

1. The fundamental human rights which President Chiang Kai-shek guaranteed to protect, namely freedom of speech, belief, assembly, residence, association and correspondence should be realized promptly.

2. A freely-elected National Assembly should be convened and the number of workers' representatives fixed explicitly.

3. The base of the government should be broadened to include representatives of all political parties and prominent democratic leaders of society on an effect-ively equal footing.

4. The causes of civil war should be eliminated. All troops should belong to the nation.

5. All corrupt officials and traitors should be strictly punished; war criminals should be condemned; enemy troops should be disarmed and repatriated as quickly as possible; all puppet troops should be disbanded.

---

35. "Battle for the Chinese Association of Labor", Hsin Min Wan Pao, Shanghai, September 5, 1946.

36. Published by the Chinese Association of Labor, Chungking.

6. The spheres of private and government enterprises should be regulated according to the "first stage of economic reconstruction." Private enterprise must be encouraged, rather than government enterprise.

7. All enemy and puppet property should be confiscated. Industrial production in the recovered areas should be restored at once.

The Land Problem

8. The land problem should be settled at once. Farm rents must be reduced and usurious loan-interest forbidden. Illegal oppression of farmers by officials must stop. The livelihood of farmers must be improved. The principle of "the soil to the tiller" must be realized.

Rights of Labor

9. The present Trade Union Law must be amended. Regulations restricting workers' rights must be repealed.

10. All workers (including those in war industries) must have the right of organization. A nation-wide workers' organization must be officially recognized.

11. Workers must have the right to strike, demonstrate and bargain collectively.

12. Workers in government enterprises must have the right to participate in plant administration.

13. A system of "labor-management" committees must be instituted to harmonize employer-employee relationships.

14. Workers must have the right to a job. The government should develop a plan to guarantee employment.

15. Minimum wage rates must be fixed according to the cost-of-living index in each place. The rule should be "equal pay for equal work" for both sexes.

16. Labor welfare must be improved. Factory inspection must be carried out effectively to improve safety and health conditions.

17. Women and child workers should be protected. Night shifts for these workers should be prohibited. Vocational education should be given to young workers at the employers' expense. Women workers should have pregnancy leave with full pay.

18. The contract labor system must be eliminated.

19. The maximum work week for the time being should be 48 hours. All workers must enjoy regular holidays with pay.

20. Vocational and technical education for workers must be promoted. The old apprentice system should be abolished.

22. Unemployed should be given temporary relief and their re-employment guaranteed.

23. Compensation should be granted at once to workers, or families of workers, wounded or killed in the war.

The 23 points were of a programmatic character and were repeatedly reprinted, for more than a year afterwards, as "The Platform of the C.A.L." 37/ It was on the basis of this program that the unity of organizations representing labor in both areas of China was secured on firm foundations. The Kuomintang government had tolerated initial steps toward such unity as a formal accompaniment to its maneuvers during the Marshall mediation. But when the mediation gave place to civil war between Kuomintang and Communists, the solidarity of labor and its spokesmen throughout China remained unimpaired -- with outspoken condemnation of civil war and U.S. intervention as its main political slogans.

7. Outlawing of the "Old" C.A.L.

Issuance of the C.A.L. "Platform" marked the decisive break between the Association and the government. The official attitude toward the organization changed at once from disapproval to harassment culminating in suppression.

In March 1946 Chu Hsueh-fan, I Li-yung (Secretary-General of the C.A.L.) and others were arraigned before the Chungking District Court on charges of "disturbing peace and order." Prosecution was afterwards suspended but interference with the organization increased during the spring and summer, notably in Tientsin and Hankow.

On August 6, uniformed and plain clothes police, accompanied by emissaries of the government-sponsored "General Labor Union", seized the Chungking headquarters of the C.A.L. as well as its American-donated Labor Hall, hospital, and hostels. More than 20 Association employees were arrested. Armed police cordons were thrown around its buildings. All records were removed. The press, as well as the public, were excluded from the immediate vicinity.

Chu's statement, made at this time, read in part.

   "Because of continual government attempts to break the unity of the workers by forcing the C.A.L. to exclude trade unions in the Liberated Areas, and because of pres-

---

37. See the C.A.L. pamphlet, The C.A.L. faces a Crisis, by P. E. Loo, Shanghai, November 15, 1946, and "Are the Workers in China Divided?" by Chu Hsueh-fan, China Weekly Review, Shanghai, March 8, 1947.

sure brought to bear on the C.A.L. to demonstrate an
anti-communism which it does not feel, I am leaving
China. The government has tried to force me to attend
a non-democratic, one-party National Assembly which I
deny is in any way representative of the wishes of the
Chinese people....

"It has planned my immediate arrest on false and trumped-
up charges. It threatens to publish, in the name of the
C.A.L., a statement denouncing the Communists and the
Democratic League, but this has never been agreed upon
and would not be tolerated by the workers..."

Two weeks after this declaration was issued, the government
"reorganized" the C.A.L. with An Pu-ting as Chairman and Shen Ting, a
Ministry of Social Affairs official, as Secretary-General. In an effort
to disrupt the continuing work of the old C.A.L. headquarters at Hongkong,
Kuomintang agents in the British colony attempted to kill Chu Hsueh-fan.
His injuries kept him in a hospital for many weeks.

The original C.A.L., however, continued to be supported by trade
unionists in both parts of China. It was also endorsed by the W.F.T.U.,
of which Chu Hsueh-fan had been elected one of the vice-presidents.
Among the resolutions adopted by the world organization at the General
Council session at Prague (June 9-14, 1947) was the following:

"The General Council of the W.F.T.U. declares that
the heroic workers of China have earned with their
blood the democratic rights of trade unionists and
declares that it will give them its wholehearted
and energetic support in the struggle for the vin-
dication of these rights.

"To this end, the General Council decides:

1. That the W.F.T.U. recognizes the C.A.L. as constituted prior to the 1946 coup of the Chinese government as the only bona-fide Trade Union Center in China.

2. That the W.F.T.U. fully endorses the following
program of the C.A.L.

a. Unity of All Chinese workers throughout China
in a single organization, without regard to
political barriers or differences.

b. The right of all workers freely to organize
themselves into trade unions, with recognition
of their right to hold public meetings, bargain
collectively, strike and engage in all other
trade union activities.

c. Complete non-interference by the government in
the internal affairs of trade unions.

d.   Realization of fundamental economic and human rights.

3.   To authorize the General Secretary to make invervention with the Chinese government demanding that the rights enumerated in Paragraph 2 be guaranteed to the workers and trade unions of China.

4.   To instruct the General Secretary to transmit a copy of this resolution with an appropriate accompanying letter to the Chinese Ambassador at Prague.

5.   To authorize the Executive Bureau to study the question of establishing an office of the W.F.T.U. in the Far East."
38/

Thus, as a result of wartime and immediate post-war developments, China once more had two labor movements. As before, a fictitious one was recognized by the government as legal. But the more representative one, made illegal in December 1946, was no longer underground, narrow in composition, or internationally unknown. On the contrary, it commanded the support of workers of all parties in all parts of the country pending formation of the still unachieved nation-wide federation. Moreover, it was this "illegal" body which was now universally recognized by trade unions in other countries, both in and out of the W.F.T.U., which refused any longer to deal with the kept "unions" that were really Kuomintang organs of control.

It was the renewed CAL, too, which participated, through Chu Hsueh-fan, in the Sixth All-China Labor Congress held in Harbin, in Communist-held Manchuria, in August 1948. The Congress, purposely numbered to show continuity with the labor movement of 1924-27, voted to re-establish the All-China Labor Federation, which had been suppressed in 1929. It united open unions in the growing Communist-led areas with underground unions in remaining Kuomintang territory and brought the Chinese labor movement back into what all previous history proved to be its main channel.

_____

38.   Information Bulletin, World Federation of Trade Unions, Paris, 1947.

SUPPLEMENT

LABOR IN NATIONALIST CHINA, 1945-48

by

Julian R. Friedman

PREFATORY NOTE

The author's experiences in China in 1945-46 provided most of the material for this paper: They were enriched through conversations with Chinese workers, employers, officials, scholars, and journalists. Mr. Cheng Hai-fong, Director, China Branch of the International Labor Office, rendered invaluable assistance and guidance.

Fortunately for the reader, this paper is free of explanatory foot notes, but unfortunately there is far too little written material on Chinese labor in recent years. Mr. Chee Hwa's article, "Shanghai Trade Unions" (China Digest, II, #2, July 1, 1947), is excellent despite its brevity. We still lack a complete translation of Professor Ta Chen's recent report on industrial labor in Shanghai.

This paper lacks extensive statistical support. It includes some data compiled by officials of the Nationalist Government and its bureaux, which reached the author through the China Branch of the International Labor Office. Those who are familiar with statistical problems in China will no doubt understand why he has used official data so sparsely. Not only are the bureaux inadequately staffed and financed for statistical work, but, as long as the Government treats statistics as politics, its work will be viewed with the deepest suspicion.

The author has made certain generalizations which a Sinologist would avoid in the absence of thorough social and economic studies. Perhaps his rash interpretations will focus attention on the need for more intensive analyses of the growth of industrial life in China.

The author is grateful to his friends who read over the manuscript in its early stages. Of course, it goes without saying that he is responsible for what is contained therein.

* * * * * *

The attention that the Pacific War directed to Chinese industrial life increased after V-J Day. Post-war events on the labor front in China invited so much additional scrutiny and publicity that industrial life can no longer be treated as a mere appendage of the agrarian economy and feudal society.

Although agriculture still sets the way of life for eighty per cent of the Chinese people, the industrial sphere with only one or two per cent exerts on the state of the nation an influence that the counting of heads alone cannot accurately measure. Today the industrial life penetrates highly strategic centers, bears the brunt of inflation, and breeds issues vitally relevant to the civil war.

With the growth of non-agricultural wage-earning groups, the usual labor problems associated with real wages and living conditions, efficiency of labor and labor costs of production, conditions of work, and bargaining power emerged in China. One might have expected Chinese civilization, so favorably reputed for its tendencies towards compromise and accommodation, to be free of controversy over labor issues. So far China has not circumvented the labor disputes common to the western industrial nations, nor has it improvised methods of settlement that are unknown in the west.

At this point it might be well to refute an assertion frequently heard in China before and after V-J Day, namely, that the approach to the study of Chinese labor problems must necessarily differ from the approach to the study of the labor problems of the United States and the European nations. We find in the nature of Chinese labor problems no peculiarities to substantiate this assertion. Of course, previous experiences and prevailing conditions in China produce a labor problem that bears marks of Chinese civilization. However, from an analytical viewpoint, the local aspects are not sufficiently basic to require new methodology. Because industrial development has taken place simultaneously with the deterioration of the older economy, its impact has been substantially more than tradition and custom could resist or dilute. Hence the "westernization" of Shanghai and Canton. However, in many instances custom dies hard; for example, the Moon Festival, a feature of agrarian life, has become a holiday occasion in industrial life.

Almost 15 years of Japanese occupation (50 in Taiwan) and more than two decades of civil war accentuated the labor issues. "Peace in the Pacific" did not automatically bring peace on the labor front. Meanwhile mere political pledges to apply Dr. Sun Yat-sen's Principle of the People's Livelihood were no adequate substitute for enlightened social reform.

Post-war labor problems existed in a China territorially united but politically divided. It was anticipated that, in many areas released from Japanese occupation, the severity of living would ease slightly. Shanghai did not suffer heavy war damage, but Canton, Hengyang, Changsha, and Hankow came out of the war in a miserable condition. Consequently, over-all improvement of industrial life would, it was understood, require forced austerity concurrently with sound reconstruction, industrial expansion, and agrarian reform over a considerable time. There could be no short cut in view of the vast poverty, lack of equipment, and political rivalries.

At the same time, living conditions in "Free China" were expected to decline following the removal of the Nationalist Government to Nanking and restoration of industry and commerce from Mukden to Canton. However, the people in the interior should have gained some relief through the decline in prices which inflationary pressure had driven sky high during the war. The Government abandoned its support of industrial projects in Szechuan and Yunnan without much foresight, and the result was a depression that magnified the labor problems in these provinces. Closing of factories led to an exodus of skilled workers, some of whom could by hurrying find jobs in the liberated zones. This migration symbolized the collapse of interior industry in favor of the pre-war concentration along the coast. Without employment, the local workers could not take advantage of the new low prices.

At the end of Soviet-Japanese hostilities, Manchuria was an economic uncertainty, but its heavy industry held out hopes of high levels of employment under relatively modern working conditions. The vast destruction of industry as a consequence of war and politics set back these hopes with a jolt and prolonged the misery and poverty of that region.

V-J Day opened an era of labor problems in Nationalist China that

offered earning opportunities in industry and occupations, exclusive
of family shops, for about three million workers. In addition to local
supplies, Nationalist China had for its industrial recovery, access to
overseas resources procured through international trade and assistance
programs. However, instead of reviving steadily from a state of war
exhaustion, it moved into a post-war depression interrupted infrequently
by fantastic spasms of prosperity for a small fraction of the population.

These circumstances were hardly conducive to emancipating the labor
scene from troublesome labor problems. Those that had their roots in
the economics of industrial growth call for little explanation. Employers sought to minimize their accountable labor costs, the workers to
maximize earnings and find more earning opportunities. As inefficiency
on both sides stifled production, each endeavored to protect profits
and "take-home" pay by charging up losses to each other.

The resulting issues were common in one form or another to all the
industrial areas. After V-J Day, management and labor had to examine
all aspects of their relations, including basic wages and price lists,
cost-of-living allowances, quantity and quality of payments in kind,
seasonal and efficiency bonuses, employee dividends, sickness and
accident grants, hospitalization with pay, clothing and uniform allowances,
purchase discounts, holidays and vacations with pay, hours of work,
working conditions, provision of tools, safety and health precautions,
arbitrary and abusive management and supervision, slacking and absenteeism, breaches of discipline, apprenticeship arrangements, hiring and
firing, discriminatory treatment, promotion and seniority, dismissal and
separation allowances.

To an extent that patently prejudiced peaceful industrial relations,
there was a lack of mutual confidence between employers and workers. The
situation could have profitably done with far less contempt for manual
laborers on the part of the non-manual managers and employees. Prior to
the Pacific War, Chinese industry had begun to accumulate experience and
acquire tradition in the labor sphere. Then, with the invasion, industry
had to utilize the inimical labor-management methods ordered by the
Japanese.

In "Free China" industrial relations developed in a crisis economy,
and, in the absence of official condemnation, such undesirable features
as guarded compounds and employer omnipotence spread. These experiences
left the post-war scene without very many precedents of industrial
democracy to follow.

The legislation of the Nationalist Government in this field was
deficient and provided little guidance, although Chinese delegations
had assisted in drafting labor conventions and recommendations of the
International Labor Organization. The Chinese labor code included the
following laws: (1) Trade Union Law of 1929, with amendments of 1931,
1932, 1933, 1943, and 1947; (2) Labor Disputes Law of 1928, with
amendments of 1931 and 1943; (3) Labor Contract Law of 1936; (4) Collective Agreement Law of 1930; (5) Factory Law of 1929, with amendments
of 1932; (6) Factory Inspection Law of 1931, with amendments of 1935;
and (7) Employment Service Law of 1935. In addition, there were in this
post-war period no end of regulations issued under some of these laws,
ministerial orders, and local ordinances, as well as authoritative

statements of policy of the government and the Kuomintang. Furthermore, as China was in a "state of emergency" the war-area armies, provincial forces, and municipal garrisons issued edicts on labor matters.

Although the laws contained some useful provisions that might have reduced local labor troubles, enforcement was noticeably infrequent and irregular. The Ministry of Social Affairs was charged with administering these laws, and it in turn relied upon the provincial, hsien, and municipal bureaux to enforce them on the spot. In some cases, the policies of the Ministry, e.g., in organization of trade unions, contradicted the law, while the lack of trained and experienced administrators, without political or economic vested interests, denied the government a constructive role in the solution of post-war labor problems.

The ordinary problems occurred most frequently, but special problems were challenging and very difficult to avoid. Such problems may be attributed to (1) the Chinese agrarian tradition; (2) the Pacific War; (3) the "take-over" policies of the Nationalist Government; (4) the relinquishment of extraterritoriality; and (5) the civil war.

Chinese agrarian tradition obstructed the modernization of the wage structure and industrial relations. It kept open the way for arbitrary management, unnecessary exploitation of labor, unwarranted demands of workers, dubious employment practices, and gangster activities.

Employers, even after the war, lorded it over the workers in an autocratic manner. They viewed manual labor with disdain and frequently paid wages consistent more with their feelings than with the value of output. Some employers imperiously imposed penalties and humiliations which the workers, lacking the usual peasant reticence and forbearance, reciprocated with non-Confucian abuse.

On the other hand, many workers refused to break with the past. They insisted that employers possessed obligations to maintain them indefinitely, as the landlords had done for the workers' agrarian ancestors. In practice, this meant that the workers looked to the employers for support in good times and bad. For example, in 1937 some foreign-owned refrigeration plants in Shanghai reduced staff and later closed during the Japanese occupation. In 1946, those workers, mostly casual laborers, who had been dismissed in 1937, returned for employment, seeking not only reinstatement but also back wages and maintenance allowances for the period of the war. When the foreign employers refused, the workers picketed the plants. Chinese employers tended to understand but resisted such demands. Non-Chinese employers found them "extreme" and infuriating.

At the same time that the workers insisted upon their traditional due, they also wanted the advantages of the modern industrial world. They demanded status in industry, especially through the recognition of their unions. In other words, in addition to security based on custom, they sought supplementary security based on collective bargaining. Unfortunately, poverty and organizational weaknesses perpetuated this dichotomy.

As one-sided as this mixture of traditional and modern practices might seem, in 1945-47 it played into the hands of the employers. The legacy of peasant life diminished rather than enhanced the fortunes of the industrial worker. He had inherited the peasant's reliance on a seasonal or annual income, natural in an agrarian economy, but quite unsuited for an urban money economy. It was not so much the rate of the job as its long-term earning potential that attracted the worker to a particular opening. Hence, he was willing to work at low weekly wages (and to live frugally in a sense, following the living cycle of the peasant) in anticipation of lucrative seasonal bonuses and handsome retirement allowances. The importance of this frame of mind might seem less where necessity and scarcity of employment curtailed the freedom of the worker to choose one or another job and forced him to take the first opening. Nevertheless, upon entering whatever employment he came by, the worker looked to the seasonal bonuses to cancel debts incurred to supplement his usually meager wage.

In prosperous years this system saved the workers from complete, perpetual poverty, in some cases even permitting a higher than subsistence level of living at Chinese New Year. However, from V-J Day to 1947-48, there was no prosperity to activate this system, and thus no windfall for the workers. On the other hand, the system made it possible for employers to earn profits or to pass on losses by charging them against the bonuses. At Chinese New Year in 1946 and 1947, many firms declared bankruptcy on the eve of the holiday; others threatened to do so unless the workers forfeited their traditional claims. This system also allowed employers who were short of cash and desirous of avoiding moneylenders to defer wage payments; It amounted to forced loans from the workers without the employers' assuming obligations to pay interest.

The bonus tradition quite frequently impaired the bargaining position of the workers. As they depended upon these irregular, indefinite payments, they could not afford to leave employment or even to strike. The employer held too heavy a weapon, for bonus claims were matters not of law but of custom torn from their original environment. Moreover, unions had difficulty in defining and specifying wage terms as long as the wage structure lacked uniformity of payments. Post-war experiences established the bonus as a symbol of vicarious prosperity rich in tradition but poor in material value, a link between the misfortunes of agrarian and industrial life.

Another practice frequently invoked after V-J Day and too readily accepted by the workers was the substitution of "loans" for wage increases, just as the landlord offers usurious loans to the peasants in lieu of higher prices for produce or lower rents and levies. These "loans" to the workers carried little, if any, interest and under inflationary conditions could be met almost without sacrifice; but the practice denied the workers increased basic wage rates and consequently an enlarged cost-of-living allowance that was fixed on the basis of these rates.

"Introductions" and labor contracting continued to function in the post-war labor scene. In the face of job shortages, "introductions" served to ration employment, but the criterion was often willingness to accept low wages and to refrain from joining trade unions or striking. Almost invariably the practice involved paying the "introducer" or a foreman. Family, provincial and local connections also figured in the arrangement. As for the contracting system, some employers after the war still obtained new workers from the countryside through agencies in preference to employing local labor directly. In this manner, employers tried to keep wages low and to prevent trade unions from gaining ground. However, with the large-scale unemployment in the coastal areas, "contracting" was losing its advantages for the employers.

Finally, the impact of tradition on the industrial scene is incompletely studied unless some mention is made of the secret societies. Of rural origin centuries ago, such societies had in a new age and different environment become employer associations of a reputable type and, in other cases, gangster and black-leg organizations. Little need be said of the former except that their concern for tradition has often been detrimental to the welfare of the workers and the efficiency of industry. The gangster societies which flourished in Central China from 1927 to 1941 extorted money from workers, intimidated them, broke strikes, attacked trade-union meetings, and pilfered goods along the waterfronts of Shanghai and Hankow. In Chungking they exacted contributions from ricksha pullers and water-carriers for the privilege of traveling from one part of the city to another. In January 1946 hoodlums attacked the strikers at the Shanghai Power Company, and immediately afterwards it was alleged in labor circles that these hoodlums belonged to the infamous Shanghai underworld. Parenthetically, it must be recorded that the growth of trade unions weakened the insidious influence of these gangs over the life of the workers. No longer could they, because of the ignorance and fear of the workers, attack with impunity.

Such conditions might have disappeared some years before had the Japanese not invaded China. The defeat of Japan in 1945 opened the way for the Chinese to eradicate many deplorable labor practices that the invader had imported or encouraged. Wherever the Japanese controlled industry on Chinese soil, they imposed the dormitory or compound system, rigidly-fixed wage rates and price lists, police controls, long hours of work, and bans on trade unions. It is not necessary to elaborate the deleterious effect of these practices. No industrial democracy could develop in China as long as they remained.

As an indispensable part of the Chinese war policy to sacrifice space in exchange for time, industrial units were constructed in the interior. Many were of modern design and afforded remarkably decent working conditions. However, too many owners, some genuinely unable to procure any but shoddy materials but others exploiting the war emergency for quick gain, built fire-traps in which the workers suffered continually from accidents and disease. Some of these working sheds survived beyond V-J Day to create a further obstacle to improved working conditions.

An adequate factory-inspection system might have minimized the social evils inherent in this situation. No effective system was instituted. The government had virtually abandoned its initial efforts at factory inspection upon the outbreak of war. The service attached to the Shanghai Municipal Council of the International Settlement failed to migrate to the interior, but Mr. Rewi Alley of that service left and did wonders with the Chinese industrial cooperative movement in that period. At the end of the war, the Ministry of Social Affairs contained a defunct factory-inspection section within its Department of Social Welfare.

Chinese workers had little chance of learning modern methods of industrial relations during the war. In opposition to the Japanese, they devised clever schemes of sabotage in the factories. Through the patriotic movements conducted by the National Salvationists and Communists they acquired experience in working together for their own and the national interest. To dissolve such solidarity, not only did the Japanese and the Chinese puppets prohibit trade unions in their areas but the Kuomintang also did the same in Nationalist China. Through the resistance movements the workers learned certain labor practices which, however commendable they might be in time of war against the enemy, were not always conducive to cooperative labor-management relations in peace.

A specific post-war problem arising directly out of the Japanese occupation concerned payment of the "Victory Bonus". The workers justified their claim to this bonus on the following grounds: (1) personal war losses; (2) achievements in resistance and sabotage; and (3) protection provided the industries at the request of evacuating employers and the government. Many contended that they had remained in the occupied areas at their own loss for the gain of the nation and investors. The bonus figures were far more than nominal and were presented before the government and employers had surveyed their economic position. Hence, payments were continually delayed, to the irritation of the workers.

Another post-war claim immediately after V-J Day concerned the question of severance pay. As industrial production diminished in the last days of the war, workers in the occupied zones were dismissed. However, no bonus was paid. When the pre-war owners and the Nationalist Government took over these factories, the workers put forth their demands for dismissal wages. They preferred employment and were prepared to abandon such claims for jobs. However, when employment failed to materialize and the workers' personal resources were exhausted, they clamored for the severance pay. These workers were joined by others who had returned from the interior with the complaint that the United States Army, which had employed thousands of Chinese had neglected to compensate them adequately at the termination of hostilities. This issue produced several demonstrations in Shanghai between September 1945 and June 1946.

The war brought about the destruction of factories and left a legacy of deteriorated machinery and displaced skilled labor. With the defeat of the Japanese, the Nationalist Government dispatched its officials to the liberated areas. Their first task was to replace the Japanese. The policies pursued to this end in this period were known as the "take-over" policies. They had a direct bearing on the labor situation.

The Nationalist Government "took over" the economy; literally it took over a large portion of industry, the properties of the Imperial Government, Japanese subjects and Chinese and foreign collaborators who forfeited their rights for having assisted the enemy. It retained these factories and entrusted their administration to the Ministry of Economic

Affairs, Ministry of War, National Resources Commission, and various public corporations, such as the Chinese Textile Corporation. The properties belonging to Chinese citizens and United Nations nationals soon passed back into the hands of their pre-war owners. In other words, the bulk of Chinese industry now belonged to the Chinese Government and to large-scale private enterprises many directors of which served in high public office.

The effect of the "take-over" policies in the economic sphere was to place small private enterprises without official connections under a severe competitive handicap. The official and "bureaucratic capitalist" employers bid up wages just when small employers, to compete effectively, would have liked to introduce economies at the expense of labor. The awkward position of small concerns drove many of them into bankruptcy in 1946 and 1947.

Not only did their size and superior equipment favor the "taken-over" enterprises, but, as part of the government, they had extraordinary access to the officially-controlled sources of raw materials, foreign exchange, machinery, and transportation supplied through UNRRA and the United States armed forces.

Employment was adversely affected by the delays that the Nationalist Government permitted in re-opening the "taken-over" factories. Despite criticism involving charges of corruption, the government could at least plead shortage of power, equipment, materials and skilled labor. However, in the re-sale of these industrial units to private owners, official policy often caused artificial shortages that compelled many factories to shut down.

There was disagreement within Kuomintang circles concerning "take-over" operations, and the resulting rivalries damaged the economic life of the recovered areas. Various cliques sought portions of the spoils, not only for economic purposes but also for political prestige.

Under the "take-over" policies, the Nationalist Government kept China in a "state of emergency". On this basis, wartime regulations concerning labor, namely compulsory arbitration and prohibition of strikes and lockouts, continued in force. To administer these regulations with a minimum of opposition, the government restricted the growth of a genuine trade-union movement, sponsoring another type of workers' organization in its place. In carrying out these policies, it relied upon the Shanghai Labor Brigade of the Loyal Patriotic Army (then under the command of General Tai Li), the war-areas armies, municipal garrisons, and police.

When the Nationalist Government "took over" the enemy and puppet properties, it also assumed control of the international settlements in Canton, Amoy, Shanghai, Tientsin, and Peiping. Perhaps out of excessive enthusiasm, Chinese troops also seized such foreign private property as the Shanghai Power Company, but a vigorous ambassadorial protest corrected this error.

The relinquishment of extraterritoriality under the 1942 treaties called for adjustment, both legal and psychological, in the industrial sphere. Foreign industry in China was now subject to the same laws and policies that the Nationalist Government promulgated for the entire nation. Now there would be uniformity of administration. Before the war there had been Chinese laws and administration for China except the international settlements, where foreign law was applied under foreign administration. The Japanese and puppet administrations removed the legal differences between the Chinese and "international" zones. Thus, the Nationalist Government was able to present a fait accompli to the foreign powers immediately after the war.

The workers gained some "freedom" through the termination of extra-territoriality. Although the Nationalist labor code curtailed freedom to organize and to bargain, the government could not enforce its legis-lation so effectively as the foreigners had applied their laws and regulations. Under the pre-war arrangements, workers in the British and American, and in some cases the Japanese, factories had received better treatment than their fellow workers had enjoyed in the Chinese-owned industries. The differences could be attributed to the differences in types of production and size of investment, the foreigners' owning mainly large-scale enterprise, the Chinese primarily small-scale. Where Chinese factories had possessed the facilities to be found in foreign circles, the workers had then enjoyed the same, if not even more suita-ble conditions of work.

Notwithstanding his superior economic position, the worker in foreign-owned industry had often felt less "free" than his compatriot in "native" industry because of the attitudes of the foreign manager. These workers had found him less "sympathetique", less flexible, and more disciplinarian with economic power, consuls, and gunboats to impose his regulations and will. Moreover, he had displayed his "superiority", thus introducing a racial factor to the discomfort of the workers. In the Chinese factory, where earnings had often been less than the workers had obtained in the foreign factories, they nevertheless had had more freedom to settle mutual questions with the employer in a local fashion which did not damage their status as the foreign method of settlement did.

In the post-war situation, the foreigner could no longer rely upon his "superiority" to dictate terms to labor, nor did it help to put the Chinese "in their place." He had to discontinue discriminatory practices in cases of promotion and to meet the workers on a basis of racial equality. In turn, the workers lost a useful excuse for slacking on the job and for demonstrating against foreign imperialism.

Of course, it would take some time to remove the humiliating atmos-phere that racism had created. The foreigners or Chinese could not be expected to adjust themselves to the new scene without some unpleasant incidents. However, the transition took place smoothly, probably because at this time more of the industrial sphere belonged to Chinese owners than to foreigners.

The racial factor now took a new form in the minds of many foreigners who were sensitive indeed to the loss of their privileged positions. When Chinese workers put forth demands for improved wages and working conditions or settlement of outstanding grievances, the foreigners were quick to wonder: Are the workers discriminating against the foreigners? Are the demands designed to squeeze foreign employers in favor of Chinese enterprise? Are the Chinese officials fair in applying the labor laws to disputes involving foreign employers?

Although the relinquishment of extra-territoriality was a historic event of extensive practical significance, Nationalist China was more concerned on V-J Day with its leading domestic problem, namely, the expanding power of the Chinese Communists. As fighting spread, the chances of reconstructing the war-torn economy became less and less. Transportation was diverted to military use at the expense of the civilian economy. In many places, rail lines were destroyed, routes from the coal and iron mines and cotton fields to the factories were blocked. Nationalist armies requisitioned factories for barracks, interrupting production and denying housing to the workers. Industries that should have joined the war against inflation manufactured products for military rather than civilian consumption.

In defense of its position, the Nationalist Government kept the nation on a war footing. Its approach to labor problems, i.e., strike prohibitions, police controls, etc., revealed that the government and employers considered the labor scene a zone of potential belligerency. As long as the Kuomintang chose to continue the war, it forced labor into politics. The anti-Communist campaigns meant more inflation and more repression behind the Kuomintang lines. More inflation and more repression drove the workers into the camp of the opposition, where the Communists had ample chance to win converts and supporters. On the other hand, had the Kuomintang decided to combat inflation and extend freedom to the workers, its powerful right-wing would have had to concede victory to the moderate and left elements, and its political reign would have ended. Therefore, as between civil war and economic reform, it chose the former in the hope of a more prolonged survival.

Without popular support, the chances of winning the civil war were slim indeed. The Nationalists attempted to appease the workers through a cost-of-living allowance policy, but under the prevailing circumstances that only accelerated the pace of inflation. At the same time, they directed the "Workers Protection Corps" and San Min Chu I Youth Corps to maintain surveillance over the workers. The government tolerated demonstrations on economic matters only when it was impossible to prevent them. It empowered the Shanghai General Labor Union to purge Communists and agitators from such trade unions as could not be suppressed. It also associated the "security" forces with the mediation and arbitration machinery.

Judging by the activities of the workers in Shanghai in this period, they understood to a large extent the economic and political crisis in China. Generally inarticulate, they responded positively to the "peace and democracy" slogans that originated within their ranks and also in the opposition political groups. However, they refrained from vigorous action that might have alienated the mercantile and professional classes, hard-pressed in the Nationalist economy. It was the strategy of the "opposition" to convince these people that capital and labor had a common stake in sound political and reconstruction policies which a coalition government would sponsor.

From this cursory examination of political, economic, and cultural factors bearing on the post-war labor situation, we may proceed to study real wages and living conditions, efficiency of labor and labor costs of production, conditions of work, and bargaining power.

Real Wages and Living Conditions

There is reason to believe that the level of real wages between V-J Day and March 1946 exceeded the level during the desperate years of 1942-45. If real wages did not appreciably increase, at least the workers felt less oppressed and the promises of better times to come excited their imagination and buoyed their hopes. The victory over Japan eliminated a formidable obstacle to the fulfillment of Sun Yat-sen's Three People's Principles. When Generalissimo Chiang Kai-shek reached Shanghai in October 1945, he received a rousing welcome from the populace.

It is not surprising, in view of the economic chaos in the occupied areas under the Japanese and puppets after 1942, that real wages since V-J Day should appear higher. However, it is startling indeed when several reputable observers contend that real wages not only increased above the 1942-45 level but even rose above the 1936 level.

This contention appealed to the Chinese Ministries of Social Affairs and Economic Affairs, the China Branch of the International Labor Office, the British Trade Mission to China, many Chinese and foreign employers, and, with few exceptions, the Chinese and foreign press. It is of far more than academic interest. It influenced the wage policy of the Nationalist Government as Minister of Social Affairs Ku Cheng-kang revealed in a speech in Shanghai on May 30, 1946. As a matter of fact, by real wages, the government estimated tension and opposition among the Chinese workers. As disaffection was actually spreading while the government held to the myth of higher real wages, the officials could only conclude that the Communists were active agitating among the workers. Consequently, it adopted fierce police measures to combat them. Of course, to the workers, whose discontent had a real economic basis, such measures appeared unwarranted and represented further oppression. Many people who might otherwise have stood by the government were alienated. On the other hand, had the real-wage contention been valid, then the post-war state of emergency should have been relaxed and the task of reconstruction should have progressed more rapidly.

Several substantial arguments were offered in support of the view that living conditions for the workers had improved. First of all, the prosperity of Shanghai and other cities was pointed to. For a few months following V-J Day, such diverse cities as Shanghai and Chungking gave the impression of prosperity. Economic activity appeared vigorous, especially with the enemy factories in operation and the United States forces employing truck-drivers, longshoremen (wharf coolies), construction crews, and guards. Well-dressed "workers" were evident in the streets; tea shops, even in the factory districts, were crowded. Flashing gold teeth found their way into the mouths of "workers". Rice and cloth disappeared from shop shelves while main-street shops filled their show windows with typewriters, tennis rackets, silverware, and colorful ornaments.

Second, the Nationalist wage policy called for adjusting wages to variations in the cost of living. The year 1936 or the months January to July 1937, far from totally depressed, were selected as "basic" or "normal". However, as there were upward revisions of the wage rates of those periods after the war, it seemed plausible that since V-J Day earnings based on new wage rates and allowances must have increased in greater proportion than the actual cost of living. Hence, the real wage of 1945-47 should have risen above the real wage of 1936-37.

Third, in an effort to remove puppet Central Reserve Bank currency from circulation as rapidly as possible, the Nationalist Government redeemed the notes at a rate of one Nationalist dollar for two hundred CRB dollars, a rate over-valuing the puppet currency. Workers with such holdings immediately exchanged their old currency for the new, and, with this windfall, then went on a brief spending spree.

Fourth, the demand for skilled labor, in Shanghai especially, exceeded the supply then avaialble, many skilled laborers being still confined to the interior, and the competition among employers enhanced wage rates for such workers.

Public enterprises offered more than private companies, while factories belonging to "bureaucratic capitalists" hoarded such personnel.

Fifth, although several delays occurred, the Nationalist Government was able soon after V-J Day to put back into operation some of the factories taken over from the Japanese. While many Chinese firms had to reduce their staffs, the government enterprises took up the slack in unemployment from V-J Day through the summer of 1946.

Sixth, it was only logical that industrial production should be resumed when UNRRA poured in large quantities of raw materials and transportation equipment. Moreover, it would be expected that living conditions should improve, what with provision by UNRRA of foodstuffs, medical supplies, powdered milk, etc. The United States armed forces also helped to alleviate distress. With cheap imports from abroad, it seemed unlikely that living conditions would decline.

Finally, the working population did not revolt against the Nationalist Government. This fact might be taken as a sign of the contentment that high real wages would induce, or at least of the lack of too severe discomforts. On V-J Day there was no attempt by the Shanghai workers to deliver their city to the Communist New Fourth Army, then on the outskirts of the city, as the workers had done during the Northern Expedition in 1924-27. In none of the Nationalist cities did the workers attempt to overthrow the government by force.

Convincing as are these reasons for suspecting a marked increase in real wages, each requires considerable qualification. The Chinese scene does not lend itself to such facile generalizations. It is too varied and contradictory. In fact, as the points set out above undergo revision, the contention that real wages between V-J Day and 1948 surpassed the real wages of 1936-37 appears less tenable.

As for the superficial impression of prosperity in certain Chinese cities, there is more to be said for the impression than the reality of prosperity. Undoubtedly the end of the war relaxed tension and stimulated optimism. Liberation brought people into the streets; it evoked the proverbial Chinese gaiety amidst discomfort and suffering.

By March 1946, however, the more flourishing cities felt the pinch of depression. Such places as Canton, Kweilin, Changsha, Hengyang, and Hankow had changed little from wartime poverty and despair.

The streets were crowded almost everywhere, but this was due to the fact that urban populations had expanded rapidly with refugees from the countryside and the interior. The purchases of commodities and precious metals represented a flow from paper money towards goods at a time when prices were relatively low. That shops exhausted the observable supply of rice and cloth with astonishing rapidity was not so much a sign of prosperity as a consequence of short supply, hoarding, and speculation. There was far more window-shopping than actual buying. Economic activity whirled furiously under the impact of optimism and apprehension, necessity, speculation and inflation. In other words, the recovered cities experienced depression and prosperity simultaneously. The super-ficial impression of the street collided in most cases with a more intimate observation of working-class homes and family conditions.

Although the United States armed services employed Chinese workers in the liberated zones, they were also dismissing their employees in the interior. Furthermore, there was a tendency in Shanghai for the United States forces to offer the more attractive positions to European refugees in preference to the Chinese.

The cost-of-living policy contained several flaws that detracted seriously from its usefulness in maintaining real wages. Two principal deficiencies concerned coverage (i.e., various types of labor) and uniformity (i.e., methods of preparation and application). The policy covered primarily industrial labor in a nation where crafts and casual work prevailed. After the summer of 1946, allowances reached fewer and fewer workers as unemployment grew. For the workers with employment, the indices were not prepared or enforced uniformly. They were calculated locally, and only in Shanghai was the cost-of-living index determined with skill and integrity, insuring at least minimum accuracy. In Shanghai, moreover, it was possible to obtain a high degree of enforce-ment, but in Wushih or Kaifeng only a low degree was reported. Only in the large factories with modern systems of accounting could one expect reliable calculation of the actual allowance.

The methods of compiling the indices varied widely, most local authorities merely estimating changes in the cost of living in terms of the prices of rice. Very few followed any scientific method for computing variations in the costs of living. Shanghai was one of the few exceptions. There the municipal secretariat adapted International Labor Office procedures to local conditions. The Shanghai index was computed monthly but on the basis of weekly prices of those commodities that appeared in a sample family budget. The general index for workers represented the prices of over fifty commodities grouped as follows: food, housing, clothing, and miscellaneous. The base year for compara-tive purposes was 1936.

Despite the careful attention that the under-staffed Shanghai office devoted to the index, it might be said that the index under-estimated the cost of living by 10 to 15 per cent. It failed to cover certain items that the workers found costly, the most important being interest on debts and pawn-brokers' fees. These burdens the workers had to meet or suffer a loss of "face" and of the material security, often the clothes and furniture, backing the loans.

The cost-of-living index could not provide for festival bonuses or dismissal allowances. These items were not included in the basic wages of 1936, although that year had had sufficient prosperity to warrant seasonal bonuses. In cases where factories had closed down in 1936, and later in 1937, the workers had received their dismissal pay or, in many cases, transportation allowances to the interior. In 1946-47 the loss of such sources of income damaged the real-wage position in the coastal cities. Moreover, the housing that employers had constructed for the workers before the war had since gravely deteriorated. As for payments in kind (excluded from the index calculations but subtracted in the application of the index), the workers gained through this method some relief from high prices and shortages. However, workers sometimes complained that the commodities were of poor quality and insufficient quantity, and that employers speculated with them, including the UNRRA provisions, and substituted inferior, often inedible produce in their place.

It is true that, under pressure of skilled-labor shortages, basic wage rates moved upwardly. This had the effect of bolstering wage rates of other workers who resented widening current discrepancies in the wage structure and therefore, put forth wage demands to remedy this matter. However, such revisions of the basic wage rate did not necessarily lead to increased real wages under the cost-of-living policy. The index was not always applied to the entire basic wage, but only to a portion of it. A sliding scale was introduced to offset marked advantages that might through the full force of the index, accrue to the workers. After May 30, 1946, the government permitted the employers to plead hardship, in which cases only a fraction of the cost-of-living index had to be applied. If the workers refused to accept this paring down of their allowance, the matter could be brought before the Shanghai Municipal Arbitration Board, established in June, 1946, which in turn was advised by the Shanghai Municipal Cost-of-Living Index Committee.

Another reason why the workers failed to obtain the full benefit of the index was the fact that the index covered the cost of living for the month previous to "take-home" payments. When the workers spent their wages and allowances, they paid the current prices which were more often above the prices of the pay-period. Shopkeepers showed a tendency to raise prices at the end of the month in anticipation of the index and again at the beginning of the next month as a result of a rising index.

When Mr. T. Y. Tsha, the Shanghai cost-of-living authority, resigned in August 1946, for reasons of "ill health", the prestige of the index declined steeply. There was criticism of the index from labor circles. The Shanghai General Labor Union also brought forth criticism but offered no alternative; at best, it could only suggest the publication of the index twice instead of once each month.

With Tsha's resignation, it was rumored that the notorious Bureau of Investigation and Statistics of General Tai Li would prepare the index in the future. This rumor, along with the secrecy imposed on the index after January 1947, made the continuation of the index policy less useful.

The Minister of Social Affairs supported this policy through 1946, but it was criticized in official and unofficial circles alike. In view of the inflation and unemployment in 1947, the policy could no longer be enforced with the aim of keeping the current real wage at par with the 1936 real wage, an aim which had certainly not been achieved in 1945 or 1946.

Third, the redemption of puppet currency at the rate of 200 CRB to one National dollar touched off only a short-lived buying spree. Whatever windfall accrued to the workers under this currency policy was dissipated under the impact of rising prices by March 1946. For example, the Shanghai index (based on prices of commodities in a sample family budget) rose from 29,923 in September 1945 to 275,422 in March 1946. In Canton the index (the basis of calculation unknown) stood at 31,302 in September 1945 and at 215,182 in March 1946 and in Peiping at 122,556 in January 1946 and at 244,130 in March.

It cannot be denied that as long as the public and large-scale private enterprises demanded more skilled labor and technicians, the wage packets expanded. Only a select few, however, benefited after the summer of 1946, when unemployment increased at a more rapid pace than employment. By March 1946, with over 2,300,000 workers employed in Nationalist China, more than 700,000 were unemployed; that is to say, about 23 per cent of the labor force with some industrial or occupation experience lacked employment. The number of unemployed in the coastal areas swelled with the arrival of workers from the interior, where the Nationalist Government had permitted wartime industries to collapse. The early gains from a tight labor market began to disappear after July 1946, and subsequently employment and wage trends were decidedly unfavorable for labor.

There is no need to recite the tragic history of UNRRA operations in China. The Chinese workers hardly knew of the activities of this international body, although they saw its labels everywhere. The responsibility for distributing work relief and emergency aid to unemployed workers in Central China rested with the Special Commissioner of the Ministry of Social Affairs. The Shanghai Bureau of Social Affairs tried to facilitate relief work, but the workers enjoyed few benefits under the UNRRA-CNRRA program.

Finally, there is the matter of loyalty to the Nationalist Government as evidence of improved living and working conditions. Although the workers in Nationalist China did not rebel against the government, they protested vigorously on many occasions and over many issues. Strikes were frequent occurrences after V-J Day, despite the numerous bans on such action. By June 1946, the workers realized that the employers could under the prevailing economic situation make few if any concessions, and that only a change in government policies could open the door to improved living conditions. On June 23, 1946 therefore they supported the famous "peace" demonstration which the Ministry of Social Affairs, Kuomintang Headquarters and the Shanghai General Labor Union denounced as subversive.

The government took precautions against uprisings in the industrial centers, but there was little likelihood that the workers would seize Shanghai or Tientsin or Hankow. In this period, the political parties were seeking peaceful means for resolving differences, and it would not have advanced the cause of labor to doom these political negotiations through rash, selfish actions. However, during the negotiations and subsequently, the government employed provocative police measures which, contrary to expectations, weakened rather than strengthened its position. The restraint displayed by the workers ought not to be interpreted as evidence of higher real wages.

Efficiency of Labor and Cost of Production

Almost every Chinese and foreign employer relished discussion of these topics after V-J Day. For example, the American-owned newspaper, Shanghai Evening Post and Mercury, contained the following comment on May 3, 1946: "China finds herself without her former great resource of manpower because though the manpower exists it is today high-priced, reluctant and inclined toward unbelievable inefficiency." Unfortunately, the lack of suitable comparative data hampered thorough analysis of such charges and assertions. However, it was widely felt in post-war China that Chinese labor was no longer "cheap".

The worker was accused of falling down on production , and hence denying commodities to the markets to offset inflation. Whatever slackness might have existed in the Chinese labor force, this factor stood very low on the list of causes of industrial inefficiency. Such a list for V-J Day China included: (1) outmoded, inferior, and worn-out machinery; (2) inadequate methods of production; (3) incompetent management and supervision; (4) poor-quality raw materials and insufficient power supply; (5) deficient facilities for training workers; (6) deplorable working conditions; and (7) subsistence living conditions.

In the absence of genuine trade-union representation, the workers had no voice in these matters. While employers and government officials demanded that the workers show greater responsibility in their work, they were reluctant to grant Chinese labor a larger role in the affairs of industry. In some cases, workers were denied positions of supervision for fear that, in case of a rebellion, the workers would be able to take over the factories.

Another charge against labor was that its economic demands were not reasonable in the face of an already suffering economy. It was suggested that labor costs had bankrupted the export trades and paved the way for foreign competition in the Chinese market. There is no doubt that labor costs figured in the exorbitant costs of production which placed Chinese goods at a severe disadvantage. However, greater damage to the Chinese trade position was caused by monetary inflation, stimulated through the addition of feebly-backed currency for military purposes, and unrealistic foreign exchange rates which invited foreign commodities to China but discouraged the sale of Chinese products abroad. Moreover, speculation and discriminatory exchange practices drove the terms of trade against China.

Business and the government had a much stronger control over costs of production than did labor, but they hesitated to take the necessary steps to lower them. On this point, the Shanghai Evening Post and Mercury of April 10, 1946, carried a most pertinent observation: "The workers know what goes on about them, they are only human, and if they apply the law of the jungle they are in a measure holding to those who should be their leaders toward better ways." Before labor could be expected to accept voluntary wage cuts, certain measures would have to be taken: governmental provision of cheap capital, elimination of arbitrary government intervention in the economic sphere, non-discriminatory distribution of UNRRA materials and foreign exchange, and proscription of official speculation. Without them, reduction in wages would have had to be imposed on the workers by force.

Despite the inflated wage situation, Chinese labor, when set to work with modern equipment, was still "cheap." A century ago it was "cheap", though slow and inefficient, as long as employers paid starvation wages and drew upon an almost endless supply of labor. When the western world industrialized, the Chinese industries could not compete in the same lines. Today it is possible to find modern equipment in some Chinese plants, and in those places labor is "cheap" enough to enable such factories to meet foreign competition.

Working Conditions

It is not possible to describe briefly yet accurately the wide variety of working conditions in post-war China. They ranged from admirable in some Yunnan and Shanghai spinning mills to deplorable in the many metal shops of Chungking and Tientsin. Obviously there were many more of the second type than of the first.

The standard of working conditions after V-J Day must certainly have stood below the level of 1936. Had favorable political conditions prevailed after September 1945, industrial reconstruction and expansion that might have followed would have been interrupted by the world-wide shortage of machinery. Re-building of factories proceeded slowly in all cities, and almost at a snail's pace in Canton, Hankow, Changsha and Hengyang.

No adequate reports on hours of work for this period are available. The official publications of the Ministry of Social Affairs stressed the hours of work in terms of legal requirements, not in terms of actual hours worked. Hours appeared to be long, in some places ten, with three to four additional hours on the premises of the employer for extra duties. However, work schedules were irregular as a result of power shortages, insufficient raw materials, and breakdown of machinery.

There are no accounts of industrial accidents and diseases for Nationalist China as a whole or even for the cities. The Ministry of Social Affairs in August 1946 established a Department of Factory and Mining Inspection, but it could not function without trained personnel. Moreover, the factory legislation, drafted before the war, required revision and to this end the Minister of Social Affairs convened a meeting of officials, employers, workers, and experts in Shanghai on August 2, and 3, 1946. However, the employers took the position that industry could not afford additional costs for safety and health measures at that time.

With such a large share of Chinese industry under the ownership or trusteeship of the Nationalist Government, there existed an unusual opportunity to establish high standards of working conditions. However, the departments in charge of these factories would not undertake "yardstick" experiments, although the Ministry of Economic Affairs, the National Resources Commission, and the public corporations created workers' welfare sections or committees.

Though few in number and deficient in funds, private projects nevertheless contributed to the welfare of the workers and their families. The most striking arrangement was the Shanghai Cooperative Industrial Hygiene Centre, under the direction of Dr. John Yui and Miss Bessie Chen. Over one hundred enterprises, principally the smaller-scale factories that often have the most hazardous working conditions, registered with this project. The employers contributed a fee per worker to the Centre, in return for which Dr. Yui and his staff provided the workers with prompt emergency attention, outpatient treatment, minor operations, and health information. The Centre consisted of a miniature hospital in the western industrial district and three clinics within easy reach of the member factories. In rendering medical aid immediately, the Centre met the needs of the employers and the workers: to reduce absenteeism and minimize the loss of earning power as a consequence of accidents and illnesses.

The Shanghai YWCA resumed its excellent pre-war activities among female workers. Its industrial section conducted night schools and disseminated information on hygiene and nutrition among its working-class students. For the welfare of the children of workers, the China Welfare Fund, of which Madame Sun Yat-sen is Chairman, opened reading rooms in the industrial districts of Shanghai.

Bargaining Power

It is necessary in conclusion to ascertain what bargaining power the employers and workers in China had after V-J Day.

Observation of the market conditions under which the products of Chinese industry were sold reveals roughly the extent to which employers could include additional labor costs in prices without losing customers. From V-J Day through the summer of 1946, a sellers' market was in existence in China. Factories had little trouble in disposing of their output on the open and black markets. There were plenty of customers, even though effective purchasing power was concentrated in the hands of only 5 to 10 per cent of the population. Deprived of goods during the war years, many bought up almost everything the market had to offer. Others hastened to exchange their currency for goods in view of the uncertain economic conditions. Moreover, the Chinese and American military forces offered a lucrative market for military and luxury products alike. However, foreign markets could not entertain ordinary Chinese commodities at fancy, inflated prices. By the summer of 1946, Chinese output had to be sold at high prices which permitted foreign products to compete on the Chinese market. Already under pressure from the government and bureaucratic-capitalist enterprises, small-scale business concerns had to reduce costs of production to preserve their role in the market. Soon the official and large-scale industries felt the pinch and, to ward off the more disastrous effects of inflation and keep up production for military purposes, set out to check rising costs of production. With these changes in market conditions during the two-year post-war period, the impact of bargaining power varied from time to time.

The source of the employers' strength in negotiating with their workers, especially the unskilled, was the vast supply of manpower. Immediately after the war, the temporary shortage of skilled men turned the tide against employers, but that situation was reversed with the arrival of workers from the interior in 1946. In certain more extreme cases, employers threatened to cease operations to bring workers "to their senses." This deterrent was employed during the disputes over the Victory and New Year bonuses. As the workers had few other job openings and employers had other attractive opportunities for investment, speculation, and money-lending, it had the effect of facilitating an agreement not too unfavorable to the employers.

The employer organizations took various forms, including provincial guilds, trade and industrial federations, and businessmen's luncheon clubs. In the crafts the employers cooperated closely to standardize wage rates and price lists.

As the largest employer in China, the Nationalist Government had a vested interest in strengthening the bargaining position of private enterprise, at least that segment of private enterprise in the hands of high officials. Its labor policies and enforcement of the labor code tended to favor the employers in disputes with labor.

The bargaining power of labor in this post-war period received a boost from the temporary shortage of skilled labor and the world shortage of labor-saving devices that might otherwise have been substituted for the absent workers. However, labor could not depend upon these advantages for very long. Bargaining power had to rest on a firmer foundation.

The growth of the trade-union movement was crucial to labor at this stage. The workers could draw from their past experiences during the initial development of trade unions in China: their expansion for political purposes in 1924-1927; the underground phase, on one hand, and the "official" trade-union phase on the other, from 1928 to 1945; and the patriotic resistance movements from 1937 to V-J Day.

When the war ended, workers in the Japanese-occupied areas formed trade unions immediately. However, the Nationalist Government refused to recognize them and insisted that they be reorganized to conform with the Trade Union Law of 1943 and the Regulations for the Re-organization of Trade Unions in Enemy-occupied areas (November, 1945). It assigned the Ministry of Social Affairs, Kuomintang Headquarters, and the provisional Shanghai General Labor Union to perform the task of reorganizing the unions in Shanghai and delegated similar bodies to do so in other cities. Ostensibly "reorganization" was intended to remove "collaborators" from the trade-union movement, but in fact "agitators", accused also of being collaborators, appeared to be the most common victims.

A union reorganized under the post-war regulations had to accept a director from Kuomintang Headquarters and a supervisor from the Bureau of Social Affairs. Before the workers could elect their officers, they had to form a "preparatory committee", which had to be acceptable to the local authorities. This committee then prepared a panel of officers and directors, which had to receive the approval of the government.

In many cases the officers and directors came from the working class and had some popularity among the workers. The situation was not the same after V-J Day as it had been before the war. In those days, the authorities and Kuomintang Headquarters had selected the union officers, when they permitted the union at all. In the post-war period, the authorities had to compromise and accept some of the choices of the rank and file. Otherwise the workers would have abstained from participating in the official trade-union movement, thus discrediting that movement and the Kuomintang in general.

After 1943 the Trade Union Law restricted the activities of official unions; that is to say, it confined union functions to certain spheres. They were encouraged to undertake welfare and educational activities, and, if they failed to do so, the authorities could utilize them for these purposes. As for relations with employers - and this is the crux of the matter - the unions had more mediation than bargaining functions; they were directed "to settle" disputes between employers and workers. In a meeting sponsored by the Ministry of Social Affairs in August 1946, suggestions were put forth to liberalize the trade union law. However, the government was not prepared to go that far at that time. The 1947 amendments failed to guarantee the independence and freedom of trade unions.

Although the official unions were far from genuine working-class organizations, the workers did not oppose them outright. In the first place, only through such unions could the workers bargain collectively with employers and petition the government. Despite their shortcomings, they also afforded the workers some experience in trade-union practices. Furthermore, at this time freedom of assembly and organization was being discussed in the political negotiations; open warfare against the government unions might have aroused opposition to this freedom of workers to belong to unions of their own choosing.

However, the workers did not meekly follow the orders of the General Labor Unions, the Kuomintang and the other authorities. Through "cells" in the official unions, some workers exercised an influence tantamount to control over the unions. They forced government-approved leaders to follow policies contrary to the explicit instructions of the Kuomintang. This they did successfully on May Day, 1946, and at the "peace" demonstration on June 23, 1946. Caught between the two opposing forces, i.e., workers and authorities, many such official leaders displayed considerable courage in sticking with the rank and file. Some were arrested for doing so.

There were some workers' organizations that refused to accept the "dictation" of the authorities and preferred an illegal status to legality with government intervention in their internal affairs. Of course they were denied official registration, and workers and employers were warned against dealing with such organizations. Their members, most of whom were unemployed, were "ineligible" to obtain from the Special Commissioner of the Ministry of Social Affairs such UNRRA relief as unemployed members of the official unions received in the winter of 1945-46. These "illegal" organizations confined their activities to welfare, education and politics. They formed a federation, the "Shanghai Workers' Federation", which gained attention through its 1946 May Day statement, its June 6, 1946 "peace appeal", its June 21, 1946 message to the Congress of Industrial Organizations (USA), and its leadership of the workers during the "anti-civil war" demonstration of June 23, 1946. Although it could not directly participate in labor-management affairs, it supported the efforts of unions in Shanghai to win concessions from employers and the government.

Unity of workers on a city-wide or national basis was virtually impossible under existing laws and regulations. Before amalgamation of any sort took place, it required the sanction of the local authorities, and, in the case of a national federation, of the Minister of Social Affairs. Despite this obstacle, the other utilities workers' unions of Shanghai formed a committee, at first within the law, later outside the law, to aid the strikers at the Shanghai Power Company in January 1946. Chinese National Air Corporation personnel struck at the same time at almost all Chinese airports, even though no nation-wide union existed.

The only national unions that existed were permitted under special laws. Postal employees, seamen, railway and tele-communications workers could maintain national organizations under the supervision of the Nationalist authorities. Although the Chinese Association of Labor represented the Chinese workers in the International Labor Organization and the World Federation of Trade Unions, it was not, strictly speaking, the equivalent of the Congress of Industrial Organizations, the British Trades Union Congress, or the French C.G.T. However, when the Chinese Association of Labor moved in the direction of these national trade-union centers, the Nationalist Government, through the Chungking authorities, seized its properties and later ousted its officers. The 1947 amendments to the Trade Union Law paved the way for a new national federation of trade unions, but the initiative still rested with the Minister of Social Affairs, not with the rank and file.

In many instances the workers cultivated the friendship and public good will, presumably for the purpose of enhancing the prestige and power of the trade-union movement. In the dispute at the Shanghai Transport Company, the workers, instead of striking and ceasing work, offered the public free transportation. The conductors refused to collect fares for several days. During the strike of employees of the Metropole Hotel in Shanghai, they accused the manager of maintaining mistresses and automobiles while starving the employees. After a settlement, the workers treated the same manager to a dinner party, at a rival hotel, and praised his generosity and understanding. Textile workers in the Shanghai western district came out in protest against the shooting of a fellow-worker by a policeman, but made up the loss of production through overtime and extra shifts. Despite prejudicial and misleading official and employer statements to the contrary, during the power-company strikes in Shanghai the workers maintained service for the public convenience.

The laws and policies of the Nationalist Government and the Kuomintang tended to weaken the bargaining power of the workers. Their

approach was based on the reasoning that, as long as the government
looked after the interests of the workers, no bargaining power
vis-a-vis employers was necessary. Officials argued that they could
lay down wage policy for the benefit of the nation, not just for a
few elements. Unfortunately, the impartiality of the government in
applying this policy was gravely in doubt. Not only was the government the greatest employer in China, but private enterprises had
their directors in the highest official positions. Moreover, labor
had no representation in the policy-making circles of the Nationalist
Government or the Kuomintang. Even if the workers had had no need
for bargaining power against the employers, they would have at least
had to use "lobbying" tactics tantamount to bargaining power within
official circles.

The Trade Union Law of 1943 (that is, the Law of 1929 with 1943
amendments) curtailed the freedom of workers to organize, strike,
picket, or boycott. This law was supplemented by no-strike edicts
issued by garrison commanders, war-area generals, and municipal
officials. Furthermore, the Labor Disputes Law of 1943 (that is)
the Law of 1928, with amendments of 1943) required that disputes be
submitted for conciliation, mediation and arbitration. In Shanghai
the municipal authorities created an arbitration board in June 1946.
Although the Shanghai General Labor Union, along with other
Kuomintang unions, secured a seat, the board consisted primarily of
representatives of the Bureaux of Social Affairs, Public Works, and
Utilities, Police Commissioner, Garrison Commander, Kuomintang
Headquarters, Chamber of Commerce, Shanghai Realty Association, and
several employers. In many cases, neither employers nor workers
preferred to have the government or the Kuomintang intervene in their
disputes, but the government and its allied agencies kept in close
touch with the labor scene. Such intervention often interposed a
political factor that delayed rather than hastened the settlement, or
at least made the solution costly to the interested parties, to the
advantage of the disinterested ones. By 1948 the Nationalist
Government no longer possessed sufficient prestige to mold the pattern
of labor-management relations.

London, June 1948

THE AMENDED TRADE UNION ACT OF JUNE 13, 1947.

Chapter I.   General Provisions

Article 1. The purpose of a trade union is to increase the workers' knowledge, skill and productive capacity, to maintain their standard of living, and to better their conditions of employment.

Article 2. A trade union shall be a body corporate.

Article 3. A trade union shall not engage in business for purposes of gain.

Article 4. The functions of a trade union shall be as follows:

(1) the conclusion, amendment and cancellation of collective agreements, which shall not be valid unless approved by the competent authority;

(2) the placing of members in employment and the establishment of employment exchanges;

(3) the establishment of savings banks, social insurance institutions, hospitals, nursing homes and creches;

(4) the organization of productive, distributive, purchase, credit and housing co-operative societies;

(5) the organization of institutions for vocational education and other forms of education for workers;

(6) the establishment of libraries and reading rooms;

(7) the issue and publication of printed matter;

(8) the organization of social gatherings, clubs and other recreational activities;

(9) the settlement of disputes between a union and its members;

(10) the settlement of disputes between workers and employers;

(11) the making of recommendations to be submitted to the administrative and legislative authorities concerning the drafting, amendment or repeal of labour legislation, and replies to the enquiries by the said authorities;

(12) the making of enquiries into the economic conditions under which working class families live, and into the recruiting and unemployment of workers, and the compilation of statistics on labour questions;

(13) any other work likely to improve the conditions of employment and to promote the interests of the members and industrial hygiene and safety;

(14) any other function provided for by law.

If a trade union in the exercise of its functions has not yet established the institutions for the benefit of the members in general which are mentioned above or provided for in its rules, the competent authority may appoint representatives to assist the union in organizing them.

Article 5. The competent authority over trade unions shall be the Ministry of Social Affairs in the case of the Central Government, the provincial government in the case of a province, and the municipal and district (hsien) authorities in the case of a municipality or hsien. Nevertheless, a trade union connected with any special purpose undertaking shall also in accordance with the law be under the direction and supervision of the competent authority in charge of the undertaking concerned.

Article 6. Salaried and wage-earning employees employed in various grades of governments, educational undertakings, and munition industries shall not form trade unions.

Chapter II. Organization

Article 7. Workers in the same locality or in the same industrial establishment who have attained the age of twenty years and are engaged in the same occupation or the same industry may combine to form trade unions in conformity with this Act, provided that the minimum number of members shall be fifty in the case of an industrial union and thirty in the case of an occupational union.

An industrial union is a union organized by the workers of various occupations in the same industry, and an occupational union is a union organized by the workers of the same occupation. Regulations shall be issued later to specify the various categories of industrial unions and occupational unions.

Article 8. The area of a trade union shall coincide with the administrative area of a municipality or hsien. Nevertheless, in special circumstances a different area may be fixed by the competent authority.

Not more than one industrial union and one occupational union shall be established by industrial workers and occupational workers in the same industrial establishment or in the same locality. Nevertheless, industrial unions formed under special circumstances by workers engaged in the same industry and in the same locality and with the approval of the competent authority shall not be taken into account.

Article 9. If it is proposed to found a union in accordance with Article 7 of this Act, an application for permission signed by the number of the members needed for the formation of the union shall be submitted to the competent authority. Having received permission, the sponsor shall elect persons to call a preparatory meeting for the purpose of reporting to the competent authority for registration.

Before the convocation of the inauguration meeting the union shall submit to the competent authority a preparatory report, together with draft rules of the union, and shall request the said authority to send a representative to supervise the election of officers.

After the organization of the union has been completed, a copy each of the list of the names of the members, particulars of the civil condition of each of the officers elected and the rules of the union shall be submitted to the competent authority for registration.

Article 10. The following particulars shall be stated in the rules of the union:-

    (1) the name of the union;
    (2) its aims;
    (3) its area;
    (4) its headquarters;
    (5) functions or enterprises of the union;
    (6) provisions respecting organizations;
    (7) conditions for the admission, withdrawal and expulsion of members;
    (8) rights and duties of members;
    (9) the number, power, term of office and election and discharge of officers;
    (10) provisions respecting the meetings of the union;
    (11) funds and other financial matters;
    (12) provisions respecting the amendment of the rules.

Article 11. The rules of the union shall be approved by more than two-thirds of the members present at the inauguration meeting.

Chapter III. Membership

Article 12. Workers of either sex who are resident in the area where the trade union is to be organized and who have attained the age of sixteen years shall join the trade union of the particular occupation or the particular industry in which they are engaged as members. But those who have joined the industrial union may not join the occupational union.

Article 13. Salaried and wage-earning employees engaged in the same industry, doing administrative work in the name of the employer, shall be qualified to be members of the union.

Article 14. Members of a trade union shall retain their qualification for membership for half a year after they have ceased to be engaged in their industry or occupation. Nevertheless, this provision shall not apply to members who have already changed their occupation.

Chapter IV. Officers

Article 15. Each trade union shall have directors and supervisors elected from among the members with their quotas fixed as follows:

    (1) from five to nine directors each for unions in or below a hsien.
    (2) from seven to fifteen directors each for unions in or above a municipality under the direct control of the Executive Yuan or an inter-hsien union;
    (3) from seven to fifteen directors for the general union of a hsien or a provincial municipality;
    (4) from fifteen to twenty-five directors for the general union of a province or a municipality under the direct control of the Executive Yuan;
    (5) from twenty-one to thirty-one directors each for national unions or national federation of unions of various industries;

(6) from thirty-one to fifty-one directors for the National Federation of Trade Unions;

(7) the quotas for supervisors of various grades of unions shall not exceed one-third of their quotas for directors;

(8) various grades of unions may have substitute directors and supervisors whose quotas are not to exceed one-half of the quotas for directors and supervisors.

When the number of the aforesaid directors and supervisors is above three, from one to nine executive directors and supervisors may be elected from among them according to their quotas.

Article 16. The board of directors shall administer the affairs of the union and represent the union in all its outside activities. The duty of the supervisors shall be to audit the accounts of the union, enquire into the progress of the affairs of the union and supervise the various officers in the performance of their duties.

Article 17. Members of a trade union who are of Chinese nationality and have attained the age of twenty-three years shall be eligible to be elected as director or supervisor of the union.

When, according to the aforesaid age limit, full quotas of directors and supervisors cannot be elected, members above the age of twenty years may be elected as directors and supervisors. Members who do not pursue the trade shall not be eligible to be elected as directors or supervisors.

Article 18. The term of office for directors and supervisors of a trade union shall be two years. They may continue to hold office if re-elected, but the number of those re-elected shall not exceed two-thirds.

Article 19. The union shall be liable for any injury caused to third parties by its directors or other representatives in the exercise of their functions, except in cases where for reasons connected with conditions of employment the directors or representatives call upon members to engage in collective action in such a manner as to entail injury upon employers.

The union shall not be liable for the personal actions of its members or officers.

Chapter V. Meetings

Article 20. Every trade union shall summon a general meeting or a meeting of representatives at least once a year. In case of necessity a special meeting may be summoned by the board of directors; notice thereof shall be given to the competent authority fifteen days in advance.

Article 21. The following matters shall be decided by the general meeting or the meeting of representatives:

(1) the amendment of the rules of the union;
(2) the estimates;
(3) reports on activities and the approval of the accounts of receipts and expenditures;

(4) the change or maintenance of conditions of employment;
(5) the formation, management and utilization of the foundation funds;
(6) the promotion of joint enterprises of the union;
(7) the organization of general trade unions and federation of trade unions;
(8) the amalgamation or subdivision of the union;
(9) dismissal of directors and supervisors in the case of dereliction or breach of law.

Article 22. The general meeting or the meeting of representatives shall not be held without the attendance of the majority of the members or representatives, and shall not adopt any resolutions without the agreement of the majority of the members or representatives present, and, in the case of resolutions relating to Paragraphs 1 and 7 of the preceding article, without the agreement of the two-thirds of the members or representatives present.

Chapter VI. Funds

Article 23. The funds of the trade union shall be derived from the following sources:

(1) admission fees and regular membership contributions;
(2) special foundation funds;
(3) occasional collections.

The above-mentioned admission fee for each member shall not exceed his daily wage at the time of his joining the union. The regular membership contribution shall not exceed 2 per cent of the member's monthly income. Contributions for the special foundation fund, occasional collections, and capital shares shall not be levied without resolutions passed to this effect in the general meeting or the meeting of representatives and without permission from the competent authority.

Article 24. For the purpose of undertaking welfare work for members, the employer shall be bound according to law to set aside a certain portion of the salaried and wage-earning employees' welfare fund for the trade union. For workers who do not work for a specified employer the union to which they belong shall appropriate welfare funds from membership fees, and if necessary, may apply to the competent authority for a subsidy.

Article 25. In each year every trade union shall report to its members on its financial situation. On a request signed by more than ten per cent of the members, a representative may be elected to check the financial situation of the union.

Article 26. The standards for the distribution of union funds and the method of payment and auditing of funds shall be drawn up by the trade union itself, but shall be submitted to the competent authority for registration.

Chapter VII. Supervision

Article 27. A trade union shall not refuse admission to any applicant who possesses the requisite qualification according to law, nor admit any person who does not possess the said qualification.

Article 28. In the event of a labour dispute, a strike shall not be declared until conciliation proceedings have been taken, nor then unless it has been decided by a majority of the total number of members on a ballot taken at a general meeting of the union. When labor disputes are being arbitrated or ought to be arbitrated according to law, no strike shall be declared.

In the event of a strike, the union shall not act to the detriment of the public peace and order, nor endanger the person or property or physical liberty of other persons.

A union shall not declare a strike to enforce the claim of its members to a wage above the standard rate.

Article 29. After approval has been secured for the establishment of a union, the union shall submit to the competent authority two blank copies of its record books, one intended for recording the names of members and the other for the accounts, to be sealed by the said authority. New books for the same purpose shall be subject to the same formality.

When these books for recording the names of members and for accounts are full, one copy shall be kept at the headquarters of the union and the other filed by the competent authority.

The list of members shall show the number of members and the name of each member, the date of his admission, his address, his place of employment and all particulars of his being placed in employment, his unemployment, his changes of address, any injuries or accidents with which he meets, and his death.

The entries of items of receipts and expenditure in the account book shall be numbered, and the vouchers or receipts shall be appended. The latter shall likewise be numbered and shall be attached to another book. If the competent authority considers it necessary, it may request the union to appoint an auditor to audit the accounts.

Article 30. In December of each year, and whenever required to do so, every trade union shall submit to the competent authority the following documents:

(1) a list of names and civil condition of the officers;
(2) the list of members who have been admitted to the union and of those who have withdrawn from the union;
(3) the accounts;
(4) a report on its activities;
(5) a report on the settlement of disputes.

Article 31. If any change is made in the rules of a union, or in the important staff, the directors or other officers, notice thereof shall be given to the competent authority and shall be published by the said authority within fifteen days. Such changes shall not take effect with respect to third parties until thus published.

Changes of the rules of a union shall not be valid unless approved by the competent authority.

Article 32. The members and officers of a trade union shall not:-

(1) close factories or business establishments;
(2) take possession of or destroy the goods and equipment of business establishments or factories;
(3) arrest or assault workers or employers;
(4) compel employers to employ only the workers recommended by them;
(5) bear arms at meetings or demonstrations;
(6) blackmail workers;
(7) order their members to commit sabotage or conduct similar action;
(8) arbitrarily levy fees or other subscriptions.

Article 33. The elections and decisions of a union may be cancelled by the competent authority if they are contrary to the law or to the rules of the union.

Article 34. If any provisions of the rules of a union are contrary to the law, the competent authority may order their amendment.

Article 35. In cases to which the two preceding articles apply, the union may appeal against the decision of the competent authority to the superior authority, provided that the appeal shall be made within thirty days of the decision.

Article 36. If any director or supervisor of a union acts contrary to the law or fails to perform his duties, the general meeting may adopt resolutions to dismiss him and the competent authority may give him warning or serve notice to the union to remove him from office.

Article 37. A trade union shall not be affiliated to a federation of trade unions in any foreign country without permission from the Government.

Chapter VIII. Protection

Article 38. Employees or their representatives shall not refuse workers employment or treat them unfairly because they are officers of a trade union. The officers of a union may ask leave of absence for attending to union business. As to hours of absence, half a day may be given to one of the executive directors and an average monthly allowance of not exceeding thirty hours each to the others.

Article 39. Employers or their representatives shall not make it a condition of employment that their workers shall not become officers of the union.

Article 40. During the period of a labour dispute, employers or their representatives shall not dismiss their workers on the ground that they have participated in the dispute.

Article 41. Trade unions shall have a priority claim on the assets of any of their debtors who go into bankruptcy.

Article 42. The following property of trade unions shall not be liable to confiscation:-

(1) office premises, schools, libraries, reading rooms, club premises, clinics, creches, hospitals, the real and personal property of cooperative societies;

(2) the foundation fund of each union.

Chapter IX. Dissolution

Article 43. The competent authority may dissolve a union in the following cases:

(1) in case of failure to fulfil the conditions as to the foundation of the union;

(2) in case of a serious breach of a law or order;

(3) in case of action to the detriment of the public peace or order or of the interests of the community.

A trade union may send a petition to the superior competent authority within three days after receiving the dissolution order if it considers the decision to dissolve the union unjustified.

Article 44. A trade union may proclaim its voluntary dissolution in the following cases:

(1) in the event of the bankruptcy of the union;

(2) when the union falls below the number of members required for its founding;

(3) in the event of the amalgamation or subdivision of the union.

Article 45. In the case of alterations of categories of industry or occupation or of the classification of organizational areas, unions shall amalgamate or subdivide and report to such effect to the competent authority. Unions of the same industry formed in accordance with the stipulation made in Article 8, Paragraph 2, may amalgamate or subdivide when the majority of the members agree and the competent authority approves.

Article 46. The amalgamated unions or newly formed unions shall succeed to the rights and duties of the original unions.

If a union is subdivided, the new unions formed by the subdivision shall succeed to the rights and duties of the original union. The decision respecting the allocation of the rights and duties among the new unions shall be taken at the same time as that respecting subdivision and shall be subject to the approval of the competent authority.

Article 47. When a union is dissolved either by a public authority or in the event of bankruptcy, a new union shall immediately be organized according to law.

Except in cases where dissolution has been ordered by a public authority, a trade union which is to be dissolved shall notify the competent authority within fifteen days of the reasons for dissolution and the date thereof.

Article 48. Except in case of amalgamation, subdivision or bankruptcy, the dissolution of a union shall be accompanied by the liquidation of its assets. The said liquidation shall be made in accordance with the provisions of the Civil Code concerning bodies corporate.

Article 49. If a trade union is dissolved, the remainder of its assets after liquidation shall accrue to the newly reorganized union. If the dissolution of a union is due to insufficient membership, the remainder of its assets shall accrue to the general trade union to which the union was affiliated, and, in case the union has not joined the general trade union, shall accrue to the Federation of Trade Unions. If the union does not belong to any general trade union or federation of trade unions, the remainder of its assets shall accrue to the local authority for the place where its headquarters are situated.

Chapter X. Federated Organizations

Article 50. A hsien or municipal general trade union may be formed upon the approval of the competent authority when there are seven industrial and occupational unions in the same hsien or municipality and when it is sponsored by one-third of them.

Article 51. A provincial general trade union may be formed upon the approval of the competent authority when general trade unions have been formed in half of the hsien and municipalities in the same province and when it is sponsored by one-third of them.

Article 52. A national federation of industrial unions may be formed by the unions of the same industry upon the approval of the competent authority when it is sponsored by seven unions.

In organizing the aforesaid national federations, the categories of industries shall be fixed by the order of the Ministry of Social Affairs.

Article 53. The National Federation of Trade Unions may be formed by the general trade unions (of the various provinces and the municipalities under the direct control of the Executive Yuan) and by the national federation of unions of various industries upon the approval of the Ministry of Social Affairs when it is sponsored by twenty-one such unions.

Article 54. To general trade unions of various grades and the National Federation of Trade Unions, the provisions of this Act shall apply, except the preceding four articles.

Chapter XI. Basic Organizations

Article 55. An industrial or occupational union may establish branches when there are more than three groups, each consisting of from five to twenty members. Branches and small groups shall be numbered.

Article 56. A branch may have an executive secretary and a group, a leader to be elected according to law from among the members belonging to it. The term of office shall be one year, but may be held continuously if re-elected.

Article 57. The executive secretary of a branch and the leader of a group shall handle all affairs under the direction of the trade union, and have no power to establish extra-union relations.

Chapter XII. Penalties

Article 58. In the case of violation of various provisions made in Article 28 of this Act, in addition to the dissolution of the trade union in accordance with Article 43, Paragraph 1, Clause 2, of this Act, if the conduct of the instigating officers and members constitutes any violation of the criminal code, they shall be dealt with in accordance with the provisions of the criminal code.

Article 59. If any members or officers of a trade union are guilty of any of the actions mentioned in Article 32 above, besides being dealt with in accordance with the criminal code for their conduct punishable under the criminal code, they shall be liable to fines according to law.

Article 60. If an employer or his representative contravenes the provisions of Articles 38, 39 and 40, he shall be liable to a fine according to law.

Article 61. If the directors of a trade union are guilty of any of the following offenses, they shall be liable to fines according to law.

(1) failure to make the requisite declaration under Articles 30 or 31, or the second paragraph of Article 47 or false declarations thereunder;
(2) contravention of the provisions of Article 29 or of the order mentioned in Article 34.
(3) contravention of the provisions of Paragraphs 1 and 2 of Article 47.

Chapter XIII. Supplementary Provisions

Article 62. Detailed measures for the enforcement of this Act shall be drawn up by the Ministry of Social Affairs and submitted to the Executive Yuan for approval.

Article 63. This Act shall come into force on the date of its promulgation.

APPENDIX B

CONSTITUTION OF THE ALL-CHINA FEDERATION OF LABOR

Approved Unanimously by the Sixth All-China Labour Congress, Harbin, August, 1948.

Section One: PREAMBLE

ARTICLE 1. - The name of the organization shall be the All-China Federation of Labor.

ARTICLE 2. - The aims of the All-China Federation of Labor shall be: to unite the workers of the whole country; to protect their interests; to fight for the liberation of the Chinese working class and for the liberation of the Chinese people in alliance with all the oppressed people of the whole country; to safeguard world peace and democracy in alliance with the workers of the whole world.

Section Two: MEMBERSHIP

ARTICLE 3. - The All-China Federation of Labor shall be composed, basically, of its affiliated organizations. Any trade union organization within the boundaries of China, whether industrial, craft or local, and which subscribes to this constitution may affiliate to the All-China Federation of Labor as a member.

Workers of the same industry or trade, who have constituted them- selves into a national organization, or workers in the same Special Municipality, Province or Border Region, who have been associated into a local organization may be members of the All-China Federation of Labor.

Individual workers' organizations, which have no general organiza- tions and apply for direct admission, require the special permission of the All-China Federation of Labor.

ARTICLE 4. - All manual and non-manual workers in enterprises, offices and schools, who get their main income by work, who have legally acquired the status of manual or non-manual workers and who subscribe to this constitution, shall be admitted as members of affiliated trade unions, of their own volition, regardless of nationality, sex, trade, religion or political opinion.

ARTICLE 5. - Affiliation and disaffiliation by trade union organiza- tions and their individual members is voluntary. Affiliated organiza- tions and members shall comply with the constitution.

ARTICLE 6. - The rights of affiliated trade union members are:
   a. On the basis of its aims, to discuss, suggest and criticize all the policies and measures of the All-China Federation of Labor.

   b. To elect and to be elected within the All-China Federation of Labor.

- 141 -

c. To share in the cultural, educational and welfare facilities established by the All-China Federation of Labor.

ARTICLE 7. - The obligations of affiliated trade union members are:

a. To comply with the aims and constitution of the All-China Federation of Labor and to carry out all its decisions.

b. To report regularly to the All-China Federation of Labor the activities of their organizations and work of the individual members.

c. To pay affiliation fees periodically.

Section Three: ORGANIZATION

ARTICLE 8. - The organizational principle of the All-China Federation of Labor is democratic centralism. Namely: the minority must submit to the majority; lower organizations submit to higher organization; affiliated trade unions submit to the decisions and directions of the All-China Federation of Labor.

ARTICLE 9. - The All-China Labor Congress shall be the sovereign authority of the All-China Federation of Labor. Its functions, powers and procedure shall be as follows:

a. The functions and powers of the All-China Labor Congress shall be to determine and amend the Constitution; to determine the policies of the trade union movement; to examine the reports of the Executive Committee; to elect the Executive Committee.

b. The All-China Labor Congress shall be convened biennially by the Executive Committee. Congress may be convened at an earlier date or postponed, as may be determined by the Executive Committee, on account of special conditions, or at the request of affiliated trade unions representing one third of the total affiliated membership.

c. Delegate representation and electoral procedure at the All-China Labor Congress shall be decided by the Executive Committee.

d. Congress is effective only with the participation of delegates representing over one half of the total affiliated membership.

ARTICLE 10. - The Executive Committee shall consist of members and substitutes elected by the All-China Labor Congress. The Executive Committee shall be the sovereign authority of the All-China Federation of Labor in the periods between Congresses. The Executive Committee shall be convened every six months by the Standing Committee. Executive Committee meetings are effective only with the participation of one half of the Executive members. The Executive Committee may meet at an earlier date or may be postponed in the case of special conditions or at the request of over one third of its members.

ARTICLE 11. - A chairman and vice-chairman shall be elected by the Executive Committee to direct the work of the All-China Federation of Labor.

ARTICLE 12. - A Standing Committee shall be formed by the chairman, vice-chairman and other members elected by the Executive Committee to conduct work at the headquarters. It shall be responsible to the Executive Committee.

ARTICLE 13. - A General Secretary shall be appointed by the Standing Committee to be in charge of the routine administrative work under the direction of the chairman and vice-chairman.

ARTICLE 14. - The following departments of the All-China Federation of Labor shall be set up:

a. Organization Department. This department shall be in charge of the organizational affairs of the affiliated trade unions and shall assist, wherever there are workers without trade unions, to organize them into trade unions.

b. Education and Culture Department. This department shall be in charge of propaganda, educational and cultural work and shall direct the cultural and educational policies of the affiliated trade unions.

c. Production Department. This department shall direct the trade unions in their participation in the administration of factories and enterprises and in the conduct of the labor competition and labor hero movements; study the problems of wages, production plans, technical experiences and other matters connected with production in the Liberated Areas.

d. Welfare Department. This department shall be in charge of and direct labor insurance; examine labor contracts and the welfare work of affiliated trade unions; assist the government in inspecting hygienic and safety services in factories.

e. Youth Department. This department shall take charge of and direct the work in connection with the juvenile workers at the various levels of the affiliated trade unions.

f. Women's Department. This department shall be in charge of and direct the work connected with women workers at the various levels of the affiliated trade unions.

g. International Relations Department. This department shall be in charge of the foreign publicity of the All-China Federation of Labor and of liaison with international and foreign national trade union organizations.

h. Secretariat. The Secretariat shall be in charge of control, clerical work and accounts.

i. Private Enterprise Committee. This committee shall be in charge of the work of the trade union movement in the privately-operated enterprises.

j. Committee for Work in the Kuomintang-occupied Areas. This committee shall study and direct the work of the trade union movement in the Kuomintang areas.

ARTICLE 15. - Each department shall have a department head; the secretariat shall have a chairman. These shall either be members of the Standing Committee or appointed by it. Each unit may have a vice-chairman. Each of these units shall have assistants appointed by the Standing Committee.

ARTICLE 16. - The All-China Federation of Labor shall set up offices at such places as may be necessary to facilitate the work. A director and assistants shall be appointed to the office. These matters shall be decided by the Standing Committee.

ARTICLE 17. - The Executive Committee shall set up whatever special committee it may consider necessary.

Section Four: FINANCE

ARTICLE 18. - Each affiliated trade union shall pay, every three months, 30 per cent of the membership fees it receives, to the All-China Federation of Labor as funds. Lower fees, or exemption from payment in cases of difficulty, require the special permission of the Standing Committee.

Section Five: ANNEX

ARTICLE 19. - This constitution shall be adopted and published by the All-China Labor Congress.

ARTICLE 20. - The All-China Labor Congress shall have the right to amend this constitution should it become necessary.

ARTICLE 21. - The right to interpret this Constitution belongs to the Executive Committee.

EXCERPTS FROM A RESOLUTION ADOPTED BY THE 6th ALL-CHINA LABOR CONGRESS,
AUGUST 1948
(as described in the China Digest, Hongkong, December 28, 1948)

With regard to trade union tasks in areas still under Kuomintang
control, the resolution stated:

"In order to realize the aims set out above, the trade union movement in the Kuomintang-occupied areas should more than ever before
increase their connections with the masses, accumulate strength and
enlarge their ranks in order to welcome the arrival of the People's
Liberation Army. They should, by every possible means and with precau-
tion, support and participate in all the revolutionary movements of the
people and hamper Chiang Kai-shek's manufacture of arms and military
transport in every possible way."

In the course of these struggles, the resolution added, workers
in the Kuomintang occupied areas should differentiate between bureaucratic and national capitalists, because national private industry and
commerce in these areas are, for the most part, also oppressed, ruined
or restricted by imperialism, and bureaucratic capital. Then the
workers should demand that their living standards be raised.

Workers in the Kuomintang occupied areas were asked to send
"suitable and skilled personnel" to the Liberated Areas to participate
in the construction of the new type of industry and commerce there.
They were instructed to "energetically protect all the publicly and
privately owned enterprises, factories, machinery and materials from
Kuomintang destruction and wreckage, especially on the arrival of the
People's Liberation Army."

"In the liberated areas the development of industry and agriculture
is the direct material basis for strengthening the people's revolutionary war and improving the livelihood of the people, not primarily of
the workers.

"The contradiction between labor and capital still exists in the
privately-owned enterprises where the workers are still exploited, but
since they occupy the leading role as masters politically and socially
in the state, they are guaranteed against any oppression and excessive
exploitation. Moreover, the existence and development of these private
productive enterprises which are beneficial to the national living
standards enhance the total economy of the liberated areas and therefore
also benefit the working class. In view of these new conditions, the
trade union movement in the liberated areas should be guided by entirely
new principles and policies.

"In the first place, the workers of the liberated areas must
thoroughly organize themselves and study, so as to raise their own con-
sciousness and fully comprehend the situation in China and all the new
conditions in the liberated areas outlined above; and to be ready to
take an active part in organized and conscious way in the manifold construction work of the new democratic state, army, economy and culture

and elect their outstanding representatives to the various leading organs of the state. Within these organs they should unite and work in concert with the representatives of all democratic classes, adhere to working-class principles and policies representing the long-term interests of the whole people, and oppose all sectional and incorrect principles and policies.

"The task of developing industrial production in the liberated areas has been raised to a position of unprecedented importance. It is a task of special importance, to the workers in the liberated areas.

"Only by developing industrial production can the final victory in the revolutionary war be ensured; the demands of the peasants following the land reform, particularly for improved agricultural technique, be satisfied; and the livelihood of workers and other sections of the people be gradually improved. Industry in the liberated areas is the industry of a new democracy. Its future development is boundless because there exists a vast fund of emancipated labor power, masses of people who willingly cooperate with all their energy, unrestricted markets for commodities, rich resources and the People's Liberation Army which will set free more cities, factories and machinery and will link up, step by step, all the liberated areas. These vital conditions for developing industry are daily increasing and growing."

Discussing the need for enduring hardship by the workers along with the rest of the people in view of the unprecedented scope of the war, the resolution stated that the working day should in general be 8 to 10 hours for factory workers, to be prolonged or lessened in specific factories or under particular conditions as may be approved by the local government.

The resolution continued: "all workers must be guaranteed a minimum standard of living, namely, their lowest wages should be sufficient to provide for the livelihood of 2 persons (including the recipient). In order to ensure labor enthusiasm and improvement of technique, however, systems of payment according to various grades and classification, time-rates and piece-rates, should be adopted.

"To guarantee the workers a minimum standard of living, the lowest wages must be increased in conformity with any increase of prices.

"The wages of factory workers should be based on an over-lapping and progressive system of grades. The division of labor and the productive process and the degree of technique should be the basis for determining the grades.

"The methods of payment, time-rates or piece-rates, and their appreciation should be determined on the basis of the actual working conditions.

"Where commodity prices are very unstable and wage adjustment difficult, the practice of subsidizing wages may be adopted to diminish such difficulties. The subsidies should also be graduated, but the differentiation should not be too great.

"Wages should be calculated on the basis of several essential commodities (food and cloth in North China and on the points system in Manchuria) and payment should be in cash and kind combined. In order still further to guarantee the real wages of the workers, the new food rationing system should be adopted, first applied experimentally, in state and publicly-operated factories and universally extended when experience has been obtained."

In the section of women and juvenile workers, the resolution stated: "all men, women and juvenile workers should receive equal pay for equal work."

"Women workers should have 60 days leave for confinement, 15 days for miscarriage up to 3 months, and 30 days for miscarriage after 3 months. Wages should be paid during this leave.

"Local governments in the liberated areas should regulate by law those industries in which employment of women and juvenile workers is prohibited and in which women and juvenile workers may not be employed in night-work. Juvenile workers should not be employed in work which is harmful to physical development."

Discussing workers' protection and welfare, the resolution called for improvement of hygienic services and safety devices in factories and regular government inspection of these; pensions, medical benefits and allowances for sickness, injury, disability and old age, to be the responsibility of the factory for the time being; social insurance of labor in cities with concentrations of factories; and workers' welfare measures in the fields of culture, education, cooperative and birth, death and sickness benefits.

Discussing the labor-hero movement and its role in the development of production, the resolution stated: "these movements should still be encouraged and correctly guided in order to give the beneficial objectives of reducing production costs, raising quality, increasing output and of collective heroism in learning and helping each other, with the minority inspiring the majority".

On the subject of collective labor contracts and labor disputes, the resolution stated: "labor should have contracts, these should be collective contracts binding both parties. The contract should state the conditions of work, engagement and dismissal, awards and penalties, workers' protection and welfare and factory regulation".

The method of dealing with labor disputes is by negotiating, conciliation and, in the last resort, arbitration.

Finally, on the general tasks of liberated areas trade unions, the resolution stated: "under the general principle of 'developing production, flourishing economy, taking into account both public and private interests and benefits to both labor and capital', the tasks of the trade unions in the liberated areas are to unite all workers to display enthusiasm in their work and observe discipline; to protect their every-day interests; educate them to raise their cultural level and particularly their technical and professional level; develop their administrative ability in the state, public and semi-public enterprises; play an overseeing role in the privately operated enterprises and encourage individual workers to improve their technique and cooperative production."

"The higher trade union organizations should have the responsibility of helping the Government in preparing labor legislation and of adopting concrete measures to guarantee the reasonable fulfilment of all points in the foregoing section.

"All men and women workers, manual and non-manual, who have legally acquired that class standing, should have the right to join a trade union of their own profession. The trade unions serve not only their members but also non-members, and encouraging the latter to join in their activities.

"By so doing, can they actually represent the workers as a whole and win over all workers to join in the trade unions.

"Within the trade unions there must be full democratic life which can truly concentrate the opinions of the mass and the daily, practical work which effectually satisfies the needs of the masses."

THE "NORTH-EAST STATE-OWNED ENTERPRISES PROVISIONAL WARTIME LABOR INSURANCE ACT"

(as described in a New China News Agency dispatch from North Shensi,
February 21, 1949).

The "Northeast State-owned Enterprises Provisional War Time Labor Insurance Act" passed by Manchuria's Democratic Government last month makes labor history in China. It marks one of the most significant victories of the present Chinese labor movement.

This act, which is designed to "protect the health of workers and employees and reduce the difficulties of life during war time," will come into force on April 1st this year. Then workers in Manchuria's state-owned industries will enjoy what Chinese labor failed to obtain in decades of hard struggle.

The Provisional War Time Labor Insurance Act stipulates that each state-owned enterprise in Manchuria is to set aside a sum amounting to 3 per cent of its total wages for labor insurance. 70 per cent of this sum is to be used in the enterprise as a labor insurance fund for its own workers, and 30 per cent deposited in the Northeast Bank as a general labor insurance fund. All state-owned enterprises are to pay two months' labor insurance fund in advance to the Northeast Bank as the general labor insurance fund.

Though limited by war conditions, this act provides the working people with sickness, accident, maternity, medical and funeral benefits as well as old-age and disability pensions. When a worker is injured through accident during work or falls sick, he gets free medical treatment in the factory's hospital, while receiving his full wages.

If he is disabled through accident or hard work, he monthly receives from the general insurance fund a pension up to 60 per cent of his monthly wages until his death.

In the event of death, the factory in which he works pays all the funeral expenses which are not to exceed two months of his wages. For the next 10 years, the immediate family of the deceased will monthly receive from the labor insurance fund a benefit up to 50 percent of the monthly wage of the deceased. Dependents of the deceased or disabled worker are to be given the first priority of work in the factory. The Government provides free schooling for the children left behind.

If sickness or injury not suffered through work invalids the worker for less than three months, he gets 55 to 100 percent of his monthly wages. All his medical fees are borne by the enterprise in which he works. If invalided for more than three months, or temporarily disabled, he is entitled to a monthly disability benefit from the labor insurance fund. The benefit is 50 percent available to workers injured through accident at work. It is available to them until he returns to work.

The act also provides pensions for aged workers. A working man reaching 60 and with a 25 year seniority of work and still working, receives monthly a health benefit from the labor insurance fund ranging from 10 to 20 percent of his monthly wage. On retirement, he gets a monthly pension up to 60 percent of his wage until death. These benefits and pensions are available to workers in mines and unhealthy occupations at the age of 55 with a 20 year seniority of work. They are available to woman workers reaching the age of 50 with a 20 year seniority of work.

By way of maternity welfare, the act provides a 45-day rest with full pay to woman workers before and after confinement. After childbirth, each woman worker is to receive a benefit from the labor insurance fund.

This act not only benefits the working man himself but his family as well. When his parents or children fall sick, they get free medical care in the factory's hospital with reduced fees for medicine. In the event of death to a member of the worker's family a funeral fee amounting to one third of the worker's monthly wage from the labor insurance fund is immediately available.

Despite war time conditions, this Provisional Labor Insurance Act is by far superior to that in any capitalist country. In the first place, all the labor insurance fund is covered by the state while in capitalist countries they are deducted from the hard-earned wages of the worker.

In liberated Manchuria, the trade unions and the workers themselves take a direct part in running the labor insurance work. But in a capitalist country it is entirely run by the government or its appointed bureaucrats who pocket huge sums from labor insurance fund.

A clause in the act states that after all insurance expenses have been covered, the balance is to go to the building of kindergartens and schools for workers' children, old workers and workers' sanitoria and rest homes, etc. This is not the case in capitalist countries. In 1946, 4.3 billion dollars from the wages of American workers went to the U.S. labor insurance fund, but only 0.8 billion dollars were actually used for their benefit.

The act provides Manchurian state-owned factory workers against such eventualities of life as sickness, injuries, disability, birth, old age and death. Before the outbreak of World War II, 41 capitalist countries did not even have pensions for aged workers, and 53 countries did not have disability pension.

For three decades the Chinese workers had gone on strikes and struggles for labor insurance, and many of their leaders had been jailed and butchered by the reactionary Kuomintang without winning anything like a labor insurance act. But today they have it in liberated Manchuria. It is only in a new democratic country like liberated China, where the working class is at the helm of the Government that such an all-embracing labor insurance scheme can come into existence during war time.

Other liberated areas are closely studying this first Labor Insurance Act in Manchuria for experience to apply to their own areas.

APPENDIX E.

Excerpts from

"THE LABOR POLICY OF THE CHINESE GOVERNMENT AND ITS REACTIONS ON INDUSTRY AND LABOR"

BY
TA CHEN
Tsing Hua University, Peiping

(from INTERNATIONAL LABOR REVIEW, Vol. LIX, No. 1, January 1949)

The social doctrines of Dr. Sun Yat-sen with regard to the welfare of the Chinese worker have been warmly supported by the Kuomintang (the National People's Party) and by the Government. Their untiring efforts to translate the idealism of the late party leader into practice have resulted in the enactment of labor laws and in the pronouncement of public policies aiming at the regulation of working conditions in modern industry and commerce.

The most fundamental and comprehensive law affecting industry and labor is of course the Factory Act, which was promulgated in 1929 and put into force in 1931. About half a year before the date originally set for its enforcement, certain groups in the country expressed serious doubts as to the extent to which the law could in fact be applied, and at their request the writer undertook a factual study of labor conditions in 228 selected factories in Shanghai in order to throw light on this subject. The results of the inquiry suggested the desirability of introducing the principle of gradual enforcement; in other words, certain provisions might, with modifications, be applied outright, others should be postponed to later dates, and still others should, for various reasons, be suspended indefinitely. These views were in general accepted by the experts of the International Labor Office who were then visiting China at the invitation of the Chinese Government, and who later assisted the Government to establish the Factory Inspection Service. ...

Another basic social measure is undoubtedly the Trade Union Act, which was first proposed by the Kuomintang in 1924, enacted as a national law and enforced in 1929, and revised several times since. This Act, more than any other social law, mirrors the social changes that have taken place in China during the last two decades. Among other things, the events of the last twenty-five years have clearly shown that those who favored extending the scope of the Act to industrial unions were too optimistic. This was one of the more controversial points at the time, and such inclusion was strongly urged by one of the original drafters of the Act on the ground that the workers should be encouraged to organize on a broader basis than their particular trade or craft, in order to accelerate the social and economic progress of the country.

Furthermore, under the original Act of 1929 any worker satisfying the conditions for membership was free to join a union and to leave it at his choice. In this respect the worker's freedom was very much curtailed during the second World War, and the restriction seems to be retained in the latest revision, made in 1947. This change of the Government's policy has evoked sharp criticism among the more enlightened workers, as well as among the liberal camps of thinkers in China and abroad. ...

THE OPERATION OF THE FACTORY ACT

If we select certain significant sections of the Factory Act for special study, we can gain a general impression as to the extent to which it has in fact been applied since it was put into force in 1931. The following analysis, ... applies to the cities of Shanghai, Chungking, Kunming, Sian and Paochi.

These cities reflect different stages of the social and economic development of the country. Shanghai is perhaps the most industrialized area. Next comes the city of Chungking, which, being the nation's capital during the war, showed rapid and worthwhile industrial growth, though before the war it was an agricultural area with some commercial importance on the Upper Yangtze. Kunming in south-west China and Sian and Paochi in north-west China are predominantly rural communities, and in these regions modern industry is just beginning. The three groups of cities reveal beyond doubt the extreme complexity of Chinese society, which is a strong argument in favor of treating as premature any attempt to enforce labor laws uniformly throughout the length and breadth of the country. ...

When the field investigation of the Shanghai factories was made in 1931, the writer's recommendation was that the enforcement of the Factory Act should properly begin with the regulations on health and safety, both because these were of paramount importance to the life of the workers and because they did not involve any substantial outlay of expenditure, thus minimizing the possible opposition from tradition-bound employers to the enforcement of the protective labor legislation. These suggestions, which were supported by the experts of the International Labor Office Mission, were accepted by the Government. That they were sound is clear from the fact that the practical enforcement program of the Act during the last sixteen years has in general been in conformity with them. The sample survey of working conditions in 240 factories in Shanghai made in 1946 under the writer's direction showed that in a number of factories there had been an improvement in the provision made for the workers' health and safety, though in more normal circumstances, even better results could have been expected. ...

Since the enforcement of the Factory Act in 1931, the situation with regard to the workers' earnings has passed through four distinct stages, but at no time have the majority of the workers obtained an income sufficient to keep them and their families in comfort, health and decency.

Up to the undeclared Sino-Japanese war of 1937, minimum wage rates should, according to the Factory Act, be based on the living conditions in the localities where the factories were situated. As family budget studies and periodical retail price reports were not available for all industrialized areas, this provision was difficult of realization.

During the war, when prices soared and inflation went from bad to worse, many factories tried to increase their workers' income by introducing a complicated system of allowances to supplement wages. Thus wages came to be relegated to a very insignificant place, and the substantial part of the worker's earnings consisted of allowances in the form of basic necessities of life, such as rice, clothing and house rent. Though still insufficient to defray his living expenses, these earnings formed the bulk of his income. This was the situation in many cities in Free China up to Japan's surrender. After that date, the workers in Shanghai in a series of demonstrations and strikes demanded that their pay should amount to the daily basic wage multiplied by the cost-of-living index number for the current month. To this, the industrialists of the city agreed. Seeing that this method of remuneration was economically advantageous to the workers, their comrades in other cities quickly imitated the Shanghai experiment. ...

Since the enforcement of the Factory Act in 1931, and especially since the establishment of the Ministry of Social Affairs in 1940, noticeable progress has been made in some forms of industrial welfare. During the war, welfare work in the south-west and north-west was undertaken on a much larger scale than had previously been attempted in similar industries anywhere in China.

However, certain intelligent and experienced industrialists are rather skeptical about the real benefit of workers' welfare. Their views have been expressed in the following terms:

> We are all agreed that welfare work is of social benefit to the workers. But we are doubtful about its economic consequences. For every type of welfare work introduced, the management has to foot the bill or the greater part thereof. But is this additional cost ultimately shifted to the consumer by an increase in the market price of the commodities manufactured? Or is an increase in welfare accompanied by a corresponding increase in the workers' efficiency to offset the additional cost to the management?

LABOR POLICY IN CHINA

THE TRADE UNION ACT

The right to organize trade unions was clearly recognized in the original Act of 1929 and is reaffirmed in the latest revision of June, 1947. Any qualified worker is free to join a union or to retire from it. In fact, the third amendment to the Act of July 1933 stipulated in section 20 that "no union can compel any worker to join it or to retire from it". During the war, however, the freedom of the workers was very much restricted. With the object of increasing the country's power to carry on the war of resistance, the Government sought to control the trade unions through an Order August 21, 1941, under which "all workers who are qualified to be members are required to join the union and are not allowed, without the permission of the Government, to withdraw from it". This compulsory membership was first applied in the craft unions in the transport and educational supplies industries, and later extended to industrial unions, such as those for the engineering and iron and steel industries. The appropriate authorities under whose jurisdiction the unions were controlled began to train personnel to serve either as secretaries or as inspectors of trade unions. Frequently, in the course of their enquiry among the unions or workers in and near Chungking, the writer and his associates came into contact with persons who had been sent by the local branch of the Party or by the city bureau of social affairs. The more observant workers condemned this practice in unequivocal terms as being "high-handed, autocratic and undemocratic".

It is to be regretted that this restriction of the workers' freedom is still retained in the Amendment Act of 1947. It is in fact disconcerting to note that, long after the conclusion of the war, the Party and the Government should consider it necessary to retain the compulsory membership feature in trade union law.

In one sense, however, the workers' right of association has apparently been extended in recent years, in that the 1947 Act permits workers to organize both federations of trade unions and a general national federation. The federation of trade unions, even on the basis of a city or a hsien (district), had been prohibited since the strike and boycott in Canton and Hong Kong in 1925-1926. Even as recently as in 1943, the amendment to the Act adopted in that year allowed the workers to organize only national federations, but not a national general labor union.

The original Act of 1929 stated that workers in the same trade might organize themselves into a craft union, and that workers in the same industry might organize themselves into an industrial union. In section 7 of the revised Act of June 1947, the same categories of unions are recognized, though different requirements are specified regarding the minimum number of members per union and the age limits for membership. Inasmuch as China today is but on the threshold of industrialization, the provision for the organization of industrial unions may be said to anticipate the socio-economic development of the country perhaps by several decades.

The functions of the union as enumerated in the Act comprise a very wide range of activities. Some of the thirteen specific items listed relate to economic and social activities of great importance, such as the conduct of workers' family budget surveys, the establishment of employment offices, the promotion of workers' education, and the submission of data to the Government as a basis for the enactment of labor laws. The inability of most of the unions to discharge their duties properly demonstrates the ineffectiveness of this agency in promoting the general well-being of the working classes.

The principal causes of the unions' failure lie in the fact that trade unionism, in theory and in practice, is a foreign concept, which few labor leaders and workers in China understand and appreciate. The activities in which many unions in China engage are but a superficial imitation of their western counterpart. About the true nature and function of the leading unions in Europe or or America, little is known and comprehended by the Chinese comrades.

According to the national Constitution adopted in December 1946 which came into force in March, 1948, there must be workers' representatives both in the National Assembly and in the Legislative Yuan, to the extent of 30 per cent of the membership of the former body and 20 per cent of the latter. In the various provinces and municipalities, the "people's political councils" must also have representatives from occupational groups, including labor. In August 1947, the principal cities and also most of the provinces already had more than 1,500 labor representatives out of a total of about 38,000 representatives from all sections of the population.

These provisions reflect the role which the Kuomintang plans that the workers should play in promoting democracy in China. The question is whether they will be able to live up to the expectations of the Party, which throughout these years has warmly supported them.

There is yet another way in which the unions are linked up with the Party and the Government. In the Trade Union (Amendment) Act of 1947, with its total of sixty-three sections, there are no less than twenty provisions which require the unions to obtain authorization from the Government before they can take certain specified steps. This governmental control ranges from the petition that must be made to the proper authorities for organizing a union to the dissolution of the union as a result of the contravention of certain Government regulations. ...

THE VIEWS OF EMPLOYERS

As contrasted with pre-war days, the war period witnessed a phenomenal increase of Government interference in industry. Often, this evoked vigorous protests from a number of industrialists. Said the experienced manager of a well-known cotton mill of Chungking:

> Many of us hope that the Government will take the laissez-faire attitude towards industry, as it used to do in the old days, when the guilds practically regulated all the trades in the country. If we sincerely tried to comply with the laws of the Government, we would have to increase our managerial staff substantially. Even for no more than the periodical submission of reports to the Government, as required under some laws, we would have to engage more clerks, which in these days of high production costs we can ill afford.

> What the entrepreneurs chiefly object to is the spirit of the law, which encourages restriction and repression. Instead, if the Government were to give more freedom, industry could flourish. But more regulations will eventually stifle individual initiative and jeopardize industry and commerce.

- 155 -

Besides, none of the labor laws is uniformly enforced throughout China. This creates unfair competition. We know that in the less industrialized areas it is easier to evade the laws. But for big cities like Shanghai, Wusih and Chungking, full compliance with the laws would put the factories in disadvantageous position, as their costs of production would be higher as compared with those of the less industrialized regions.

In our conversations with managers and the heads of personnel sections, we invariably asked them questions as to the suitability of the Chinese laborer for factory work. The Government, in its efforts to regulate modern industry, tends to assume that the Chinese worker is an exact counterpart of the worker in the Occident, and to expect that labor legislation in China will produce identical results. Is this a valid assumption? An engineer of considerable industrial experience in Yunnan and Szechuan states:

We may have to re-evaluate the Chinese workman, after our long experience with him in Kunming and Chungking. In the first place, the Yunnanese worker is small and light, and usually has a weak constitution. He cannot handle heavy machines and has no endurance. He is easygoing, happy and playful and he lacks the steadfastness which is essential for many types of industrial work. Of course, in Kunming the climate is unusually mild and not much subject to variations; the temperature ranges from about 8° C. in January to 18° C. in August. This monotonous climate makes one lethargic and slow-moving.

Another factor we must study is the social background of the Yunnanese workman. He is an agricultural worker originally. On the farms, he needs no technical skill and does not have to speed up his work, as he is sometimes compelled to do in a factory when working at a machine.

Regarding the modern worker's skill, the same engineer made the following observation:

Some workmen were formerly connected with the local handicrafts and they are skilled workers in a sense. In the guilds, the masters and journeymen are ordinarily dextrous with their hands. In the factories, however, the worker must be concise in perception, quick in judgment, and correct, careful and precise in handling machines. In industrial work, the worker's skill is often associated with machinery. This expertness must be learned, and learning usually takes time.

He continued by relating his experiences with workers in and near Chungking. With slight modifications, the above characterization of the Yunnanese worker still holds good.

As for my experience in Shanghai before the war, I was also in charge of labor gangs and our workmen came from the villages of the Shanghai hinterland. The Shanghainese worker, though - like the Yunnanese - not

of strong physique, is more intelligent, learns more
quickly and is a hard worker. In our factories we
often assigned them jobs that required technical
knowledge and experience, and they usually turned out
to be satisfactory workmen.

In the judgment of an experienced administrator of labor of an iron
and steel works in Shanghai, the chief questions affecting the relations
between management and men could be summed up in the following terms:

At the risk of some oversimplification, the problems
of capital-labor relations may be categorically divided
into three groups; (1) economic problems, including
those relating to the workers' earnings; (2) social
problems, including the workers' demand for social
status; and (3) psychological problems, including the
workers' unconciliatory attitude towards the management. Of these groups, I would consider the last
as being the most significant during the war and after
it.

With regard to the effect of the war, he continued:

The war has certainly aroused a more active senti-
ment among the workers towards all classes of people,
especially towards those who give them jobs. They
generally tend to be emotional and shiftless and to
feel dejected at times. We should go a long way
towards improving the relations between the management and the men if we could be patient and sympathetic
towards the workers, who are, after all, co-partners
with us in industrial production.

Members of the managerial staff of large factories who had direct
contact with the workers frequently expressed definite opinions about
them. Furthermore, those who had had industrial experience throughout
these years could often compare the workers' behavior before, during and
after the war. The manager of a wool spinning and weaving factory in
Shanghai and Chungking analyzed his experience with his workers as
follows:

Before the war, my largest factory was operated in
Shanghai. For many years, half of our labor troubles
arose from the workers' demand for increased wages or
for a bonus at the end of the year. So long as their
income was sufficient to maintain them and their
families, they were satisfied and worked steadily.
But during the war, their attitude changed perceptibly,
as shown by the labor disputes in our plants near
Chungking. There they frequently demanded a voice in
discussing questions relating to their position in the
factory and also relating to the conduct of our business.
Occasionally they expressed the wish to participate in
the activities of the factory by electing workers'
delegates to talk over matters of mutual interest with
the representatives of management.

A large number of our interviews with workers and labor leaders in several cities have revealed their psychological reactions to the policies of the Government, to their relations with the members of the management, and to their evaluation of the trade unions. The following analysis is limited to Shanghai, and sets forth briefly the results of 201 interviews.

In 38 cases the workers displayed a friendly attitude towards the employer, whether as the result of an old friendship with him, or because they were related to him, or because they had been in his employment for a long time. The attitude of 11 workers was indifferent towards the employer, they alleged that the relationship between them hardly went further than that expressed by "we give him labor and he gives us money". The remaining members of the group of 201 workers expressed ill-feeling towards the employer, though the intensity of that feeling differed with the individual: "The capitalist has no feelings. He is not sympathetic towards us. There is a wall between him and us." Or: "The employer and other members of the management are generally apathetic towards the workmen. They consider us lowdown and keep us at a distance from them."

The following statement illustrates the attitude towards the overseer or foreman:

The foreman is not considerate. He is often obsequious to the employer and shows no fellow-feeling for us. He shows favoritism to his friends and relatives, but does not treat us justly on the basis of meritorious work.

... A total of 98 workers, who were intelligent, articulate and had had long experience of industrial work, demanded social equality with the management. To them, the relations between management and men could be considerably improved. ...

Of the 71 workers who gave reasons for joining a union, 50 stated they did so of their own free will, while the remaining 21 had been forced to become members by external pressure. In the view of this group, the functions of the union must be: (a) to fight on behalf of the workers and to present their demands to the management when necessary; (b) to improve the conditions of employment; (c) to work for security of employment; (d) to give the workers an opportunity to air grievances; (e) to increase their power through organization. ...

A considerable number of the more intelligent workers, both men and women, frankly declared that the trade union movement today was quite defective, but that they had high aspirations as to the directions in which the unions should develop in the future. ...

Among the more observant workers, there was a general conscious-ness of the fact that the labor movement today is weak and ineffect-ive. The 37 persons who outlined their views on this point, 28 of whom were union officials or ex-officials, enumerated various obstacles to trade union progress, which can be summarized as (a) the tricks of an unsympathetic employer, - (b) the lack of group

spirit among the workers, - (c) the difficult position of the union
official, - (d) the pressure of politics, - (e) the insecurity of the
union official's job, - (f) the heterogeneity of the workers, - and
(g) the incompetence of some labor leaders. Some workers see the
important role that the labor leader can play in the organization and
conduct of the unions. If the union is in the hands of an incompetent
leader, it can naturally make little headway in unionist activities. ...

CONCLUSIONS

The preceding summary of certain basic data on industry and labor
in contemporary China may suggest a few concluding remarks.

In the first place, the enforcement of the labor laws has produced
uneven effects on the urban centres at different stages of industrial
and socio-economic development. This reinforces the writer's contention
that the national laws of China should be comprehensive and elastic,
and confined to the enunciation of general principles only. On the
basis of these principles, detailed regulations should be issued by the
Ministry of Social Affairs, or by the provincial or municipal governments, as the case may be, in accordance with the actual conditions
prevailing in the localities in which the regulations are to be applied.

Secondly, in order that this legislation may be more effective,
its adoption must be preceded by much more thorough-going socio-economic
investigation than has hitherto been attempted. No social law should be
enacted or promulgated without previous social study. Today, the ineffectiveness of most social legislation in China is due to the fact
that it is largely a superficial imitation of similar legislation in
the Occident and not the result of fact-finding enquiries in the country
itself or designed to meet its changing economic and social situation.

Thirdly, the Government's labor policy should be framed realistic-
ally with reference to the considered opinions of the industrialists
and workers whose conduct such policy is intended to regulate.

Fourthly, it seems clear that both employers and workers desire to
have a reasonable degree of freedom, so that they can freely take the
initiative in tackling problems concerning their welfare and their lives.
In this task, they are quite ready to co-operate with the Government in
giving effect to its policies.

Fifthly, industry is quite aware that a new social situation has
arisen, but is still uncertain in what direction to cope with the change
and what techniques to adopt.

Lastly, the recent war has given the Chinese labor movement an
unprecedented impetus, and the workers have grasped this opportunity to
demand social ascendancy in Chinese society. In their persistent struggles they have frequently come into conflict with the Government and
also with the employing class. In time, it is hoped, they will be able
to improve their social status and thus make an even more useful contribution to the effort to introduce democratic ways of life throughout the
whole nation.